THE
KNITTED
ALPHABET

First edition for the United States and Canada
published in 2014 by Barron's Educational Series, Inc.

Copyright © 2013 Quid Publishing

All inquiries should be addressed to:
Barron's Educational Series, Inc.
250 Wireless Boulevard
Hauppauge, New York 11788
www.barronseduc.com

ISBN: 978-1-4380-0295-8

Library of Congress Catalog Card No. 2013941173

Conceived, designed and produced by
Quid Publishing Ltd
Level Four
Sheridan House
114 Western Road
Hove BN3 1DD
England
www.quidpublishing.com

Printed by 1010 Printing International Limited, China

9 8 7 6 5 4 3 2 1

THE KNITTED ALPHABET

How to Knit Letters from A to Z

Kate Haxell & Sarah Hazell

BARRON'S

CONTENTS

INTRODUCTION

If you love to knit, and you like to speak your mind,

then this is the book for you. A peruse of *The Knitted Alphabet*, some

completely perfect yarn, your favorite knitting needles, and a little

time are all you need to spread your message, stitch by stitch. Whether you like

your letters plain and simple, fancy and florid, big and bold, modern, retro,

traditional, eccentric, elegant…there are 800-plus letter, number, and symbol charts in

this book, so you're bound to find something to suit what you want to say. And there

are so many ways to say it in knit: wear it on your sleeve, on your head, across your

heart; carry it, cuddle up in it, chill out on it; share it, gift it, or keep it close—you can

add a name, a message, a motto, or just a discreet monogram, to any knitted project.

Color knitting is going to be most knitters' preferred writing medium, and if you are a

novice—or want to brush up on your techniques—then check out the helpful

instructions on pages 242–253. And if color knitting isn't your thing, then you can

bead, sequin, embroider, texturize, or appliqué letters, and you'll find some techniques

alongside the color knitting methods. Throughout the book, there are knitted

letter swatches with ideas and advice on techniques and yarn choices, and

there are ten projects that we hope will inspire you to create your

own knitted notes. Enjoy using this book as much

as we did making it.

Kate and Sarah

HOW TO USE THIS BOOK

In this book, you will find 26 charted alphabets covering a wide range of styles. Three of them have both lower and uppercase letters (Calligraphy, see page 52; 50s Retro, see page 104; and Chalked, see page 218), and five have numbers that go with the letters (Elegant Handwriting, see page 12; Typewriter, see page 64; Sans Serif, see page 120; Tall and Thin, see page 178; and Chalked). There are letters at a variety of scales, from eleven stitches high (Computer, see page 30), to 57 stitches high (Poster, see page 232). Plus, there is a selection of punctuation marks and dingbats to decorate, punctuate, and create emoticons with (see page 156).

As well as 26 charted letters, each alphabet features ten knitted letters, worked in a variety of yarns and techniques, while each set of numbers has four knitted numerals. At the end of every alphabet, and with every set of numbers, is information on how each swatch was worked and what yarns were used; information that we hope will be both inspirational and instructional.

Knitting charts are often shown on squared graph paper. However, the shape of a knitted stitch is rectangular—it's wider than it is deep—so a square-grid chart is deceptive. So that you can tell exactly how the letters, numbers, punctuation, emoticons, and dingbats will look knitted in to your own projects, all the charts in this book are given on knitter's graph paper, which has rectangular boxes. For more information on the charts and how to read them, see page 242.

Lowercase letters have ascenders and descenders (see opposite), and the charts within an alphabet are all the same size—large enough to accommodate any letter in that alphabet—so you can see how the letters relate to one another in terms of size and position "on the page."

When it comes to positioning and spacing the letters that will make up your chosen word/name/phrase, you will need to experiment a little to decide on the best arrangement, but that's easy to do with the help of a photocopier. First, photocopy the blank sheet of knitter's graph paper on page 253 (taping several together if needed), and the letters you would like to use. You might need to enlarge or reduce either the sheet or the letters so that the grid boxes match in size: a perfect match isn't essential, though the boxes need to be quite similar for the process to work. Cut the letters out roughly, allowing a narrow border of a blank grid box or so all around (all the letters have at least one blank box around them). Then lay the letters out on the blank sheet and arrange them as you wish, matching the borders to the grid of the blank sheet. Tape all the pieces together to make your chart.

Also in *The Knitted Alphabet* are ten projects (for example, see page 20), with instructions and the chart used to knit them. Although you will almost certainly want to use different words to those we have chosen, each chart has some information on how the letters we used are positioned and spaced, information that will be useful to you when it comes to creating your own chart.

THE ANATOMY OF A LETTER

Calligraphy is an expressive, gorgeous, ancient, recognized, and popular art form that happens to be related to writing, though a beautifully drawn letter doesn't need to "say" anything to justify its existence. The various parts of letters (even knitted ones!) have proper names, and while there is no real need to learn them, they are interesting to know.

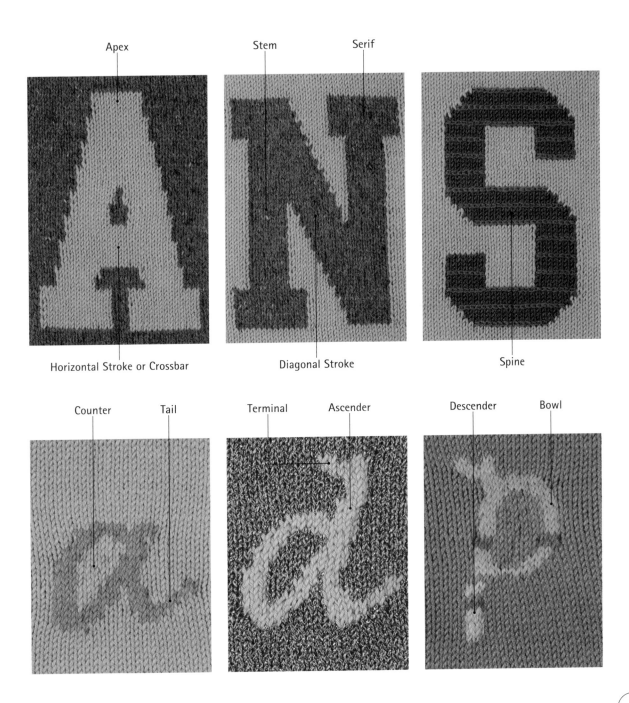

Apex

Stem   Serif

Horizontal Stroke or Crossbar

Diagonal Stroke

Spine

Counter   Tail

Terminal   Ascender

Descender   Bowl

THE KNITTED ALPHABETS

1 Elegant Handwriting

2 Celtic

3 Computer

4 Graffiti

5 80s Retro

6 Calligraphy

7 Typewriter

8 Flower Power

9 Stamped

10 3-D

11 Blackletter

12 50s Retro

13 Sans Serif

14 Quirky Handwriting

15 70s Retro

16 Curly

17 20s Retro

18 Stencil

19 Hearts

20 Tall and Thin

21 Brushscript

22 Digital Display

23 60s Retro

24 Classic Serif

25 Chalked

26 Poster

1

ELEGANT HANDWRITING

The swooping shapes of these letters are classically elegant, while the informality of the handwritten style keeps the alphabet looking fresh. This is a useful and versatile alphabet as the color palette you choose will strongly affect the look: this vibrant and contemporary combination of hot pink and tangerine orange rubs out any lingering old-fashioned feel here, but knitted in more muted colors the letters would have a lovely vintage look. Turn to the baby blanket project (see page 20) for other color ideas for this alphabet. There is also a full set of numbers to match these letters (see pages 18–19). As the strokes of the letters are thin, you may find it easiest to strand (see page 246) the background yarn right across the backs of the letters, as was done here.

Yarns used
- Cotton 4ply yarn in orange
- Fine mohair yarn in orange
- Metallic yarn in pink
- Variegated sock yarn in oranges
- Wool/cotton blend 4ply yarn in orange and pink

Other materials
- Pink beads

Techniques used
- Intarsia (see page 243)
- Stranding (see page 246)
- Knitted-in beading (see page 251)
- Duplicate stitch (Swiss darning; see page 252)

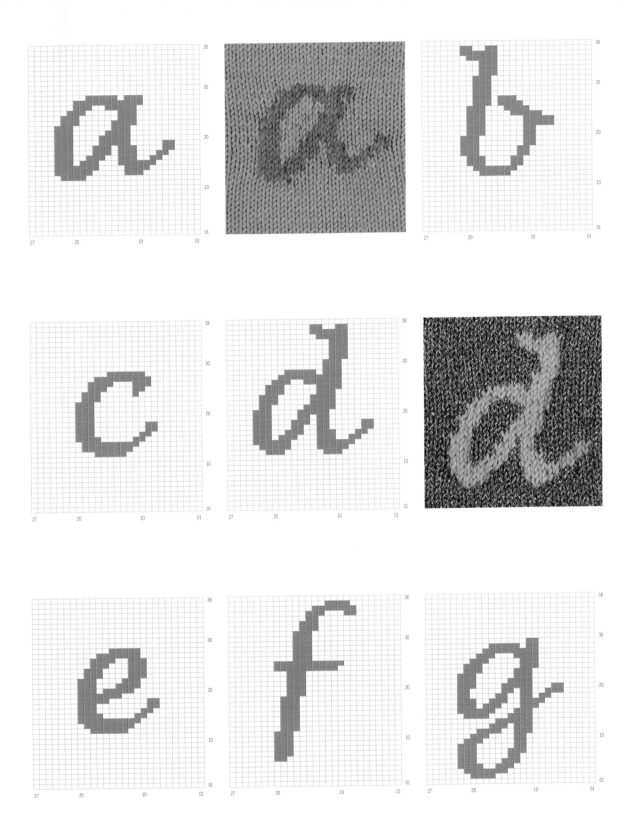

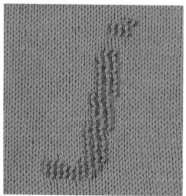

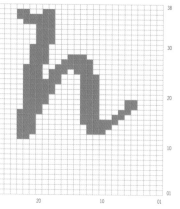

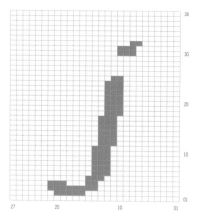

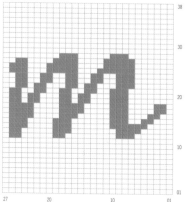

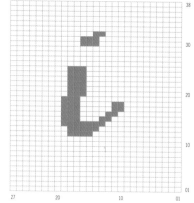

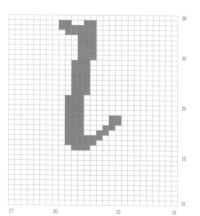

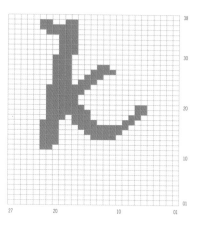

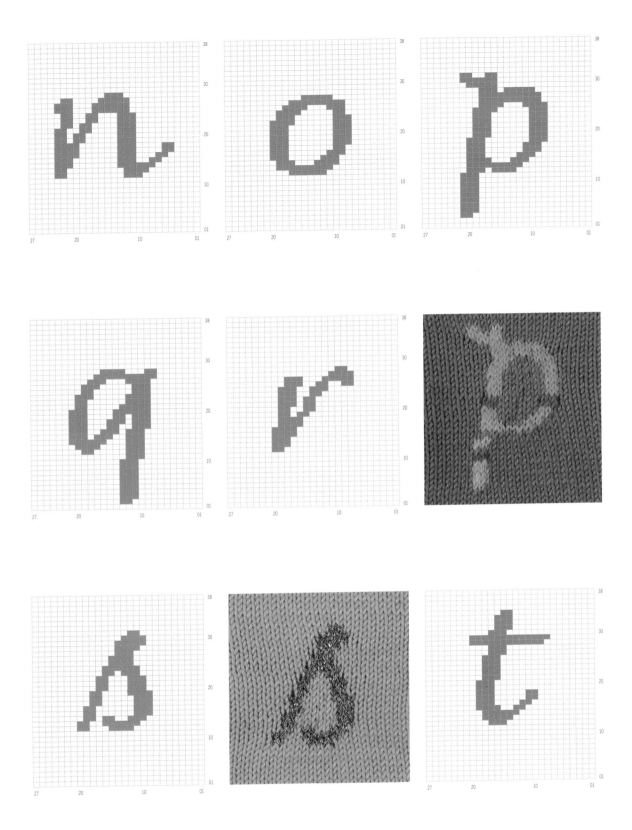

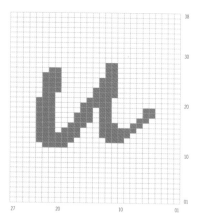

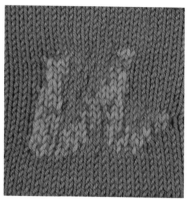

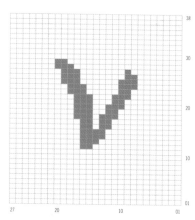

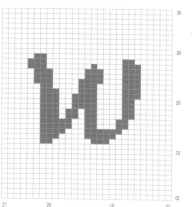

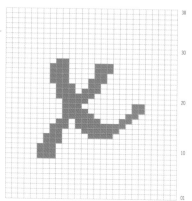

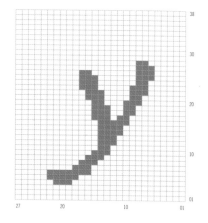

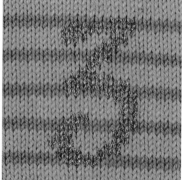

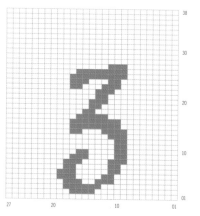

The Knitted Swatches

A This swatch is knitted in two colors of wool/cotton blend yarn. Working the thin, looping strokes of this alphabet will be a test of getting the tension of the floats right in stranded knitting (see pages 247–248), but small irregularities in tension can be eased with the tip of a knitter's sewing needle (see page 249) once the knitting is complete.

D Here, a metallic yarn is used for the background and a cotton 4ply for the letter. Metallic yarns might look a bit tricky to knit with, but they are actually easy to handle and the wriggly, sparkly surface is visually very forgiving of any uneven stitches, so this can be an excellent yarn to use if you are a color knitting novice.

H Here, the same yarns as letter "A" have been used, but the positions are reversed and the letter is duplicate stitched (Swiss darned; see page 252). Swapping colors like this works very well on an afghan: choose a limited palette and work blocks in all the possible variations to create a finished piece that's colorful, but also restrained.

J This letter is beaded using the knitted-in technique (see page 251), where a bead can be added to every stitch on every row as needed. These beads are color-lined: that is, they are made of clear glass and the color is added inside the bead hole. If you are using this type of bead, there are a couple of things to check: first, that the color doesn't flake off onto the yarn as the beads are slipped along it; second, that you can launder the beads without the color vanishing—both of these problems can occur with cheaply made color-lined beads.

M A two-tone, textural combination: the background is two strands of mohair held together and the letter is a single strand of cotton 4ply yarn. Used this way, the weights of the two yarns are similar, though you need to take a bit of care to get the tension of the stitches even at the color changes, especially since any uneven stitches tend to show on cotton yarn.

P Variegated yarns work great with letters, adding an extra sprinkle of color for no extra effort on your part. They are usually only available in sock weight. Be careful of those with long color changes as you can end up with a letter almost entirely one color, as here, which may not be the effect you had hoped for from a multicolored yarn.

S This swatch uses the same yarns as letter "D," but reversed. If you find metallic yarns a bit gaudy in quantities, try them as smaller accents; just one or two letters in a name or word, with the other letters knitted in a non-metallic yarn of the same color.

U Here, the background is wool/cotton and the letter one strand of wool/cotton and one of mohair held together. The fine mohair adds soft texture, but only a little extra bulk, so used over a small area the overall gauge (tension) and drape of the fabric shouldn't be affected.

X This swatch has a metallic yarn background and doubled mohair yarn for the letter. The combination might sound a bit intimidating, but both yarns are quite forgiving of uneven stitches—the fluffy yarn hides them and the wriggly metallic yarn disguises them—so this is actually something that a beginner to color knitting might try.

Z This letter is duplicate stitched (Swiss darned; see page 252), which allows you to easily experiment with working on a patterned background. Here, it's a simple stripe pattern, but you can duplicate stitch onto any stockinette (stocking) stitch knitting. Of course, if you are an expert color knitter, then you can knit a patterned background together with letters, but duplicate stitching like this is a great alternative option.

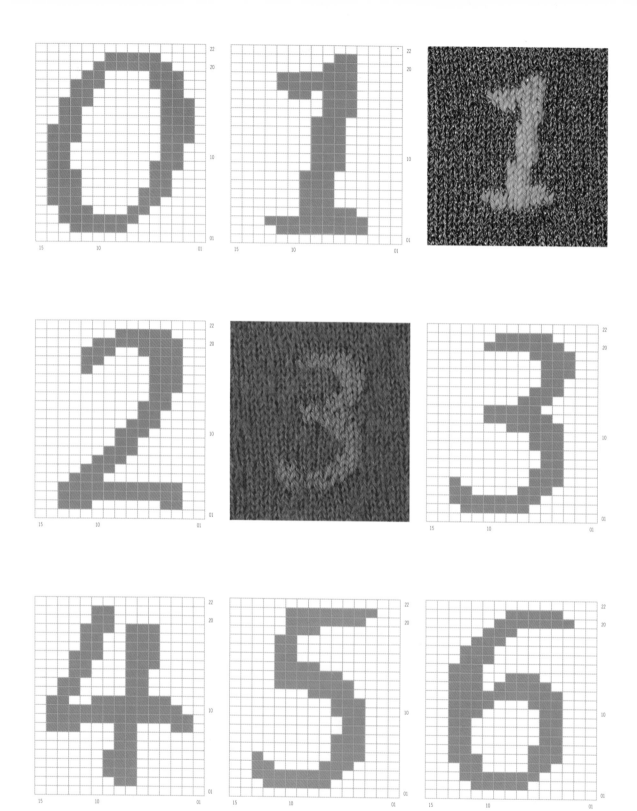

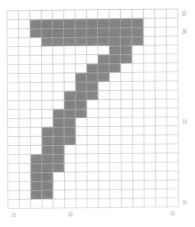

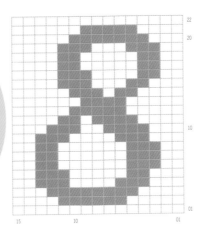

Numbers

Although these numbers have been charted to suit the style and scale of the Elegant Handwriting letters on pages 13–16, they will also work well with the Calligraphy alphabet (see pages 52–63).

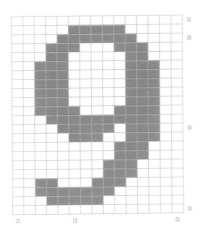

1 } This numeral uses the same yarns as letter "D." Remember to check that two yarns have compatible laundering requirements before knitting them together. A lukewarm hand wash in a no-rinse detergent will usually overcome any potential shrinkage issues, but it's worth washing a swatch before starting a sweater that you may never be able to clean.

3 } The background yarn of this swatch is a fine mohair and it's been used double to make it a similar weight to the wool/cotton 4ply yarn that the numeral is knitted in. If you have never worked with doubled yarn, don't be put off: the strands twist around one another as you work, making it easy to treat them as a single strand, and with fluffy yarn such as this, it won't show if you miss one strand in a stitch.

7 } This letter is beaded using the knitted-in technique (see page 251). However, as the beads are a little larger than the stitch, they are placed on different "legs" of the stitches on alternate rows. To do this, work the purl rows as normal, then before starting the knit row, slide all the beads along the stitch they are on and over the needle to the back. Then knit the row, placing the beads in the usual way. The beads that were moved will be sitting on the left-hand "leg" and those knitted on the right-hand "leg." This gives each bead a bit more room, and produces the herringbone pattern.

9 } You can also work letters in texture, though it might take a bit of planning: simpler textures and bolder shapes will usually work best. This numeral is knitted in reverse stockinette (stocking) stitch, and while the effect is quite subtle, it works perfectly well.

PROJECT 1

BABY BLANKET

Welcome a new baby to the world with a crib blanket spelling out its name and birthday. This version is worked in seed (moss) stitch with stockinette (stocking) stitch panels for the letters and numbers, but you could easily work it in stockinette with just a seven-stitch seed border if you prefer.

Yarns
◎ **Rowan Cotton Glace:**
5 x 1¾ oz (50 g) balls in Clear (941) A
1 x 1¾ oz (50 g) ball in each of
Flower (943) B, Elf (946) C,
Café (980) D, and Pier (983) E

Letters
◎ Elegant Handwriting (see page 12)

Tools
◎ Pair of US 3 (3.25 mm) knitting needles
◎ Knitter's sewing needle

Measurements
◎ Approximately 18 x 28 in (46 x 70 cm)

Gauge (tension)
◎ 24 sts and 32 rows to 4 in (10 cm) over st st
using US 3 (3.25 mm) needles

Abbreviations
◎ See page 254.
◎ Note: use the intarsia method
(see page 243) throughout.

KEY

- A
- B
- C
- D
- E

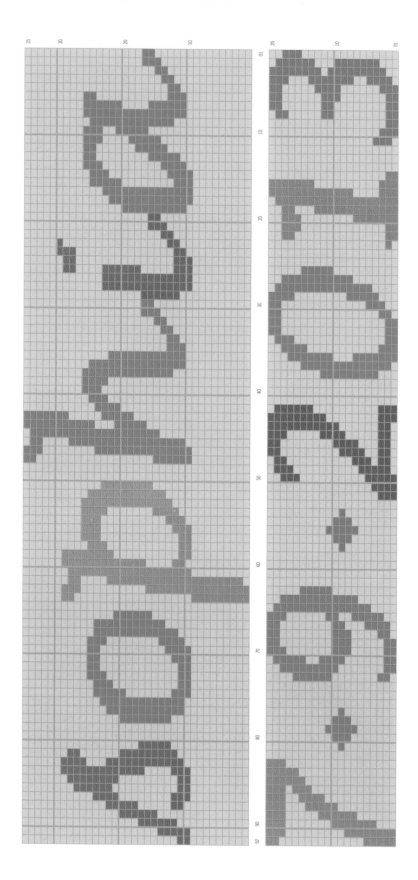

POSITIONING THE LETTERS

Some of the letters of Elegant Handwriting have little flourishes so that when the letters are butted up together, joined-up handwriting is formed. Those letters without the flourishes can just be equally spaced so that they fit in visually. With lowercase letters that have ascenders and descenders, you can refer to the original charts to see how they sit on a baseline in relation to one another. Simply adjust the width of the blanket or panels to accommodate the letters you require.

BLANKET

Using yarn A, cast on 112 sts.

Row 1 (RS): [K1, p1] to end of row.

Row 2: [P1, k1] to end of row.

Rows 1–2 form seed (moss) st.

Work 58 rows more in seed (moss) st.

Row 61: Seed (moss) 7, k to last 7 sts, seed (moss) 7.

Row 62: Seed (moss) 7, p to last 7 sts, seed (moss) 7.

Rep rows 61–62 once more.

PLACE CHART

Row 63: Seed (moss) 7, k3, place row 1 of date chart over next 92 sts, joining in separate balls of yarns B, C, D, and E as required, k3, seed (moss) 7.

Row 64: Seed (moss) 7, p3, place row 2 of date chart over next 92 sts, p3, seed (moss) 7.

Cont in patt as set until row 20 of date chart is completed.

Break yarns B, C, D, and E, and cont in yarn A.

Rep rows 61–62 twice more.

Work 44 rows in seed (moss) st only.

Work rows 61–62 twice more.

PLACE CHART

Row 215: Seed (moss) 7, k3, place row 1 of name chart over next 92 sts, joining in separate balls of yarns B, C, D, and E as required, k3, seed (moss) 7.

Row 216: Seed (moss) 7, p3, place row 2 of name chart over next 92 sts, p3, seed (moss) 7.

Cont in patt as set until row 24 of name chart is complete.

Break yarns B, C, D and E, and cont in yarn A.

Rep rows 61–62 twice more.

Work 60 rows in seed (moss) st.

Bind (cast) off.

TO MAKE UP

Weave in loose ends.

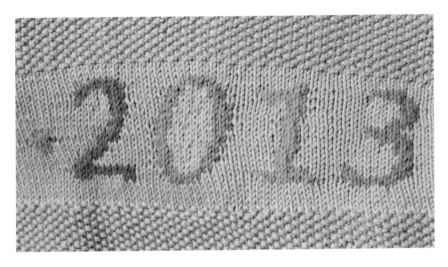

2

CELTIC

This alphabet is based on traditional Celtic handwritten letters, but styled and simplified a little to make them suitable, and easy, to knit. Developed by monks in the first centuries of Christianity, there are two main types of Celtic letters: angular and rounded. The ones shown here are the latter. Such bold shapes don't need a vibrant color palette; shades of just one color will work well, and what better color choice than green for Celtic letters. As these letters are quite open, the color-knitted swatches are worked using intarsia (see page 243) throughout, though you can strand (see page 246) across small gaps if you prefer.

Yarns used
◎ Cotton 4ply yarn in pale green
◎ Cotton DK yarn in apple green
◎ Fine mohair yarn in lime and dark green
◎ Metallic yarn in emerald
◎ Variegated sock yarn in greens
◎ Wool DK yarn in lime and dark green

Other materials
◎ Green cube beads
◎ Green large delica beads

Techniques used
◎ Intarsia (see page 243)
◎ Knitted-in beading (see page 251)

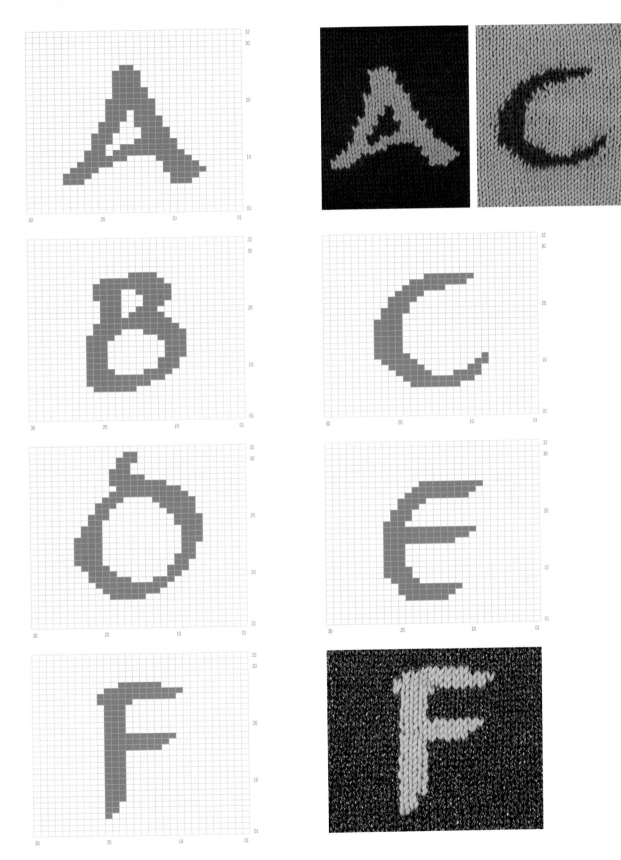

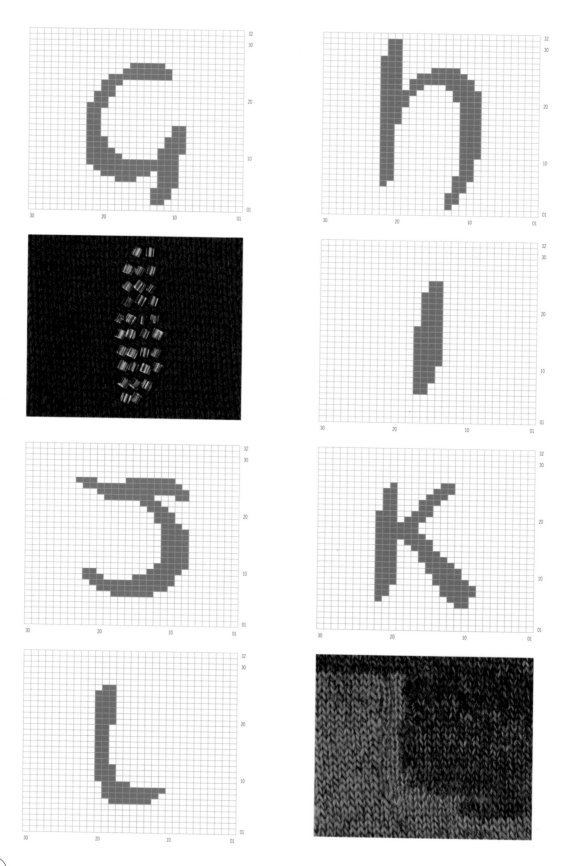

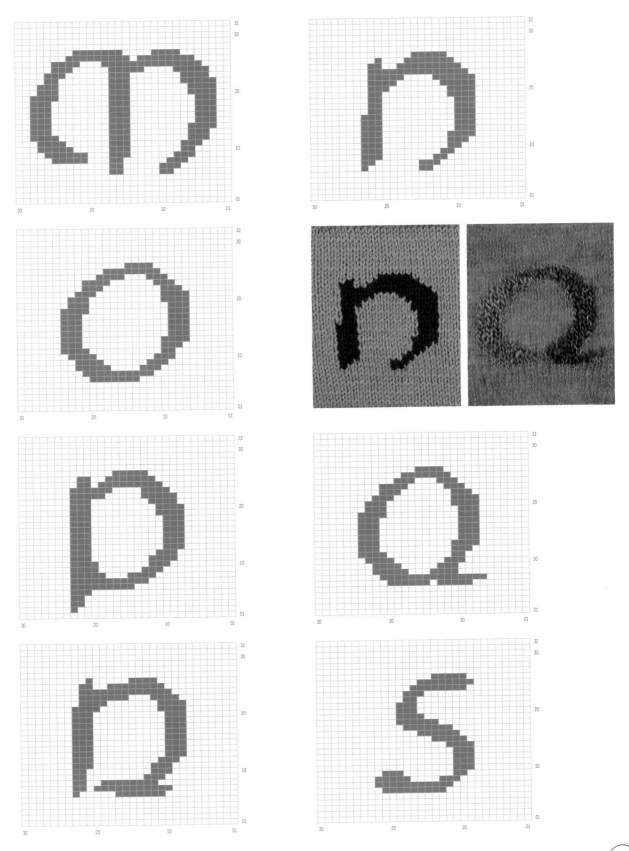

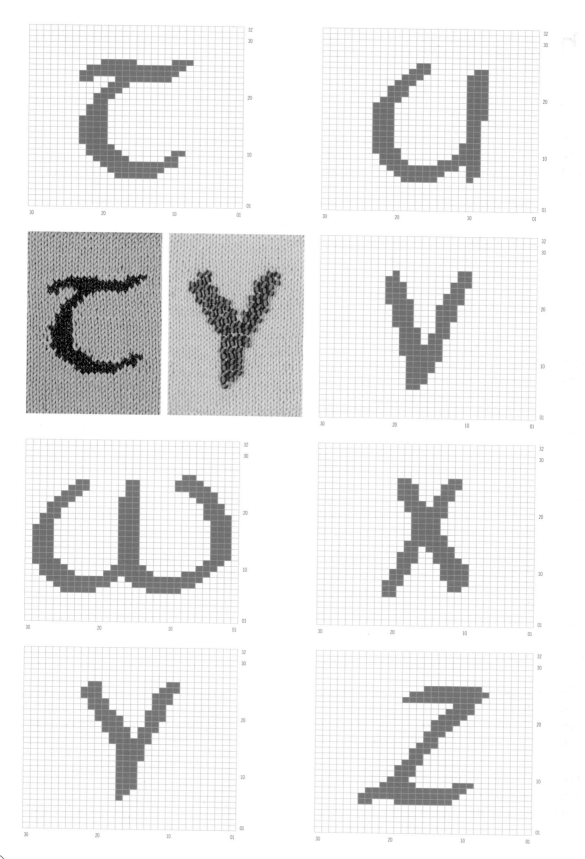

The Knitted Swatches

A This swatch is worked entirely in wool DK yarn. Wool is a naturally slightly elastic fiber, so it's easier to adjust the tension of individual stitches than it is with cotton yarn. Once the knitting is complete, any slightly uneven stitches can be eased out with the tip of a knitter's sewing needle (see page 249), and blocking the knitting will also improve the finish.

C Mixing fibers can make any project more visually interesting: here, a smooth cotton yarn is used for the background and a doubled fine mohair for the letter. The light texture of the mohair contrasts well with the smooth surface of the cotton, and the simple, bold, letter shape isn't blurred by the fuzzy yarn.

F This background is a metallic yarn and the letter a cotton 4ply yarn, which are similar enough in weight to be knitted together without having to double up either one. Remember to check that two yarns have compatible laundering requirements; a lukewarm hand wash in a no-rinse detergent will usually overcome any potential shrinkage issues, but it's worth washing a swatch before starting a sweater that you may never be able to clean.

I This letter is beaded using the knitted-in technique (see page 251), where a bead can be added to every stitch on every row as needed. There are only three restrictions on beads you can use (and shape isn't one of them, as these cube beads show): the hole in the bead must be large enough for doubled yarn to pass through, the bead cannot be larger than the knitted stitch, and if the project is going to need laundering, then the beads must be able to stand that.

L For this swatch a doubled fine mohair yarn is used to knit a letter on a background of a variegated sock yarn, one that has a very long color change; that is to say, the color changes very slowly along the length of the yarn. As this swatch was worked in intarsia, with a separate ball of yarn for each side of the letter (see page 243), the color difference either side of the letter is pronounced. Stranding (see page 246) the background yarn behind the letter would get around this problem.

N This swatch uses the same yarns as letter "A," but reversed, and the results look very different. Here, the dark letter recedes into the bright background instead of a bright letter floating on the dark background. Color and shade relationships can be subtle and complex, and it's always worth swatching two colors together before starting a project, just to check that the results are as you anticipated.

Q This is the same yarn combination as "L," but the background yarn is the fine mohair used as a single strand. This makes it a very different weight to the sock yarn used to knit the letter, and it takes serious color-knitting skills to achieve such a good-looking result as this. The main issues come when tensioning the stitches either side of the intarsia color change (see page 244), and weaving in the ends invisibly (see page 248).

T You might think that metallic yarns are stiff and unyielding—as the name suggests—but in fact they are usually very fluid and drape well. You can use them with stiffer yarns, such as the cotton 4ply used for the background here, but you should swatch the two together before starting a project to check that the different knitted fabrics will work together.

W The background yarn of this swatch is a fine mohair yarn that has been used double to make it a similar weight to the cotton yarn that the letter is knitted in. If you have never worked with doubled yarns, don't be put off: they twist around one another as you work, making it easy to treat them as a single strand, and with fluffy yarns such as this, it won't show if you miss one strand in a stitch.

Y This type of bead is called a delica; instead of being round or oval like a seed bead, they are tube-shaped. This means that, when used for knitted-in beading (see page 251) as here, they look quite wriggly, but as it's an overall wriggliness—rather than just an occasional bead askew—the result doesn't look as though you've knitted badly.

3

COMPUTER

The square shapes of these letters fit neatly into a grid and so allow this to be a very small-scale alphabet. Reminiscent of the early days of computers—blinking letters and chunky graphics—it has a pleasingly retro feel that's popular today, even with those not old enough to understand the origins of the letters. All the letters are based around a rectangle, so there are lots of straight vertical lines that need neat color changes to make them stand out clearly. If you struggle with this on the one-stitch lines, then knit the thicker lines and horizontals, stranding (see page 246) the background yarn behind them, and duplicate stitch (Swiss darn; see page 252) the thin lines.

Yarns used
◎ Cotton 4ply yarn in pale gray
◎ Metallic yarn in silver and black
◎ Variegated sock yarn in grays
◎ Wool/cotton blend 4ply yarn in pale gray and dark gray

Other materials
◎ Black beads
◎ Silver beads

Techniques used
◎ Intarsia (see page 243)
◎ Stranding (see page 246)
◎ Knitted-in beading (see page 251)
◎ Duplicate stitch (Swiss darning; see page 252)

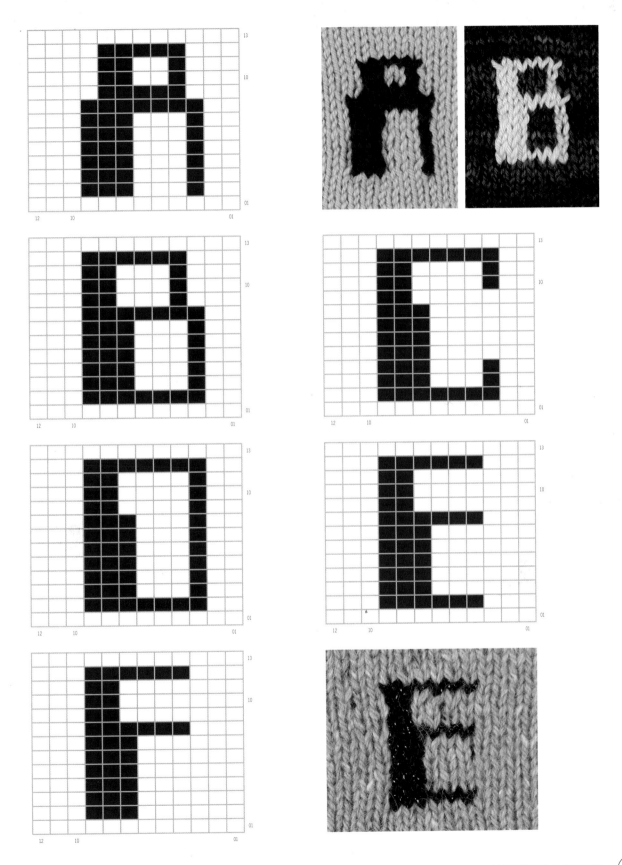

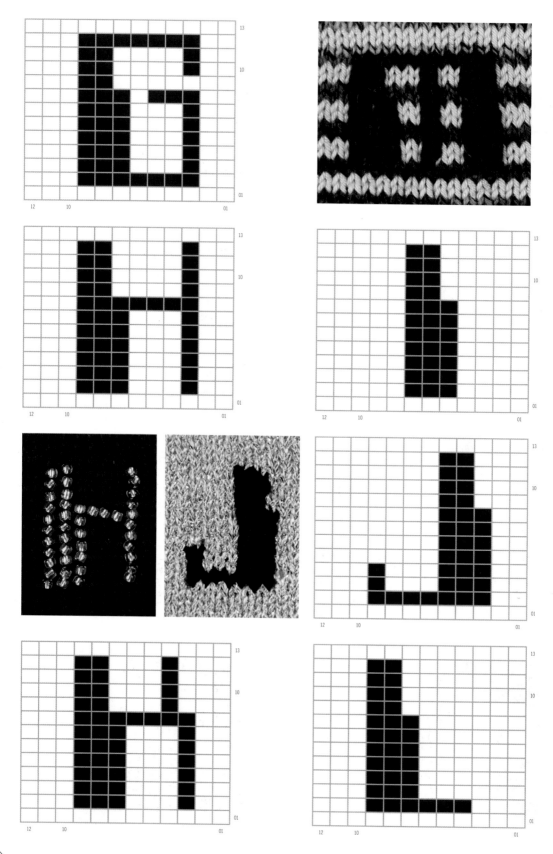

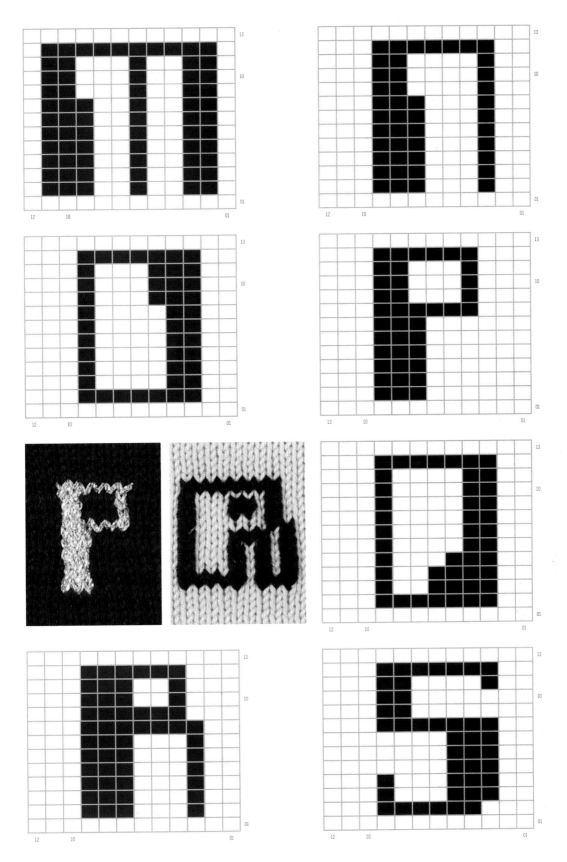

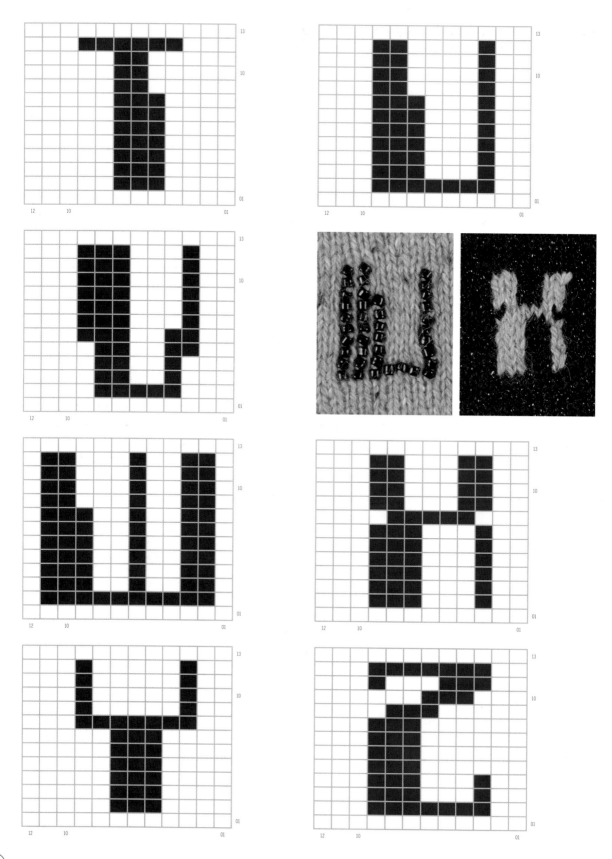

The Knitted Swatches

A A wool/cotton blend yarn in 4ply weight is used for the background and letter in this swatch. Using two yarns of the same type does make it relatively easy to tension the stitches evenly at the color changes, and so work neat color knitting, especially when the yarn has a little elasticity, as this wool/cotton does.

B The background of this letter is a variegated sock yarn and the letter is cotton 4ply, and as both yarns are about the same weight, they knit up well together. As the background yarn is stranded across the back of the letter, the stripes of color—which are short and random—continue either side: if the letter is worked in intarsia, this doesn't happen (see letter "C," Graffiti, page 37).

E The metallic yarn and felted tweed yarn used here are similar weights, but very different in texture and appearance, and the contrasts work well. They are also a good combination for beginners to color knitting, as the flecked surface of the tweed yarn and the glittering, wriggly surface of the metallic yarn are both very forgiving of any uneven stitches.

H This letter is beaded using the knitted-in technique (see page 251), where a bead can be added to every stitch on every row. With this technique, the beads sit at a slight angle on one "leg" of the stitch, so the columns look a bit wriggly, but that's the nature of this style of beading.

J Looking at it you might think that metallic yarn is scratchy against the skin, but this one is actually very soft. In addition, it has a lovely fluid drape and so would work well as a garment if you like a bit of sparkle. The letter is knitted in wool/cotton 4ply yarn that is a similar weight to the metallic background.

M The striped background of this swatch is made by knitting two-row stripes of plain pale gray wool/cotton 4ply and two-row stripes of variegated sock yarn, the latter making the result "extra stripy." The letter is duplicate stitched (Swiss darned; see page 252) in black wool/cotton 4ply.

P This is the same yarn combination as letter "J," but reversed. If you find full-on metallic yarns a bit much used in quantities, try them as smaller accents in a project; just one or two letters in a name or word maybe, with the other letters knitted in a non-metallic yarn of the same color.

R Duplicate stitch (Swiss darning; see page 252) can be used just to outline a shape, as well as to fill it in. Outlining like this can change the look of a letter quite a lot, so it's always worth working a sample letter on your gauge (tension) swatch if you're contemplating outlining on a project.

U Beads come in many varieties, but as long as they conform to three rules, you can knit with them: the hole in the bead must be large enough for doubled yarn to pass through (see page 249); the bead cannot be larger than the knitted stitch; and if the project is going to need laundering, the beads must be able to stand that. These beads are handmade and vary slightly in shape and size, making the letter look a little wobbly.

X This swatch uses the same yarn combination as letter "E," with the positions reversed. Today, many yarns are treated to be machine washable, but check that two different fibers can be laundered together. If in doubt, machine wash a swatch. = more than the other it will be very visible, and you'll need to hand wash the project.

4

GRAFFITI

Scrawled across grimy walls or daubed onto buildings, these letters may well cause frowns, but knitted in bold colors they are much more likely to be appreciated. The contemporary, urban styling makes them suitable for projects for boys as well as girls, and the chunky shapes and random angles make them very easy to knit. The limited yarn palette used shows the variety that can be achieved with just a few different fibers, and the vibrant variegated yarn—reminiscent of crazily sprayed paint—gives lots of colors with just plain knitting. If you are color knitting, work the letters in intarsia (see page 243), although you can strand (see page 246) across small gaps if you prefer.

Yarns used
◎ Fine mohair yarn in green
◎ Variegated sock yarn in multicolors
◎ Wool/cotton blend 4ply yarn in black and green

Other materials
◎ Black beads
◎ Multicolored beads

Techniques used
◎ Intarsia (see page 243)
◎ Stranding (see page 246)
◎ Knitted-in beading (see page 251)
◎ Duplicate stitch (Swiss darning; see page 252)

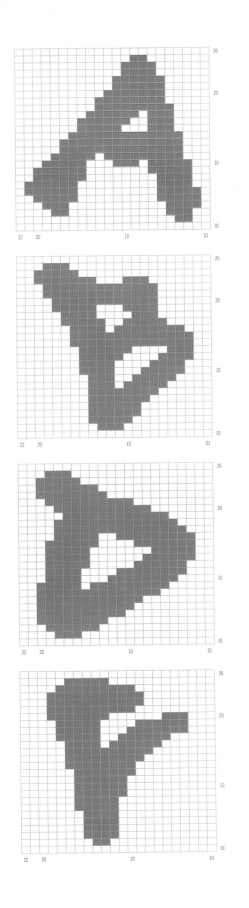

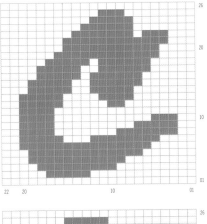

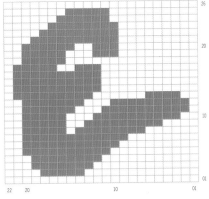

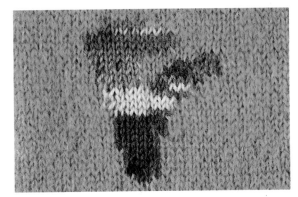

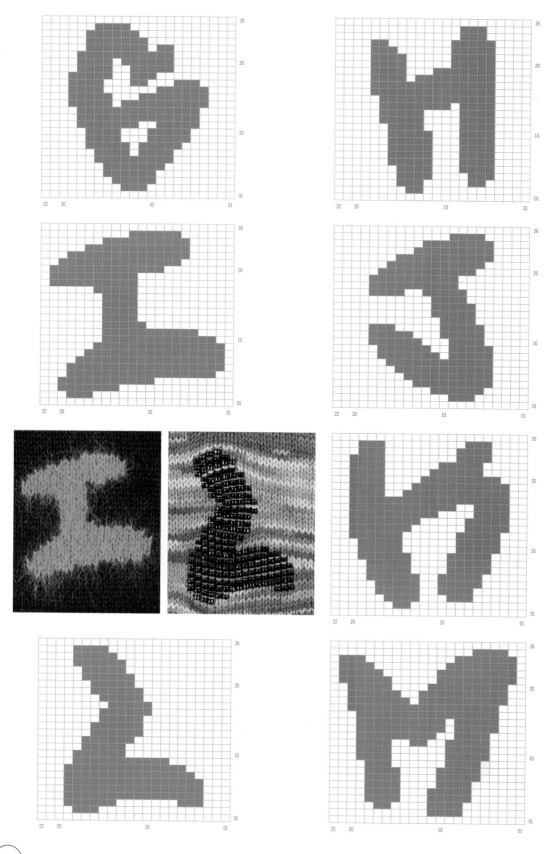

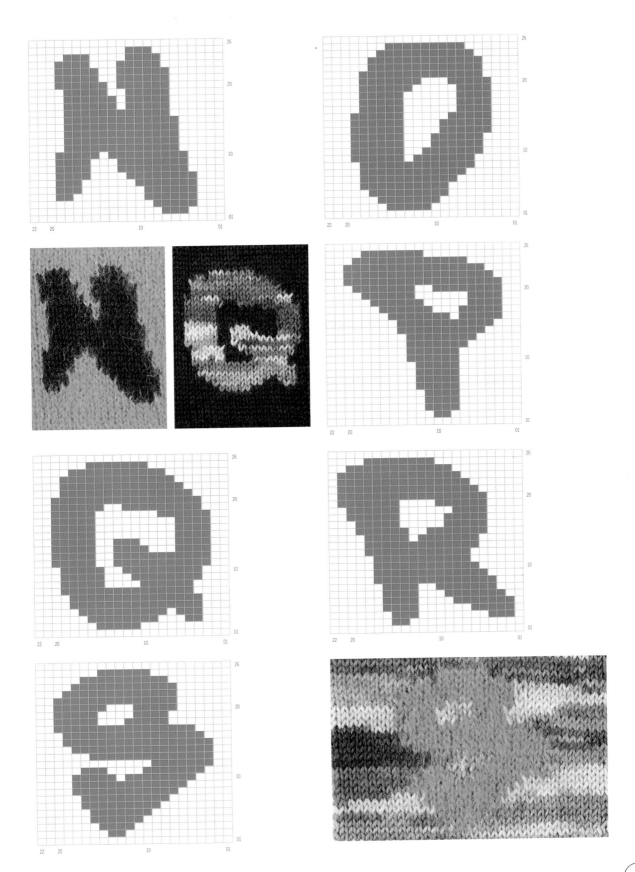

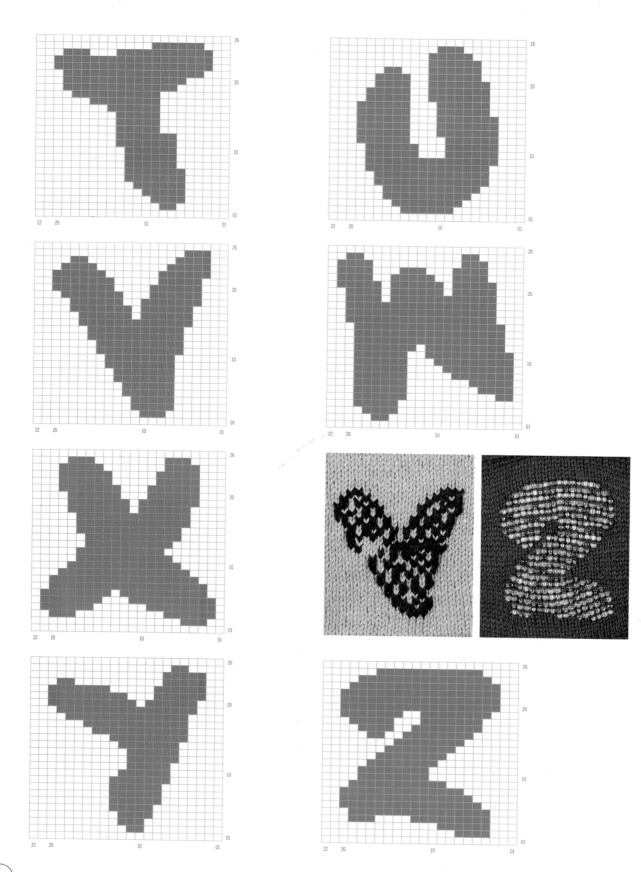

The Knitted Swatches

A } The chunky shapes of these letters make them easy to knit. There are no single color stitches to try to tension correctly, so knitting this alphabet in relatively unforgiving smooth yarns is very doable. Here, two colors of a wool/cotton 4ply yarn have been used, although these letters would also work well in thicker yarns (see Messenger Bag, page 42).

C } This vivid variegated yarn knits up to give a feel of spray-painted walls where newly sprayed tags overlap old ones, and so it suits Graffiti very well. As this letter is worked in intarsia (see page 243), the background colors don't continue either side of the letter, but the striping is so random that it doesn't look odd. You need a strong solid color to make a letter stand out on this background.

F } The background yarn of this swatch is a fine mohair and it's been used double to make it a similar weight to the sock yarn that the letter is knitted in. If you have never worked with doubled yarns, don't be put off: they twist around one another as you work, making it easy to treat them as a single strand, and with fluffy yarns such as this, it won't show if you miss one strand in a stitch.

I } Here, the fine mohair is doubled, as in the previous swatch, and is used to knit a letter on a background of wool/cotton 4ply yarn. The light texture of the mohair contrasts well with the smooth matte surface of the wool/cotton, and the chunkiness of the letter shape isn't blurred by the fuzz.

L } This letter is beaded using the knitted-in technique (see page 251), where a bead can be added to every stitch on every row. The beads are a little too large for the stitches so there is some distortion of the knitting: you can see how the variegated stripes bend at the top and bottom of the letter. The effect on the randomly colored background looks okay, but generally it is better to use a bead that is a little smaller than the stitch.

N } Here, the same yarns as letter "I" have been used, but the positions are reversed. Today, many yarns are treated to be machine washable, but check that the two different fibers can be laundered together. If in doubt, machine wash a swatch. If one fiber shrinks more than the other it will be very visible, and you'll need to hand wash the project.

Q } This swatch reverses the positions of the yarns in letter "C," producing a very different look. Instead of a bold shape floating on a colored background, this letter looks as though a Q-shaped hole has been cut in the black background and the colors are peeking through it. It's always worth swapping the positions of planned colors when swatching, just to see what happy accidents might occur (and to avoid less-than-interesting combinations).

S } Here, the variegated yarn is used for the background, but the letter is worked in doubled fine mohair. The green color is just about strong enough to make the letter visible, but only just: a stronger or more contrasting color would be better. This can often be a problem with variegated yarns, as they look quite different knitted up to how they do in the ball, and what works with them in the ball might not in the knitting.

V } For this swatch the yarns used on the letter "A" are swapped over, so that the green is the background. The letter is duplicate stitched (Swiss darned; see page 252) in black, but the whole shape is not filled in: the effect is scratchy, although the letter is recognizable enough as the outline is almost solid and the color contrast is very strong.

Z } For this gorgeous letter, different colored beads were threaded onto the yarn at random, then the letter was beaded using the knitted-in technique (see page 251), so a bead appears on every stitch and row where it is needed. As long as all the beads are a similar size—these are not identical—then the technique will work beautifully.

PROJECT 2

MESSENGER BAG

Put graffiti to good use by using it to lay claim to a good-looking and practical bag. This version is lined with striped ticking fabric to make it super-sturdy, although any medium-weight fashion or furnishing fabric would work well, and the strap can have an extra lining layer of cotton tape or webbing (placed between the knitting and the fabric) for strength if needed.

Yarns
◎ **Rowan Summerspun**
4 x 1¾ oz (50 g) balls in Holborn (110) A
◎ **Rowan Handknit Cotton**
1 x 1¾ oz (50 g) ball in Rosso (215) B

Letters
◎ Graffiti (see page 36)

Tools
◎ Pair of US 5 (3.75 mm) knitting needles
◎ Knitter's sewing needle
◎ Approximately 35 x 20 in (90 x 50 cm) of
medium-weight cotton fabric for lining
◎ Sewing machine
◎ Sewing thread to match yarn A

Measurements
◎ Approximately 13½ in (34 cm) wide
and 17¼ in (44 cm) deep

Gauge (tension)
◎ 21 sts and 30 rows to 4 in (10 cm) over st st using
Rowan Summerspun and US 5 (3.75 mm) needles

Abbreviations
◎ See page 254.
◎ Note: use the intarsia method
(see page 243) throughout.

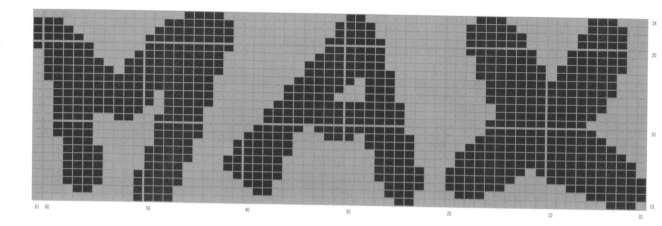

61 60   50   40   30   20   10   01

KEY

 – A

– B

POSITIONING THE LETTERS

The varying angles and sloping sides of the letters in Graffiti mean that you need to consider how to space them. Here, the "M" and "A" overlap by a stitch, whereas there's a clear two-stitch gap between "A" and "X." To position your own choice of letters, photocopy them then cut them out roughly, allowing a border of chart squares all around. Lay the letters out and slide them into the best positions, aligning the rows of the border squares as desired. Tape them together to make your chart.

BAG

(worked in one piece starting at front flap)

Using yarn A, cast on 75 sts.

Row 1 (WS): K1, [p1, k1] to end of row.

Rep row 1, 6 more times.

Row 8 (RS): [K1, p1] twice, k to last 4 sts, [p1, k1] twice.

Row 9: K1, [p1, k1] twice, p to last 5 sts, [k1, p1] twice, k1.

Rows 8–9 set patt of st st with 5-st seed (moss) stitch border.

Rep rows 8–9 twice more.

PLACE CHART

Row 14: [K1, p1] twice, k3, place row 1 of chart over next 61 sts, joining in separate balls of yarn B as required, k3, [p1, k1] twice.

Row 15: K1, [p1, k1] twice, p2, place row 2 of chart over next 61 sts, p2, [k1, p1] twice, k1.

Cont in patt as set until row 24 of chart is complete.

Break yarn B and cont in yarn A.

Rep rows 8–9 until work measures 17 in (43 cm).

BASE OF BAG

Next row: K1, [p1, k1] to end of row.

Rep last row 7 more times.

FRONT OF BAG

Rep rows 8–9 until work measures 29 in (73 cm).

Bind (cast) off knitwise on WS of work.

STRAP

Using yarn A, cast on 7 sts.

Row 1 (RS): K1, [p1, k1] to end of row.

Rep row 1 until work measures 68 in (174 cm) or length desired.

Bind (cast) off knitwise on WS of work.

TO MAKE UP

- Weave in loose ends.
- Block knitted pieces.
- Cut a rectangle of fabric 1¼ in (3 cm) longer and 2 in (5 cm) wider than the knitted bag piece. Set this aside.
- Join strips of fabric to make a strap lining ¾ in (2 cm) wider and longer than knitted strap piece. Press under ³/₈ in (1 cm) at each short end and ½ in (1.2 cm) along each long edge of the lining, so that it is slightly narrower than the knitted strap. Wrong sides facing, pin the lining to the strap and machine sew or hand sew it in place (we machine sewed using a narrow zigzag stitch for strength and a walking foot to help feed the layers through evenly).
- Using yarn A, the knitter's sewing needle, and whip stitch, and with RS together, sew one end of the strap to one end of the seed (moss) base of the bag. Sew the front of the bag to one side of the strap, sewing from the bag base to the bound (cast) off edge. Sew the back of the bag to the other side of the strap, stopping level with the bound (cast) off edge. Repeat at the other end of the strap. Turn bag RS out.
- Press under ⅝ in (1.5 cm) at each short end of the bag lining, then fold it RS together to match the shape of the knitted bag. Taking a ³/₈ in (1 cm) seam allowance, machine sew the side seams. Press the seam allowances under along the edges of the flap lining to fit the width of the flap.
- WS together, put the lining inside the bag. Using a sewing needle and thread, slip stitch the lining in place all around.

5

80s RETRO

The 80s—sometimes called "the decade that taste forgot," sometimes called "the designer decade"; I guess it just depends on where you were standing fashionwise. Whichever your perspective, these letters, and the primary color palette, are reminiscent of a decade of high tech and sleek shapes. Other palettes that would work well would be black and white—white letters on a black background, especially—and hot pink and cool gray. As the strokes of the letters are thin, you may find it easiest to strand (see page 246) the background yarn right across the backs of the letters, as was done here.

Yarns used
◎ Fine mohair yarn in red and yellow
◎ Metallic yarn in red
◎ Tweed DK yarn in yellow
◎ Wool/cotton blend DK yarn in red
◎ Wool DK yarn in red and yellow

Other materials
◎ None

Techniques used
◎ Intarsia (see page 243)
◎ Stranding (see page 246)

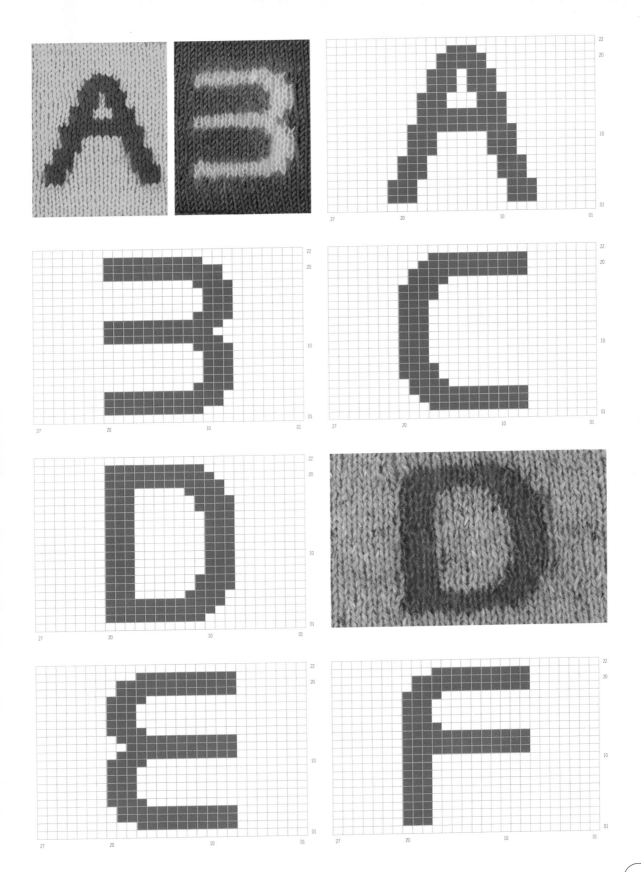

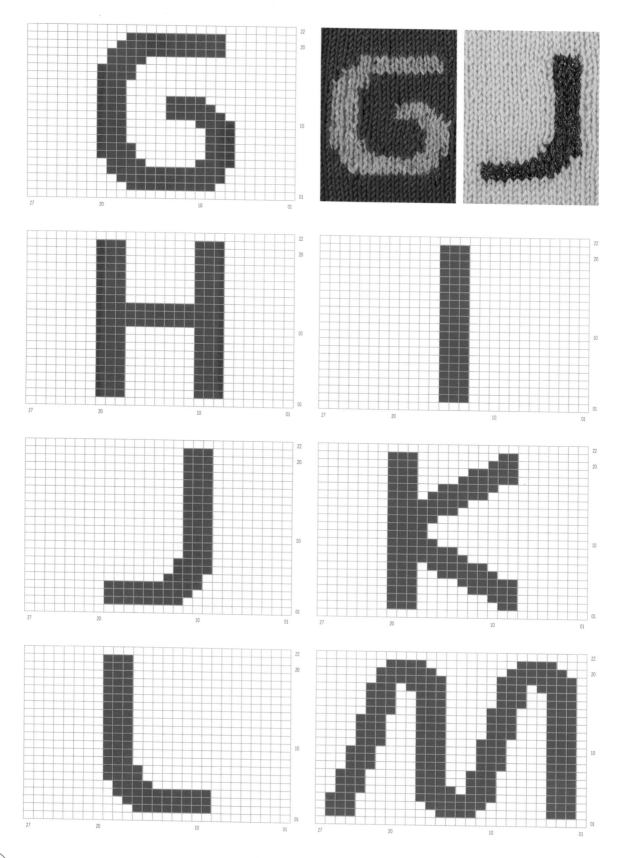

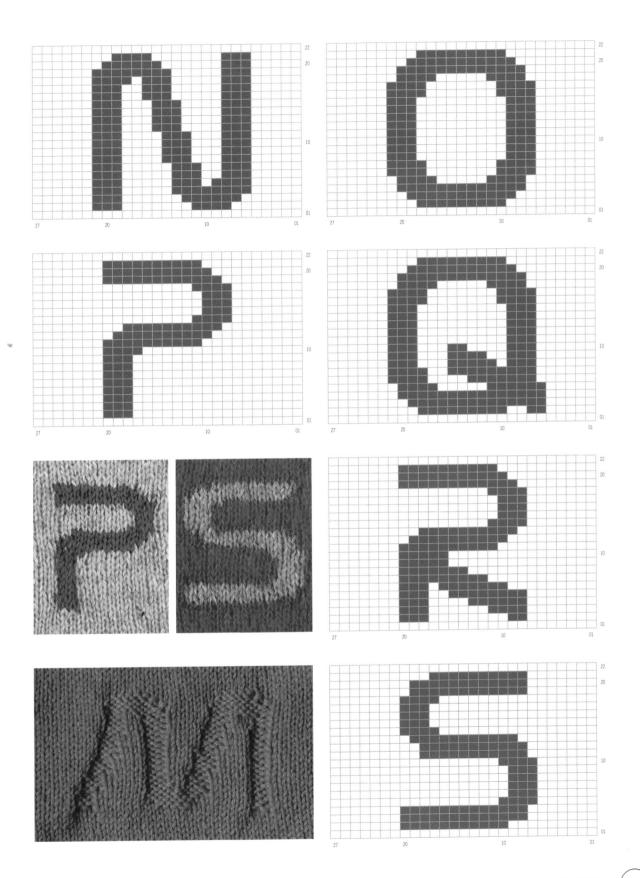

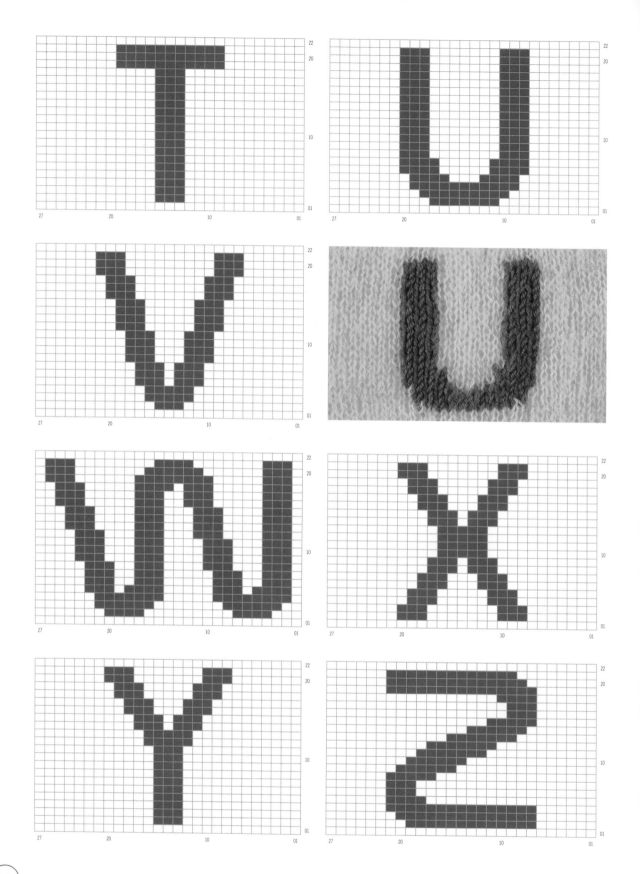

The Knitted Swatches

A This swatch is worked entirely in wool DK yarn. Wool is a naturally slightly elastic fiber, so it's easier to adjust the tension of individual stitches than it is with cotton yarn. Once the knitting is complete, any slightly uneven stitches can be eased out with the tip of a knitter's sewing needle (see page 249), and blocking the knitting will also improve the finish.

B The light texture of the mohair used for this letter contrasts well with the smooth matte surface of the wool/cotton background, and the simplicity of the letter shape isn't blurred by the fuzz.

D The letter of this swatch is knitted in a fine mohair and it's been used double to make it a similar weight to the tweed yarn of the background. If you have never worked with doubled yarn, don't be put off: the strands twist around one another as you work, making it easy to treat them as a single strand, and with fluffy yarn such as this, it won't show if you miss one strand in a stitch.

G Here, the letter is in tweed and the background in a wool/cotton blend yarn. Today, many yarns are treated to be machine washable, but check that the two different fibers can be laundered together. If in doubt, machine-wash a swatch. If one fiber shrinks more than the other it will be very visible, and you'll need to hand wash the project.

J Metallic yarns might look a bit tricky, but they are actually easy to knit with, and the wriggly, sparkly surface is visually very forgiving of any uneven stitches, so this can be an excellent yarn to use if you are a beginner to color knitting. Here, the letter is in a red metallic on a plain wool DK background.

M You can also work letters in texture, though it might take a bit of planning: simpler textures and bolder shapes will usually work best. This letter is knitted in reverse stockinette (stocking) stitch, and is subtle but effective.

P Tweed yarns are usually one dominant color with flecks of other colors, sometimes very bright, contrasting flecks. You can use these flecks to pick up colors used in another part of a project, or in another garment or accessory worn with a knitted tweed piece.

S This swatch uses the same yarns as letter "D," but reversed. This combination is quite forgiving of uneven stitches—the fluffy yarn hides them and the flecked tweed yarn disguises them—so it's one to try if your color knitting is still at the improving stage.

U For this swatch the same yarns as letter "B" are used, but the positions are swapped. Mixing fibers can make any project more visually interesting, but when making a large project with different fibers, always buy just a ball of each yarn first and knit a swatch to check that the combination works as you hope.

Y Here, the same yarns as letter "J" have been used, but reversed. Swapping colors like this works very well on an afghan: choose a limited palette and work blocks in all the possible variations to create a finished piece that's colorful, but also restrained. You can use different fibers to add textural variety.

6

CALLIGRAPHY

Calligraphy is, in essence, handwriting made art, and the gloriously elegant, swooping letters of this alphabet interpret that art into knitted stitches. Simplified from the intricacies of some calligraphy in order not to drive knitters entirely crazy, the letters are no more tricky to knit than any others in this book. There are both uppercase and lowercase letters here, in scale to one another so that they can be combined easily into a single word or message. The color-knitting swatches were knitted in intarsia (see page 243), although you can strand (see page 246) across small gaps if you prefer.

Yarns used
- Cotton/linen blend yarn in purple
- Fine mohair yarn in plum
- Metallic yarn in silver
- Tweed DK yarn in gray
- Wool/cotton blend DK yarn in pale gray
- Wool DK yarn in purple

Other materials
- Purple beads

Techniques used
- Intarsia (see page 243)
- Stranding (see page 246)
- Knitted-in beading (see page 251)
- Duplicate stitch (Swiss darning; see page 252)

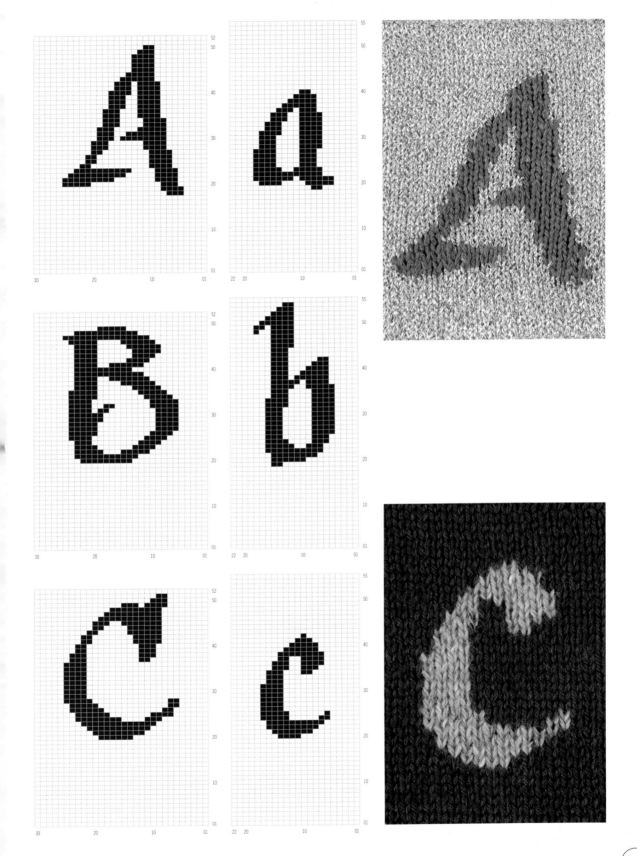

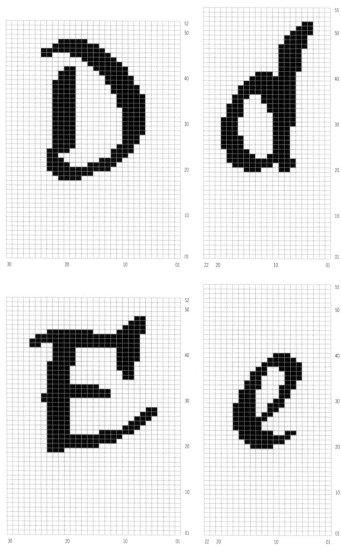

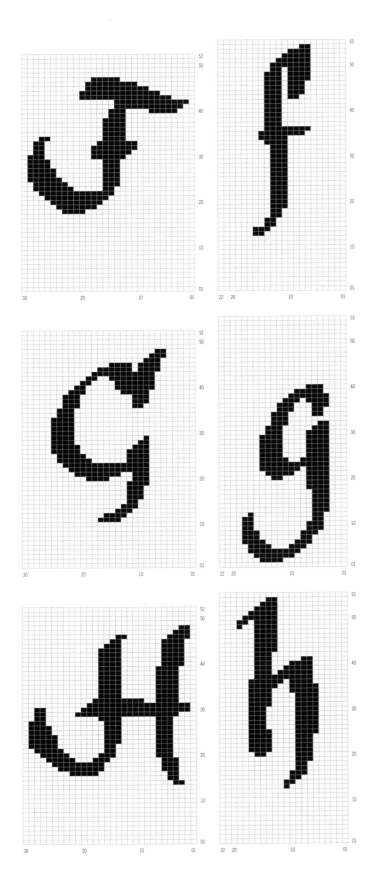

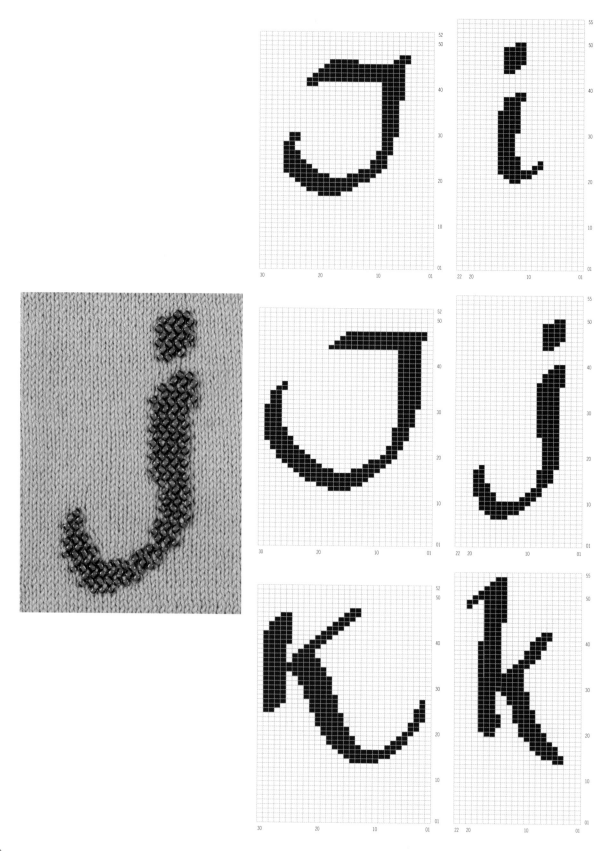

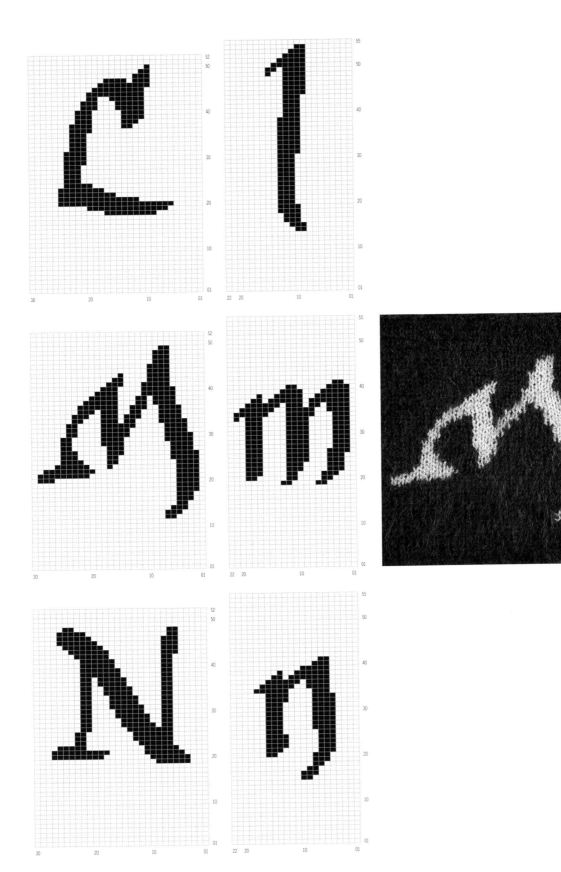

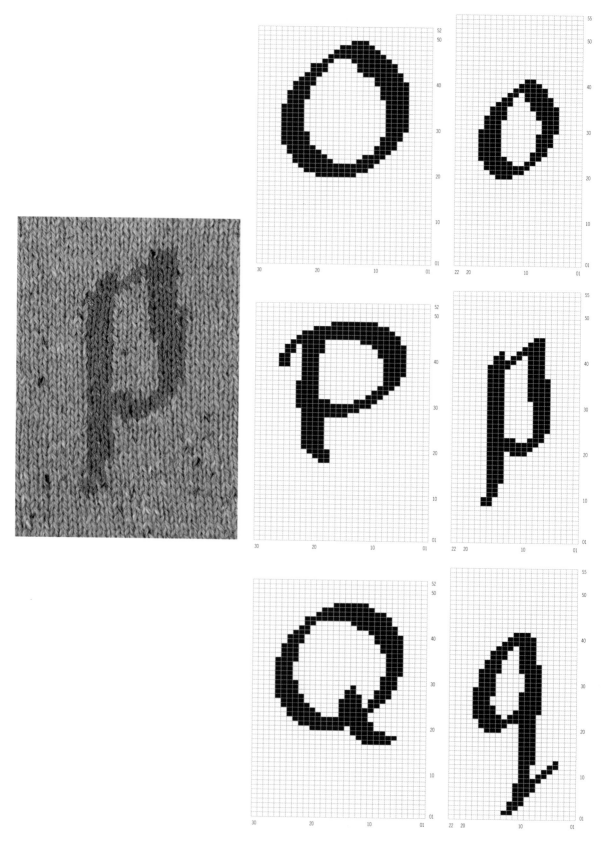

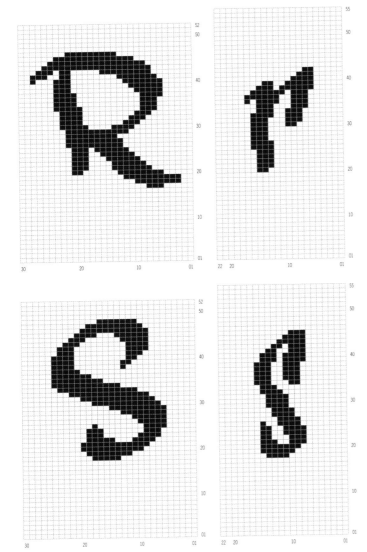

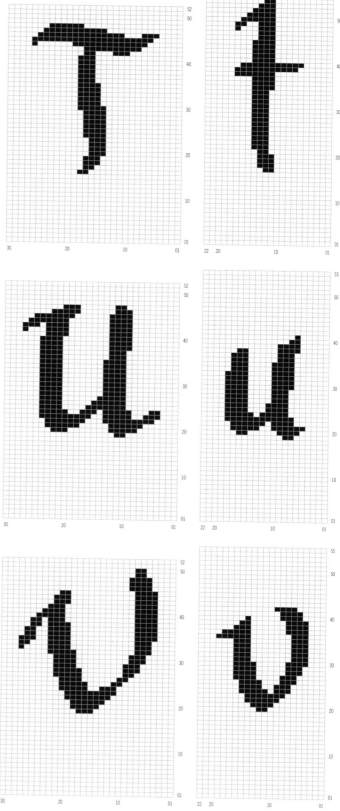

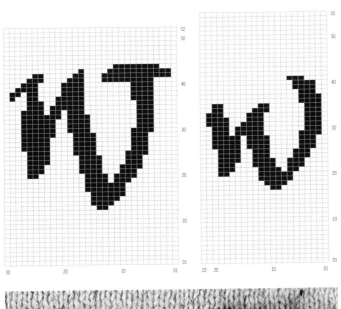

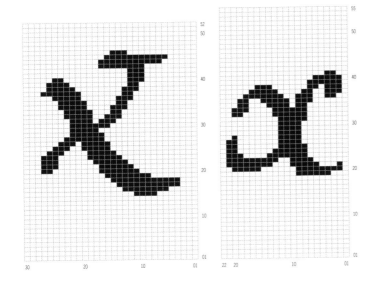

The Knitted Swatches

A The uppercase "A" is in a cotton/linen blend yarn that has a sheen that enhances the naturally rather uneven fabric because it reflects the light. The background is metallic yarn, which has a glittering, wriggly surface. Both yarns are quite forgiving of uneven stitches as they just get lost in the natural irregularities, so this is a combination a novice color knitter might try.

C Double-knitting weight yarns are probably the most commonly available weight and there are many, many fiber and textural variations. Here, the background is a plain wool DK yarn and the lowercase "C" is knitted in a wool tweed DK. Using two yarns of the same weight does make it relatively easy to tension the stitches evenly at the color changes, and so work neat color knitting, especially when the yarn has a little elasticity, as these wool yarns do.

F The background of this swatch is knitted in one strand of fine mohair and one strand of metallic yarn held together, which is a thick enough combination to work with the wool DK used to knit the uppercase "F." Mixing the mohair with the metallic tones down the bling factor quite a bit, but allows for a subtle sparkle that's very pleasing.

J This lowercase "J" is beaded using the knitted-in technique (see page 251), where a bead can be added to every stitch on every row. However, as the beads are a little larger than the stitch, they are placed on different "legs" of the stitches on alternate rows. To do this, work the purl rows as normal, then, before starting the knit row, slide all the beads along the stitch they are on and over the needle to the back. Then knit the row, placing the beads in the usual way. The beads that were moved will be sitting on the left-hand "leg" and those knitted on the right-hand "leg." This gives each bead a bit more room, and produces the herringbone pattern.

M This swatch has a background of fine mohair used double to make it a similar weight to the metallic yarn used for the uppercase "M." This is another combination that is quite forgiving of uneven stitches—the fluffy yarn hides them and the wriggly metallic yarn disguises them—so it's one to tackle if your color knitting is still at the improving stage.

P This swatch is knitted in a tweed DK with a cotton/linen blend that is a slightly lighter weight for the lowercase "P." Remember to check that two yarns have compatible laundering requirements before knitting them together. A lukewarm hand wash in a no-rinse detergent will usually overcome any potential shrinkage issues, but it's worth washing a swatch before starting a sweater that you may never be able to clean.

R This uppercase "R" is worked in the same yarn combination as letter "F," but the positions are swapped. If you've never knitted with two different yarns held together, don't be scared by the idea: they will quickly twist around one another to create a single strand, and the naturally mottled surface means that should you miss one of the yarns for a stitch, it won't show.

T For this swatch, the same yarns as letter "A" are used, but the positions are swapped so the lowercase "T" is in the metallic yarn. If you find metallic yarns a little gaudy in quantities, try them as smaller accents in a project; just one or two letters in a name or word, with the other letters knitted in a non-metallic yarn of the same color.

W Doubling up a finer yarn—or using two fine yarns held together—to make a strand the same weight as a thicker yarn is perfectly viable. Here, the uppercase "W" is knitted in doubled fine mohair on a background of DK tweed. The doubled mohair is a little lighter in weight than the tweed, but not enough to make the knitting very tricky; just be careful when tensioning the stitches at the color changes.

Z This lowercase "Z" is duplicate stitched (Swiss darned; see page 252) in a wool/cotton blend yarn onto a background of a cotton/linen blend yarn. This embroidery stitch can be worked horizontally or vertically, and it's worth experimenting on a swatch of stockinette (stocking) stitch to see if you find one direction easier to work than the other.

7

TYPEWRITER

Those of us of a certain age will feel very nostalgic looking at this alphabet: we'll remember little keys that you had to strike really quite hard to make a metal stalk shoot up and whack onto your paper to produce a printed letter that looked just like those shown here. However, despite the fact that typewriters are no longer part of our daily lives, this is a truly timeless font and to make it extra-versatile, there are numbers to go with it (see page 70). As the strokes of the letters are quite thin, you may find it easiest to strand (see page 246) the background yarn right across the backs of the letters, depending on the yarns you are using.

Yarns used
- Cotton 4ply yarn in orange
- Fine mohair yarn in orange and blue
- Merino/silk blend DK yarn in orange and blue
- Metallic yarn in blue
- Wool/cotton blend DK yarn in orange and blue

Other materials
- Blue beads

Techniques used
- Intarsia (see page 243)
- Stranding (see page 246)
- Knitted-in beading (see page 251)
- Duplicate stitch (Swiss darning; see page 252)

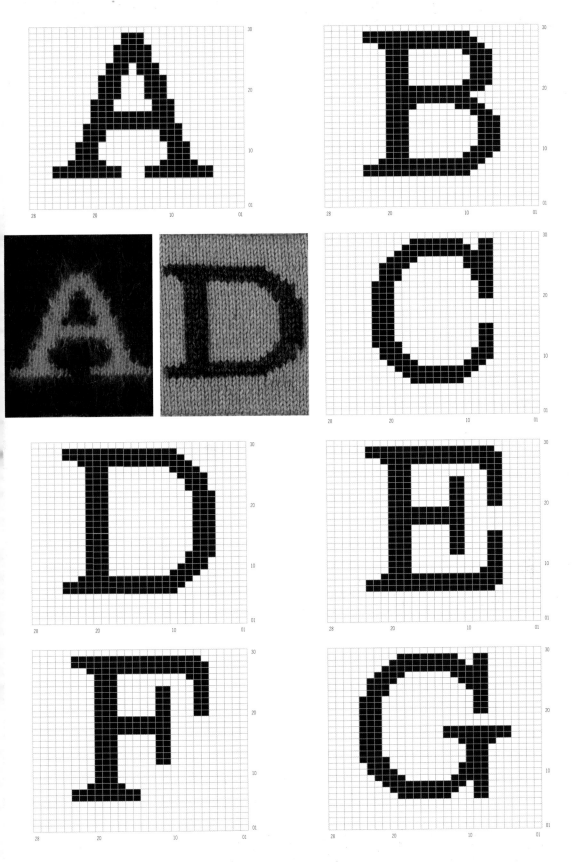

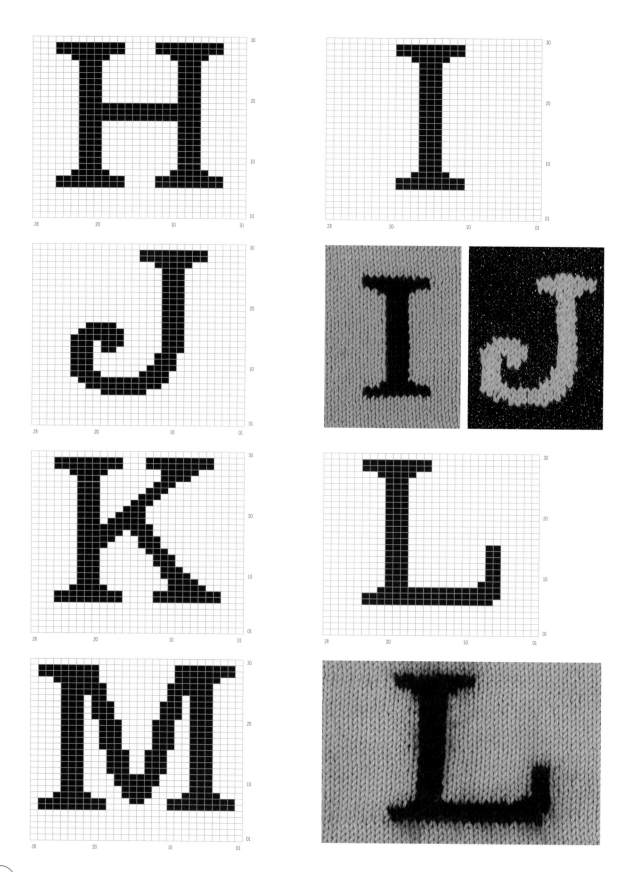

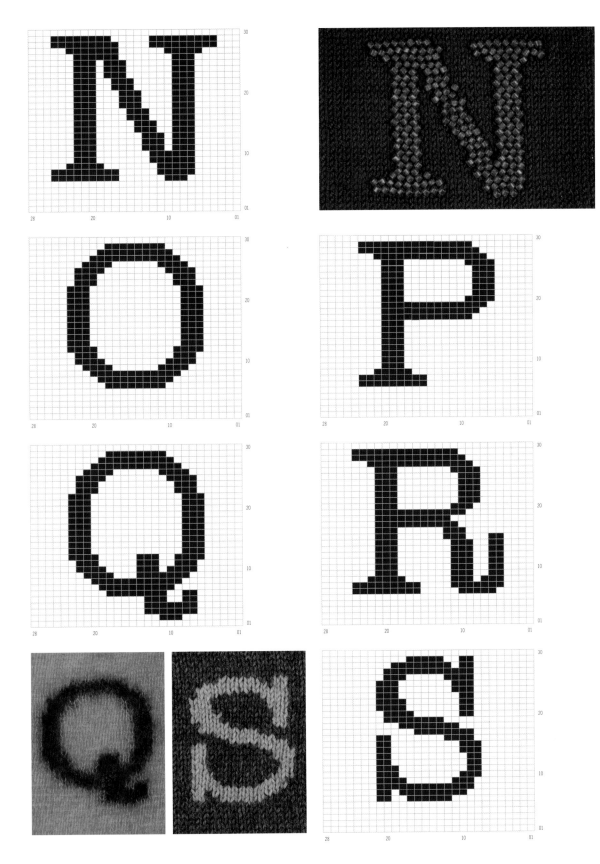

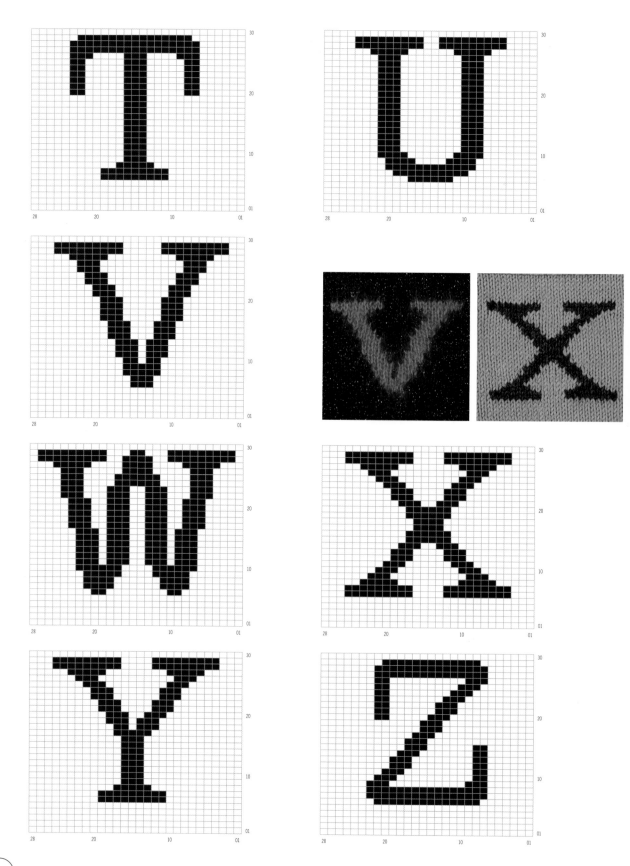

The Knitted Swatches

A This swatch is knitted entirely in fine mohair yarn used doubled. When you are knitting with fuzzy yarns, it's best to work using the intarsia method (see page 243) and not strand either yarn across the back of the other. This is because the fuzz of the stranded color can creep through the stitches and show as a blur on the front of the knitting.

D This letter is duplicate stitched (Swiss darned; see page 252) in the same weight yarn as was used to knit the background: both are merino/silk DK with a slightly mottled finish. When working a whole letter in duplicate stitch, be careful to keep the embroidery at a similar tension to the knitting; if you pull the embroidery yarn too tight, it won't cover the background neatly and the fabric will be distorted.

J Mixing fibers can make any project more visually interesting: here, a smooth cotton yarn is used for the letter and a metallic for the background. The smooth sheen of the cotton contrasts well with the sparkle, and as both yarns are a similar weight they knit up easily together. When making a large project with different fibers, always buy just a ball of each yarn first and knit a swatch to check that the combination works.

I A wool/cotton blend yarn in DK weight is used for the background and letter in this swatch. Using two yarns of the same type does make it relatively easy to tension the stitches evenly at the color changes, and so work neat color knitting, especially when the yarn has a little elasticity, as this wool/cotton does.

L Doubling up a finer yarn to make a strand the same weight as a thicker yarn is perfectly viable, and here the letter is knitted in doubled fine mohair on a background of cotton 4ply. Used this way the weights of the two yarns are similar, though the nature of them is entirely different and you need to take care to work the color changes neatly, with no baggy stitches.

N This letter is beaded using the knitted-in technique (see page 251), where a bead can be added to every stitch on every row. However, as the beads are a little larger than the stitch, they are placed on different "legs" of the stitches on alternate rows. To do this, work the purl rows as normal, then before starting the knit row, slide all the beads along the stitch they are on and over the needle to the back. Then knit the row, placing the beads in the usual way. The beads that were moved will be sitting on the left-hand "leg" and those knitted on the right-hand "leg." This gives each bead a bit more room, and produces the herringbone pattern.

Q For this swatch, the same yarn combination as letter "A" is used, but the positions of the yarns are swapped, and only one strand is used. Working with such a fine yarn takes serious color-knitting skills to achieve a result as good-looking as this, and you have to be extra careful when weaving in the ends to prevent any contrast showing in the wrong place on the front.

S Here, the same yarns as swatch "D" are used, but the colors are reversed and the letter is knitted rather than duplicate stitched (Swiss darned). Swapping colors like this works very well on an afghan: choose a limited palette and work blocks in all the possible variations to create a finished piece that's colorful, but also restrained. You can choose a two-color palette and use different fibers to add variety.

V A glitter and texture combination: the letter is two strands of mohair held together and the background is a single strand of metallic yarn. Remember to check that two yarns have compatible laundering requirements before knitting them together. If in doubt, machine wash a swatch. If one fiber shrinks more than the other it will be very visible, and you'll need to hand wash the project.

X This swatch uses two wool-blend yarns: a wool/cotton and a merino/silk. If you are a beginner to color knitting, then choosing yarns with a wool content is a good idea as it is a naturally slightly elastic fiber, so it's easier to adjust the tension of individual stitches than it is with cotton yarn. Once the knitting is complete, any slightly uneven stitches can be evened out with the tip of a knitter's sewing needle (see page 249).

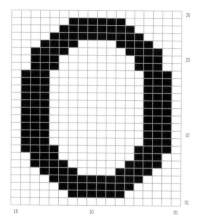

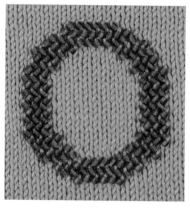

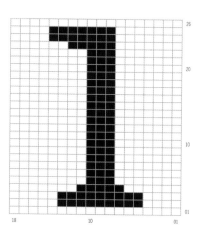

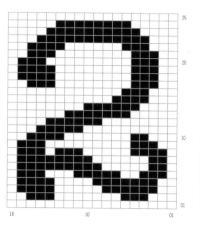

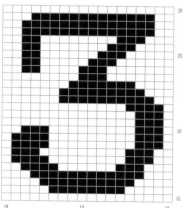

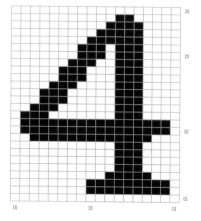

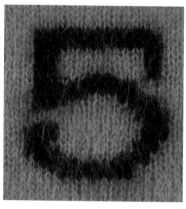

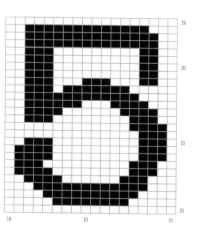

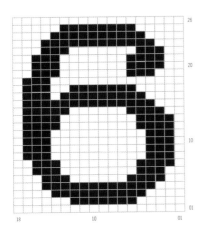

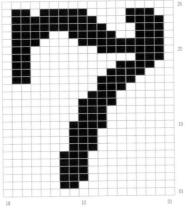

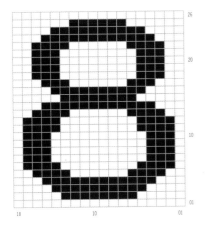

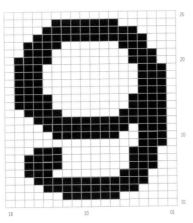

O} This swatch is worked in the same way as letter "N," using the same beads. However, as the beads are translucent, the color of the yarn passing through them changes the bead color. In this instance the result works, but depending on the colors of both elements, and how translucent the beads are, you can end up with an unattractive result, so work a swatch before starting a project.

3} Metallic yarns might look a bit tricky, but they are actually easy to knit with, and the wriggly, sparkly surface is visually very forgiving of any uneven stitches, so this can be an excellent yarn for beginner color-knitters to use. Here, it's combined with a cotton 4ply for the knitted number.

5} This swatch uses the same fine mohair yarns as letter "Q," but the yarn is used doubled, making it much easier to work with when color knitting. If you have never worked with doubled yarn, don't be put off: the strands twist around one another as you work, making it easy to treat them as a single strand, and with fluffy yarns such as this, it won't show if you miss one strand in a stitch.

Dates

Use one of the punctuation marks on pages 156–161 to separate numbers in dates: the slash, full point, or colon will all work well, or you could use an asterisk or a heart for a quirkier look.

9} This numeral is duplicate stitched (Swiss darned; see page 252) onto a stockinette (stocking) stitch background. One great advantage of this technique is that it can be added once the knitting is complete. So if you have finished your project, but it looks a little plainer than you imagined, you can easily add detail and color. It's best to use the same weight yarn as used for the knitting, and be aware that a contrast background will show through a bit between stitches.

PROJECT 3

DOG COAT

A personalized coat for Elvis the Bedlington terrier. This is an easy-to-knit project and you can just add or take away stitches and/or rows to make it fit a different-sized dog. We have added a little embroidery in metallic gold to highlight the letters.

Yarns
◎ **Rowan Cotton Glace**
2 x 1¾ oz (50 g) balls in Winsor (849) A and
1 x 1¾ oz (50 g) ball in Mineral (856) B
◎ **Anchor Artiste Metallic**
Small amount of gold (300) C

Letters
◎ Typewriter (see page 64)

Tools
◎ Pair of US 3 (3.25 mm) knitting needles
◎ Knitter's sewing needle
◎ Two buttons
◎ Sewing needle and thread

Measurements
◎ Approximately 17 in (42 cm) from nape to tail
and 12 in (31 cm) wide

Gauge (tension)
◎ 23 sts and 32 rows to 4 in (10 cm) over st st using
Rowan Cotton Glace and US 3 (3.25 mm) needles.

Abbreviations
◎ See page 254.
◎ Note: use the intarsia method
(see page 243) throughout.

KEY

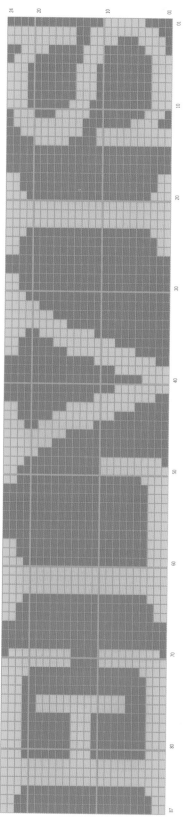

■ – A

□ – B

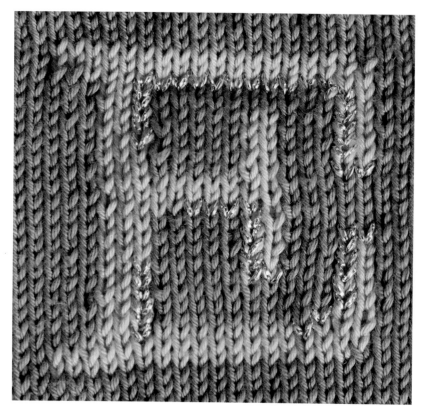

POSITIONING THE LETTERS

You need to consider how to space the letters in Typewriter to balance the different widths and angles and the long serifs. Here, the "L" and "V" overlap by three stitches, whereas there are gaps between the other letters. To position your own choice of letters, photocopy them then cut them out roughly, allowing a border of chart squares all around. Lay the letters out and slide them into the best positions, aligning the rows of the border squares as desired. Tape them together to make your chart.

COAT

(worked in one piece, starting at lower left edge)

TEXTURE PATTERN

Row 1 (RS): [K2, p2] to last 2 sts, k2.

Row 2: [P2, k2] to last 2 sts, p2.

Row 3: [P2, k2] to last 2 sts, p2.

Row 4: [K2, p2] to last 2 sts, k2.

These 4 rows form patt.

BORDER

Using yarn A, cast on 104 sts.

Rows 1–3: Knit.

Join in yarn B.

Rows 4–5: Knit in yarn B.

Rows 6–7: Knit in yarn A.

Rep rows 4–7, 4 times more.

Break yarn B and cont in yarn A.

Row 24: Knit.

Row 25 (WS): Cast on 12 sts, k to end. (116 sts)

SHAPE SHORT NECK STRAP

Work rows 1–4 of patt twice, then row 1, once more.

Next row: Bind (cast) off 12 sts, cont in patt to end of row. (104 sts)

BODY

Starting with a row 3 of patt, work a further 12 rows in patt, ending with a row 2.

Next row: K2, p2, k to last 4 sts, p2, k2.

Next row: P2, k2, p to last 4 sts, k2, p2.

Rep last 2 rows once more.

PLACE CHART

Next row: K2, p2, k4, place row 1 of chart over next 88 sts, joining in separate balls of yarn B as required, k4, p2, k2.

Next row: P2, k2, p4, place row 2 of chart over next 88 sts, p4, k2, p2.

Cont in patt as set until row 24 of chart is complete.

Break yarn B and cont in yarn A.

Next row: K2, p2, k to last 4 sts, p2, k2.

Next row: P2, k2, p to last 4 sts, k2, p2.

Rep last 2 rows once more.

Return to texture patt and starting with a row 3, work 11 rows in patt, ending with a row 1.

SHAPE LONG NECK STRAP

Next row: Cast on 38 sts, and then work in patt as set to end of row 2. (142 sts)

Work 5 more rows in patt, ending with a row 3.

Buttonhole row: K2, p2, k2, yo, p2tog, [k2, p2] to last 2 sts, k2.

Work 3 more rows in patt.

Next row: Bind (cast) off 38 sts, work in patt to end of row. (104 sts)

BORDER

Rows 1–3: Knit.

Join in yarn B.

Rows 4–5: Knit in yarn B.

Rows 6–7: Knit in yarn A.

Rep rows 4–7, 4 times more.

Break yarn B and cont in yarn A.

Row 24: Knit.

Bind (cast) off.

TUMMY STRAP

Using yarn A, cast on 75 sts.

Knit 3 rows.

Buttonhole row: K70, yo, k2tog, k to end of row.

Knit 3 rows.

Bind (cast) off.

TO MAKE UP

- Weave in loose ends.
- Block knitted pieces.
- Using yarn C, duplicate stitch (Swiss darn; see page 252) highlights onto the letters as desired.
- Sew one end of tummy strap to inside of coat, where border meets texture pattern. Sew button to align with buttonhole to same position on other side of coat.
- Sew button to short end of neck strap to align with buttonhole.

8

FLOWER POWER

This alphabet offers you various ways of adding flowers to finish the letters. You will notice that letters such as "A" and "E" don't have holes in them; instead, you can either sew on a made or purchased flower of one sort or another, or embroider a flower to form the hole. Patterns are given for the knitted flower used on letter "A" and the crochet flower used for letter "O." The chunky shapes of these letters make them perfect for intarsia knitting (see page 243), though it would be easier to strand (see page 246) the letter color across the backs of the small gaps than introduce another bobbin.

Yarns used
◎ Fine mohair yarn in lime green
◎ Fine mohair yarn with integral tiny sequins in white
◎ Variegated sock yarn in pink/brown/purple
◎ Wool/cotton blend 4ply yarn in white, pink, and lime green

Other materials
◎ Embroidery floss
◎ Flower button
◎ Flower sequins
◎ Pink and green beads

Techniques used
◎ Intarsia (see page 243)
◎ Stranding (see page 246)
◎ Slip stitch beading (see page 250)
◎ Knitted-in beading (see page 251)
◎ Embroidery (see page 251)
◎ Duplicate stitch (Swiss darning; see page 252)

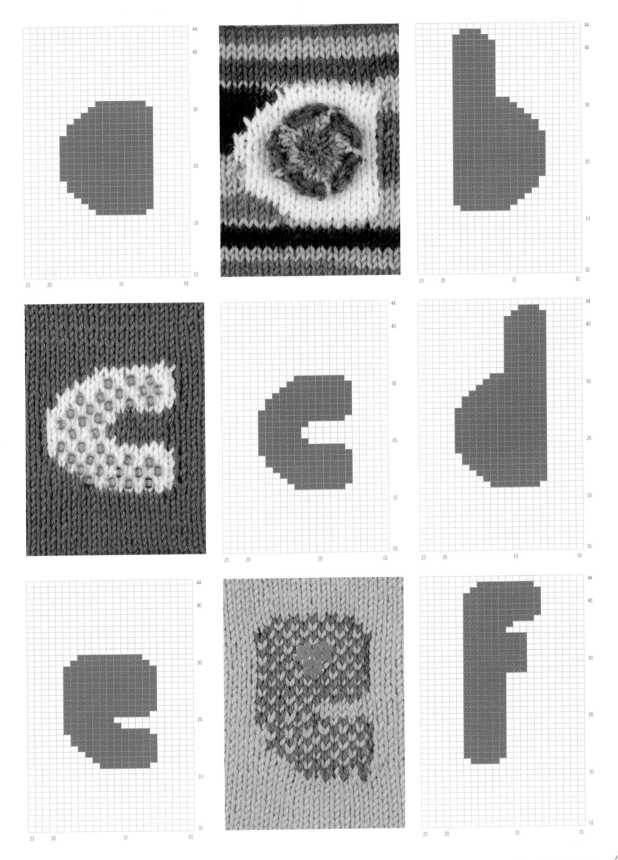

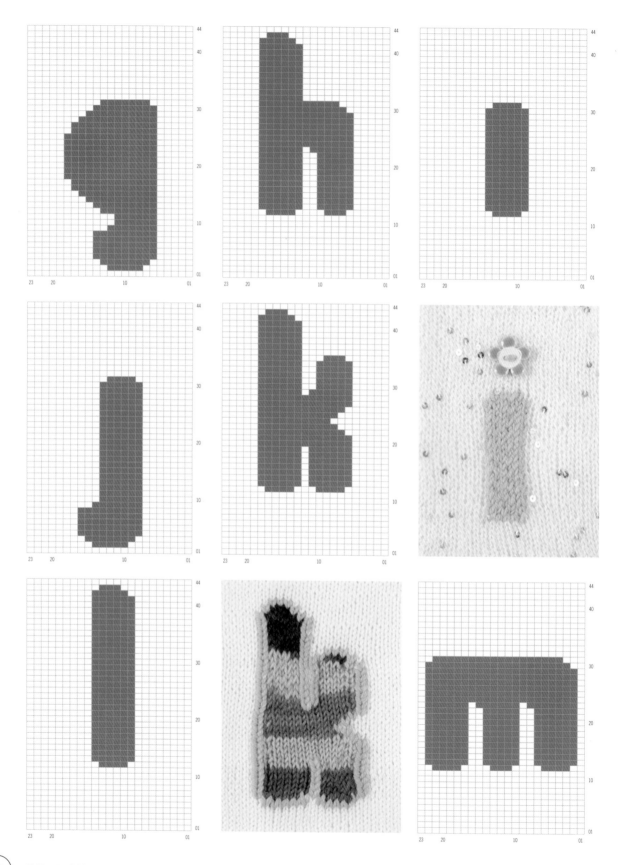

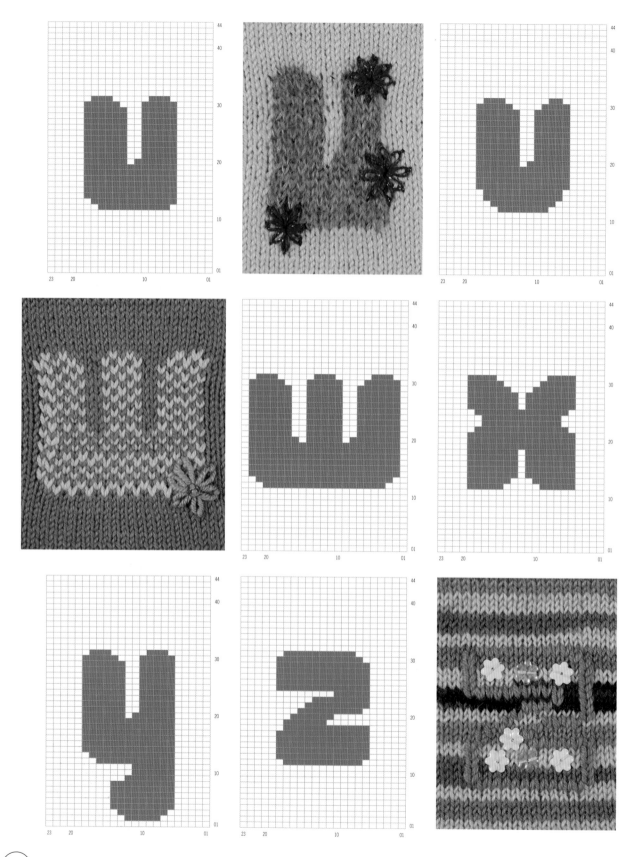

The Knitted Swatches

A } The flower that makes the hole in this letter is simple to knit. Leaving a long tail, cast on 27 sts. Beg with a p row, work 3 rows in st st.
Row 4 (RS): K3, twist the left-hand needle down under the knitting and back up into position, putting a twist in the knitting itself, [k5, twist] 4 times, k4.
Row 5: Purl.
Row 6: K1, [k2tog] to end. (14 sts)
Row 7: [P2tog] to end. (7 sts)
Break yarn and thread through 7 sts, pull up tight and fasten off.
Use tail left from cast on to sew seam. Sew flower to middle of letter.

C } These beads are color lined: they are made of clear glass and the color is added inside the bead hole. Check that the color doesn't flake off onto the yarn as the beads are slipped along it, and that you can launder the beads without the color vanishing—these problems can occur with cheaply made color-lined beads. Here, the beads are placed using the slip stitch method (see page 250).

E } This letter is knitted in alternating stitches of the background color and letter color, in classic Fair Isle fashion. If you can strand with one yarn in each hand (see page 247), this is a quick and easy effect to work. Sequins are stitched on to form the hole.

I } The background of this swatch is a fine mohair yarn that has tiny sequins strung on it. It's doubled to make it a similar weight to the wool/cotton 4ply yarn the letter is knitted in. The flower-shaped button replaces the dot; you can also use buttons to create the holes in letters where needed.

K } Variegated yarns work great with letters, adding a sprinkle of color for no extra effort on your part. This letter is outlined with duplicate stitch (Swiss darning; see page 252) in lime green yarn the same weight as the background. Outlining like this is an effective and decorative way of disguising any baggy edge stitches should your color knitting not turn out as well as you'd hoped.

O } If you are knitting a whole word with an "O" in it, you can replace that letter with the crocheted flower shown at the bottom of this page.
Using a B/1 (2 mm) crochet hook and 4ply yarn, ch6 and join with ss to form ring.
Round 1: Ch3 (counts as 1dc (tr)), 1dc (tr) into the ring, [ch6, 3dc (tr) into the ring] 5 times, ch6, 1 dc (tr) into the ring, join with ss to 3rd of ch-3.
Round 2: *Ch1, [1sc (dc), 1hdc (htr), 7dc (tr), 1hdc (htr), 1sc (dc)] into next ch-6 sp, ch1, miss next dc (tr), ss into next dc (tr); rep from * 4 more times, ch1, [1sc (dc), 1hdc (htr), 7dc (tr), 1hdc (htr), 1sc (dc)] into next ch-6 sp, ch1, miss next dc (tr), join with a ss to base of beg ch-1. Fasten off.

R } Outlining a letter rather than filling in the whole shape can be very successful if the letter shape is bold and simple enough, and this can be done with beads. Place the beads using the knitted-in technique (see page 251), where a bead can be added to every stitch on every row as needed, on the outside squares of the charted letter.

U } You can add simple embroidery to decorate a letter once the knitting is complete. Here, a glittery pink embroidery floss is used to make lazy daisy flowers (see page 251) on a letter knitted in doubled fine mohair on a background of wool/cotton 4ply yarn. The secret to successful embroidery on knitting is getting the stitch tension right. If you pull the embroidery stitches tight, as you might on woven fabric, you will distort the knitting, so pull them taut gently and adjust individual stitches as necessary.

W } This letter is knitted using the same yarns and techniques as letter "E," but the colors are reversed. A lazy daisy is also added to this letter, worked in the same yarn used for the knitting. You can make the petals of a flower different sizes and sew on a bead to make a center for your flower.

Z } You can also create a letter by outlining the shape with duplicate stitch (Swiss darning; see page 252). Here, the background is a variegated sock yarn, the duplicate stitch is worked in a wool/cotton 4ply yarn, and the letter is filled with sewn-on sequins for a flowery finish.

9

STAMPED

These letters are a little trickier to knit than some of the other alphabets in this book because they require three colors to be used on most rows. However, the letter shapes themselves are fairly simple to count and knit, and the broken edges of the stamped backgrounds are irregular, and therefore very forgiving if you make a small mistake there. This alphabet is best knitted in intarsia (see page 243); use short, cut lengths of yarn for the openings in letters (see page 243 for how to judge the amount of yarn needed) and bobbins for the letter and background colors.

Yarns used
◎ Fine mohair yarn with integral tiny sequins in blue
◎ Metallic yarn in bronze and blue
◎ Mohair DK yarn in blue, brown, and cream
◎ Wool 4ply yarn in brown and cream
◎ Wool/cotton blend 4ply yarn in blue
◎ Wool DK yarn in brown and cream

Other materials
◎ Bronze beads

Techniques used
◎ Intarsia (see page 243)
◎ Stranding (see page 246)
◎ Knitted-in beading (see page 251)

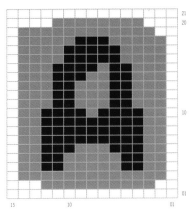

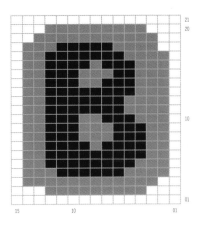

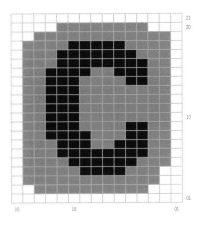

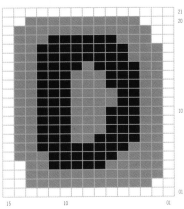

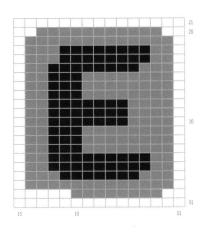

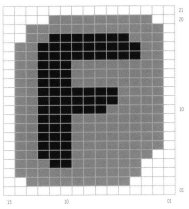

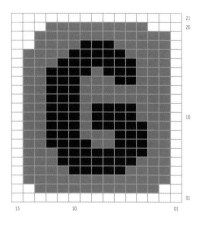

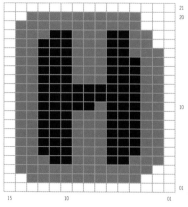

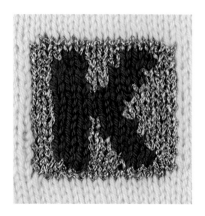

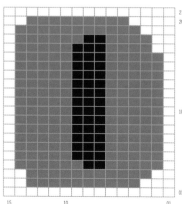

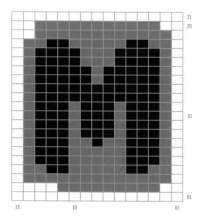

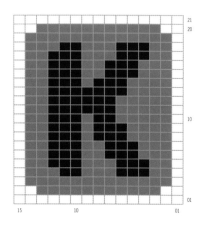

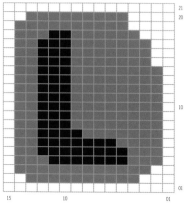

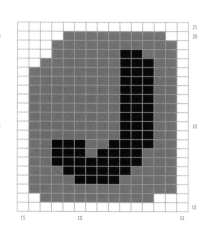

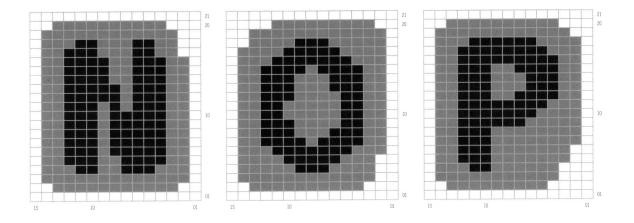

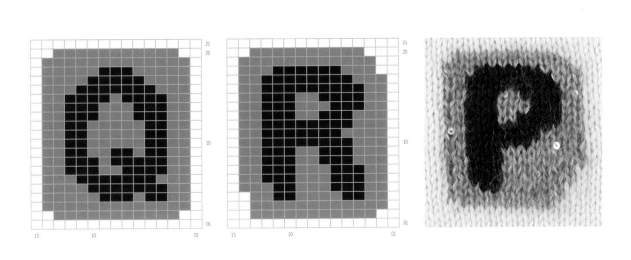

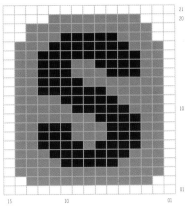

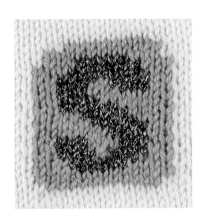

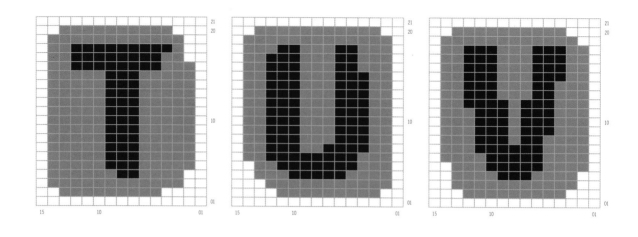

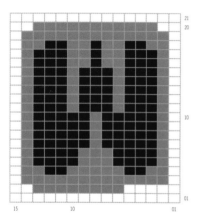

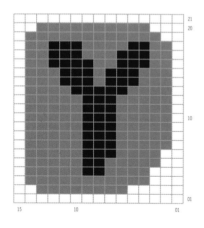

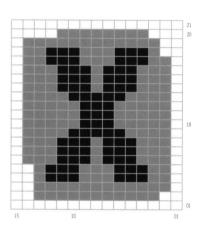

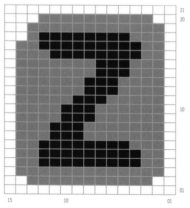

The Knitted Swatches

A Double-knitting weight yarns are probably the most commonly available weight and there are many, many fiber and textural variations: this yarn is a lambswool and mohair blend, so it's both soft and fluffy. Using two yarns of the same weight does make it relatively easy to tension the stitches evenly at the color changes and so work neat color knitting, especially when the yarn has a little elasticity, as this wool yarn does.

B This letter is knitted in a fine mohair with tiny sequins, used double here to make it a similar weight to the wool DK used for the background. The sequins are actually strung onto a very fine, smooth strand that's twisted with the mohair, so the sequins don't slide around. This is good in that they don't get pushed together by the fingers that you tension the yarn over.

F This letter is beaded using the knitted-in technique (see page 251), where a bead can be added to every stitch on every row. Be aware that a lot of beads can affect gauge (tension), stretch the stitches, and change the drape of the knitting, so while a few beaded letters is probably fine, a whole beaded motto might be too much for the yarn to take.

H If you find metallic yarns a bit gaudy in quantities, try them as smaller accents in a project; just one or two letters in a name or word, with the other letters knitted in a non-metallic yarn of the same color.

K This letter is knitted in two colors of 4ply wool and a metallic yarn. The two yarns are similar enough in weight to be knitted together without having to double up either one, but check that yarns have compatible laundering requirements before knitting them together.

M Here, the same yarns as letter "A" have been used, but the positions are reversed. Swapping colors like this works very well on an afghan: choose a limited palette and work blocks in all the possible variations to create a finished piece that's colorful, but also restrained. You can choose just a two-color palette and use different fibers to help ring the changes.

P One potential problem with beaded/sequined yarns is that it can be tricky to persuade the embellishments to appear on the right side of the knitting. You can sometimes wriggle beads/sequins along a yarn to make them appear on the right side, but the construction of this yarn means that the sequins don't move easily.

S Metallic yarns might look a bit tricky, but they are actually easy to knit with, and the wriggly, sparkly surface is visually very forgiving of any uneven stitches, so this can be an excellent yarn to use if you are a beginner to color knitting.

W Looking at it, you might think that metallic yarn is scratchy against the skin, but this one is actually very soft. In addition, it has a nice fluid drape and so would work well as a garment if you like a bit of sparkle. The background is knitted in wool/cotton 4ply yarn that is a similar weight to the metallic letter.

Z These beads are a pale ice blue, but the background color is so dark and strong that they are rather overpowered and have ended up looking silver. They are perfectly pretty, but this does demonstrate the need to swatch all choices to check how the finished result will look.

PROJECT 4

BUNTING

Shout "Bravo!" with colorful customized bunting! Choose letters from one or more alphabets in this book to spell out your message, and knit the pennants in your favorite colors. The tape that the pennants hang from can be crocheted, knitted, or made from fabric, as you prefer.

Yarns

◎ **Rowan Handknit Cotton**

1 x 1¾ oz (50 g) ball in each of Gooseberry (219) A, China Rose (366) B, Yacht (357) C, Rosso (215) D, Linen (205) E, Blue John (365) F, Bee (364) G, and Bleached (263) H

Letters

◎ 80s Retro (see page 46)
◎ Blackletter (see page 98)
◎ Quirky Handwriting (see page 128)
◎ Punctuation (see page 156)
◎ Brushscript (see page 190)
◎ Digital Display (see page 196)

Tools

◎ Pair of US 6 (4 mm) knitting needles
◎ Knitter's sewing needle
◎ F/5 (4 mm) crochet hook

Measurements

◎ Each pennant approximately 7 in (18 cm) wide at top and 5 in (13 cm) long

Gauge (tension)

◎ 19 sts and 28 rows to 4 in (10 cm) over st st using US 6 (4 mm) needles

Abbreviations

◎ See page 254.
◎ Note: use the intarsia method (see page 243) throughout.

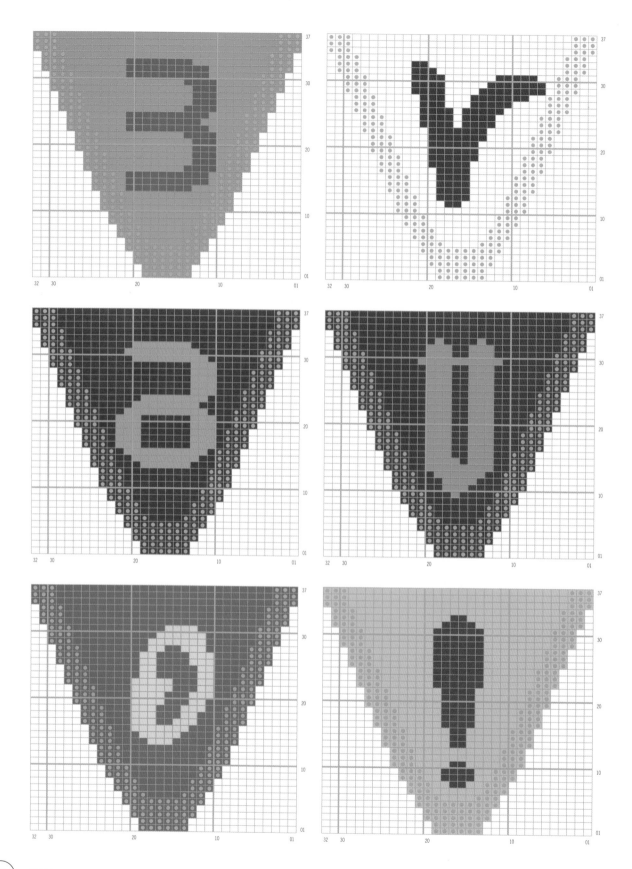

KEY

- ■ – A
- ■ – B
- ■ – C
- ■ – D
- ■ – E
- ■ – F
- ■ – G
- □ – H
- ⊡ – Knit every row

POSITIONING THE LETTERS

Quite a lot of the letters in this book will fit onto these pennants, and if you want to use a large letter, you can simply add more rows to the top of the pennant chart. To position letters, photocopy them and the pennants to the same scale. Cut out the letters roughly, allowing a border of chart squares all around. Position them on the pennants, aligning the grids of the letters and pennants. Tape them together to make your chart.

PENNANT

Use two colors of your choice.

Using US 6 (4 mm) needles, first color, and the thumb method, cast on 6 sts.

Work chart, working 3 sts at each end of every row in garter stitch and center of pennant in st st, and joining in second color as required.

Bind (cast) off.

TO MAKE UP

- ◎ Weave in loose ends.
- ◎ Block pennants.

TAPE

You can crochet the tape as here, or pick up and knit a garter stitch tape working back and forth on a circular needle, or sew the pennants to a fabric tape.

CROCHET TAPE

Using F/5 (4 mm) crochet hook and yarn G, ch15.

Row 1 (RS): *Work a row of sc (dc) into the top of pennant !, ch5, rep from * working across the top of pennants O, V, A, R, and B in sequence, ch15, turn.

Row 2: Ch1, 1sc (dc) in every ch or sc (dc) to end of row, changing to yarn H at the end of the row.

Row 3: Ch1, 1sc (dc) in every sc (dc) to end of row, changing to yarn F at the end of the row.

Rep row 3 in yarn A.

Fasten off.

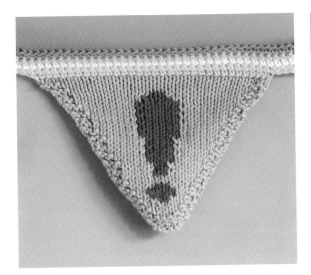

10

3-D

This is one of the more complicated alphabets to knit in that you need three colors for each letter, but the actual letter shapes are chunky and quite straightforward. You will need to pick your color palette quite carefully to make the most of the three-dimensional effect: two shades of one color and a contrast background work well, and the shadow section can be lighter or darker than the letter itself. This is a great alphabet with which to experiment with mixing yarns. This alphabet is best knitted in intarsia (see page 243); use short cut lengths of yarn for the openings in letters (see page 243 for how to judge the amount of yarn needed) and bobbins for the letters and shadows.

Yarns used
◎ Cotton DK yarn in purple and yellow
◎ Cotton/linen blend yarn in pale green
◎ Fine mohair yarn in purple
◎ Metallic yarn in gold
◎ Tweed 4ply yarn in mauve and yellow
◎ Wool 4ply yarn in yellow
◎ Wool/cotton blend 4ply yarn in lilac, yellow and pale green

Other materials
◎ Lilac beads

Techniques used
◎ Intarsia (see page 243)
◎ Knitted-in beading (see page 251)
◎ Duplicate stitch (Swiss darning; see page 252)

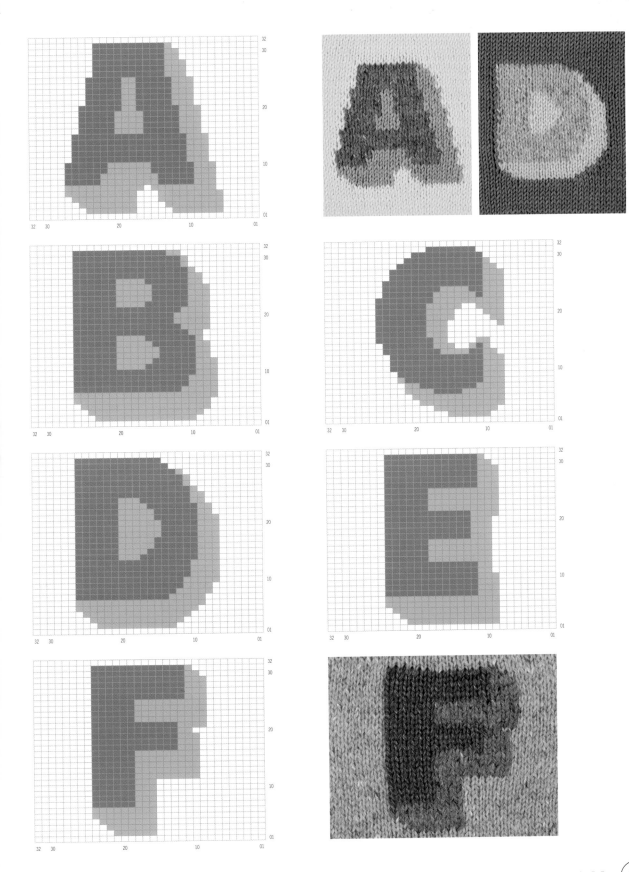

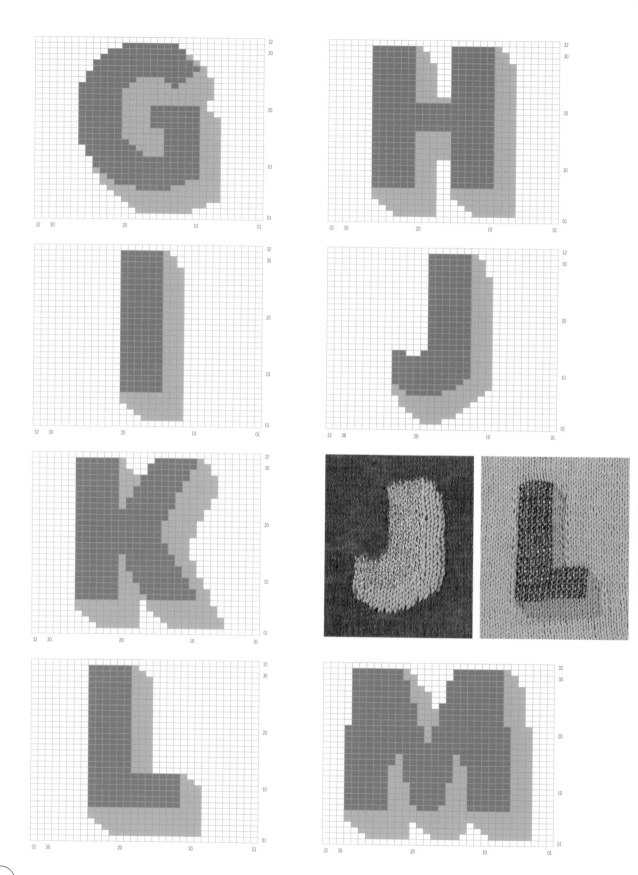

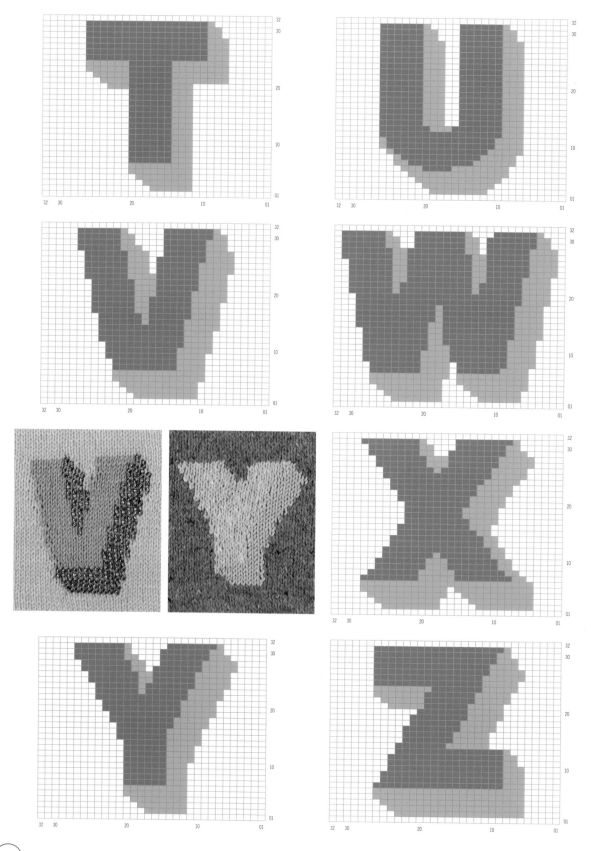

The Knitted Swatches

A This letter is knitted in a tweed yarn with wool/cotton in a lighter tint as the shadow, on a contrast background of wool/cotton. Although the yarns are not all the same type, they are of the same weight, so there are no problems knitting them together. A knitter's tip: tweed yarns are forgiving if you are a beginner at color knitting, as the flecked colors help to hide any uneven stitches.

D This swatch also uses a tweed yarn for the letter, with wool for the shadow and cotton for the background. With the yarns used this way, the three-dimensional effect isn't very strong, but swapping positions would make it work better; see letter "N."

F The simple, blocky shapes of these letters make them ideal candidates for being embroidered with duplicate stitch (Swiss darning; see page 252) instead of being knitted. Here, a tweed yarn is used for the letter and a fine mohair is used doubled to embroider the shadow. When duplicate stitching over a large area of knitting, be careful to keep the embroidery yarn at an even, and not too tight, tension for a neat finish.

J Three yarns of entirely different fibers are used here: the letter is in a man-made fiber metallic yarn, the shadow in cotton and the background in mohair/silk blend. Remember to check that yarns have compatible laundering requirements before knitting them together. A lukewarm hand wash in a no-rinse detergent will usually overcome any potential shrinkage issues, but it's worth washing a swatch before starting a sweater that you may never be able to clean.

L This letter is beaded using the knitted-in technique (see page 251), where a bead can be added to every stitch on every row. With this technique, the beads sit at a slight angle on one "leg" of the stitch, so the long columns look a bit wriggly, but that's the nature of this style of beading.

N Here, the same yarns used to knit letter "D" and its shadow are swapped, and the three-dimensional effect is excellent: the paler background yarn also helps with this. It's always worth swapping the positions of planned colors when you are swatching, just to see what happy accidents might occur (and to avoid less-than-successful combinations).

Q This letter and the background are knitted in the same cotton DK yarn, and the shadow section is knitted in three strands of fine mohair held together to make a strand thick enough to match the cotton. If you have never worked with multiple strands of yarn, don't be put off: the strands twist around one another as you work, making it easy to treat them as a single strand, and with fluffy yarn such as this, it won't show if you miss one strand in a stitch.

S Even relatively complex letters can be just outlined—rather than filled in—and still be effective. The best way to outline is to use duplicate stitch (Swiss darning; see page 252). In this swatch, the letter is embroidered with two strands of mohair held together and the shadow is a single strand of metallic yarn.

V The beads and type of yarn used to knit letter "L" are used again here, though the beads are on the shadow and the background is a different color. As the beads are physically prominent and visually more eye-catching than the yarn, the letter looks debossed. This is one of those happy accidents that comes about through experimentation, so try crazy ideas as swatches, just to make sure they aren't actually brilliant ideas.

Y This swatch also features a debossed letter, though it is worked in yarns only. The effect is created partly by the shadow being a stronger shade than the letter, and partly because the cotton/linen blend yarn used to knit the letter is thinner than either the shadow or the background yarns.

11

BLACKLETTER

Sometimes called Old English, this style of lettering is centuries old: the Gutenberg Bible, the first printed Bible in the world, used a blackletter typeface. There are various versions of it, and these letters are based on a simple one. Lots of straight uprights make this a quick and easy alphabet to knit, but you need to be careful to tension the yarn properly to make the tiny one-stitch serifs at the base of the letters visible. They can always be boosted with duplicate stitch (Swiss darning; see page 252) once the knitting is complete. If you are color knitting, work the letters in intarsia (see page 243) overall, stranding (see page 246) both the background yarn and letter yarn within the letter shape, as needed.

Yarns used
◎ Fine mohair yarn with integral tiny sequins in cream
◎ Metallic yarn in black
◎ Tweed yarn in dark gray and pale gray
◎ Wool 4ply yarn in cream
◎ Wool DK yarn in cream and gray

Other materials
◎ Gray beads
◎ Matte charcoal beads

Techniques used
◎ Intarsia (see page 243)
◎ Stranding (see page 246)
◎ Slip stitch beading (see page 250)
◎ Knitted-in beading (see page 251)
◎ Duplicate stitch (Swiss darning; see page 252)
◎ Cable (see page 253)

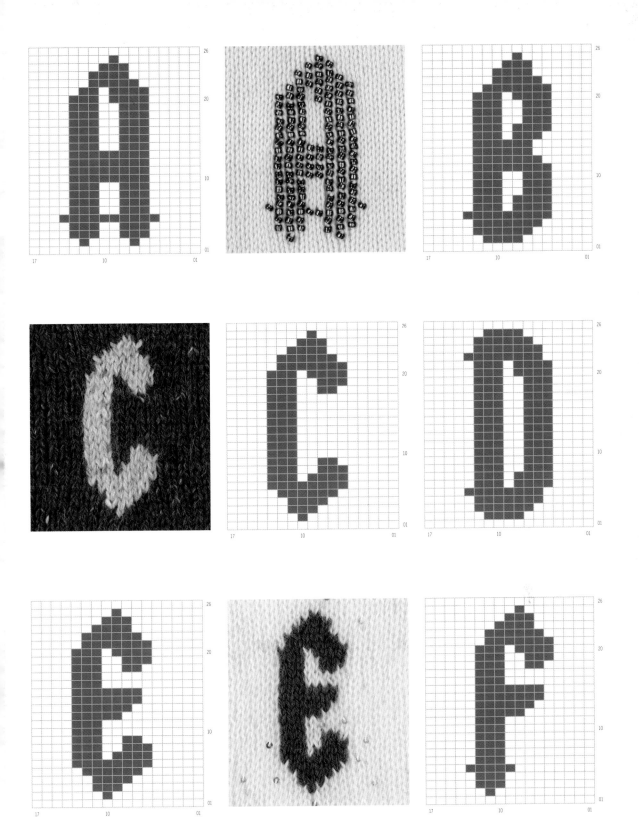

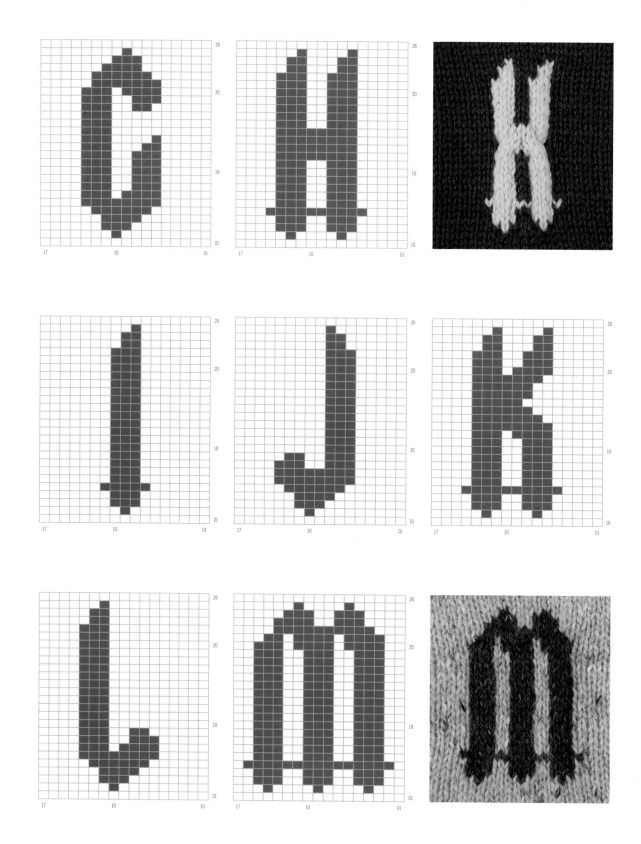

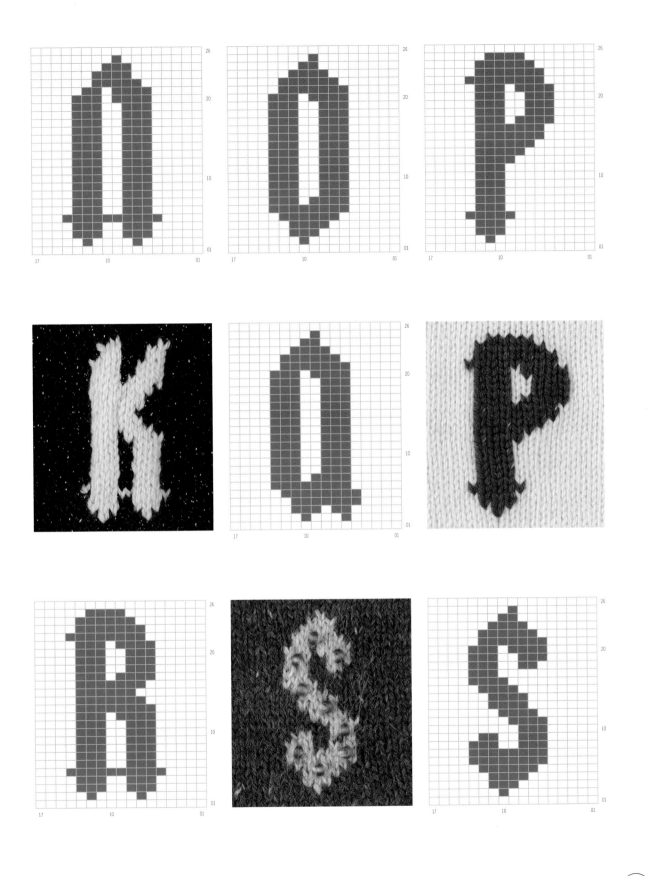

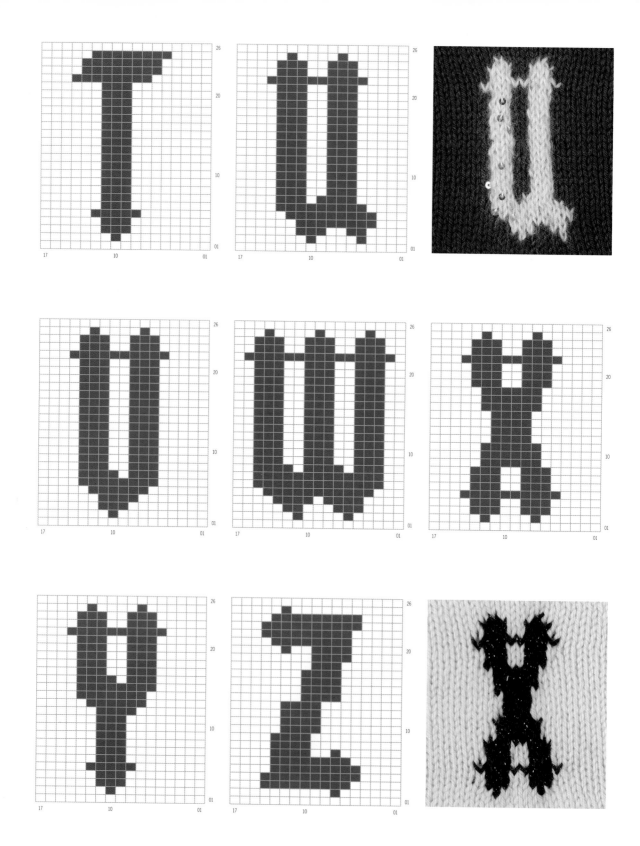

The Knitted Swatches

A This letter is beaded using the knitted-in technique (see page 251), where a bead can be added to every stitch on every row as needed. The yarn is a wool DK and the beads are size 6 seed beads; perfect for knitting. With this technique the beads sit at a slight angle on one "leg" of the stitch, so the long columns of beads look a bit wriggly, but that's the nature of this style of beading.

C Two colors of tweed yarn are used in this swatch: the soft blue flecks appear in both shades and the light color flecks into the dark color, so the two work really well together. Also, tweed yarns are forgiving if you are new to color knitting, as the flecked colors help to hide any uneven stitches.

E The background yarn of this swatch is a fine mohair with tiny sequins strung onto it, and the letter is DK wool. Both yarns have been used as a single strand, so the letter is thicker than the background, giving it a slightly embossed look that suits the nature of the typeface. When using two different-weight yarns together, you have to be careful to tension them both neatly at the color changes to avoid distortion.

H This swatch is knitted entirely in DK wool yarn. To add interest, there is a cable twist (see page 253) in the middle of each leg. It's a four-stitch cable, using the three stitches of the leg and one stitch from the middle cross stroke; it is worked on the third row of the cross stroke. Working a front cable on the right and a back cable on the left makes them bend towards one another.

K Metallic yarn is combined with wool 4ply yarn in this swatch; both as single strands as they are of similar weights. However, the wool is a little stiffer than the metallic, which has a very soft drape. The metallic yarn is—like the tweed yarn in letter "C"—forgiving if you have any uneven stitches as they tend to disappear on the glittering, wriggly surface.

M Here, the same yarns as letter "C" have been used, but the positions are reversed. Swapping colors like this works very well on an afghan: choose a limited palette and work blocks in all the possible variations to create a finished piece that's colorful, but also restrained. You can choose just a two-color palette and use different fibers to help ring the changes.

P This letter reverses the positions of the yarns in letter "H," and the letter is duplicate stitched (Swiss darned; see page 252). On the straight stroke, the darning is worked vertically; on the bowl of the letter, it is worked horizontally. Small flecks of the background color appear, but not much of it considering the tonal difference between the colors.

S This swatch uses the same yarns in the same positions as swatch "C," but the letter is decorated further with beads placed using the slip stitch method (see page 250). When you are planning where to place beads in this way, remember that they lie across the base of the slipped stitch and so sit low on the row of knitting. If you put them on the first row of a new color, they will overlap onto the last row of the previous color.

U For this swatch, the background yarn of "E" was used to knit the letter. One potential problem with beaded/sequined yarns is apparent here: the sequins have appeared almost entirely on one leg of the letter (the other leg has just one tiny sequin). You can sometimes wriggle beads/sequins along a yarn to make them appear on the right side, but the construction of this yarn means that the sequins don't move easily.

X Swapping the positions of the yarns used in letter "K" gives a glittery letter on a plain cream background. It's quite a subtle effect, but rather elegant. If you find full-on metallic yarns a bit much used in quantities, try them as smaller accents in a project; just one or two letters in a name or word.

12

50s RETRO

These streamlined, chunky letters have a fabulous 50s feel: picture them on the side of a convertible Cadillac with fins, or in black and white over the door of a diner that has a zinc counter and red banquette seats. And there are both upper and lowercase letters to indulge yourself with. Here, they are knitted in a bright red and pale blue palette that's typical of the period, but try them in other retro shades, such as mint and pale pink, or tangerine and white. The chunky shapes of these letters make them perfect for intarsia knitting (see page 243); use short cut lengths of yarn for the openings in letters (see page 243 for how to judge the amount of yarn needed) or strand across them as you prefer.

Yarns used
◎ Cotton 4ply yarn in red and turquoise
◎ Metallic yarn in turquoise
◎ Wool DK yarn in red and turquoise

Other materials
◎ Red beads
◎ Turquoise felt

Techniques used
◎ Intarsia (see page 243)
◎ Stranding (see page 246)
◎ Knitted-in beading (see page 251)
◎ Bobbles (see page 252)
◎ Duplicate stitch (Swiss darning; see page 252)
◎ Cable (see page 253)

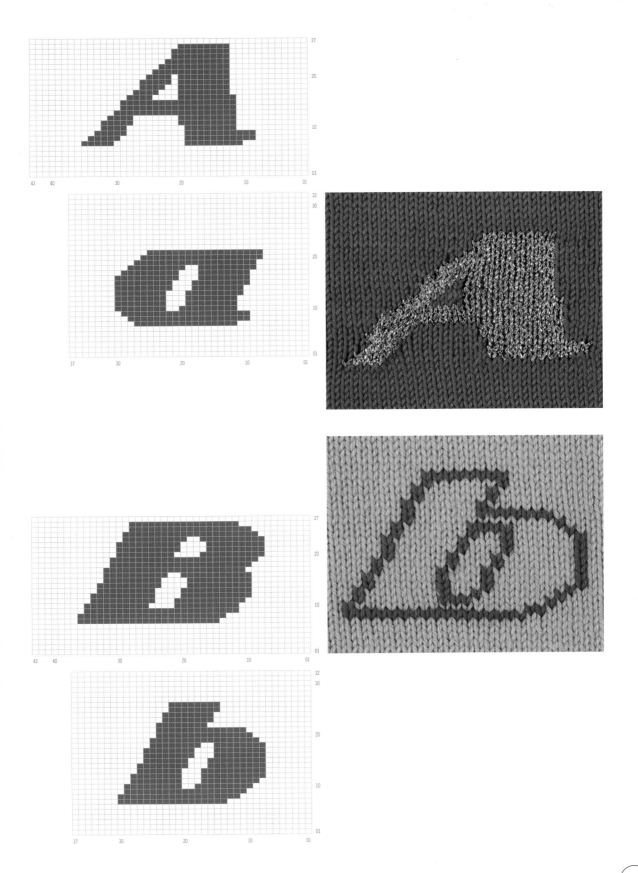

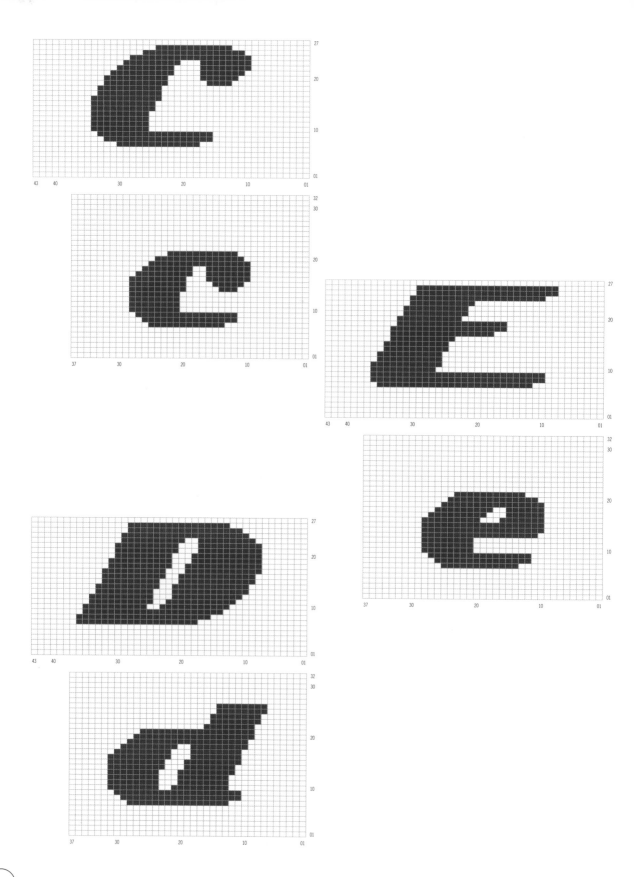

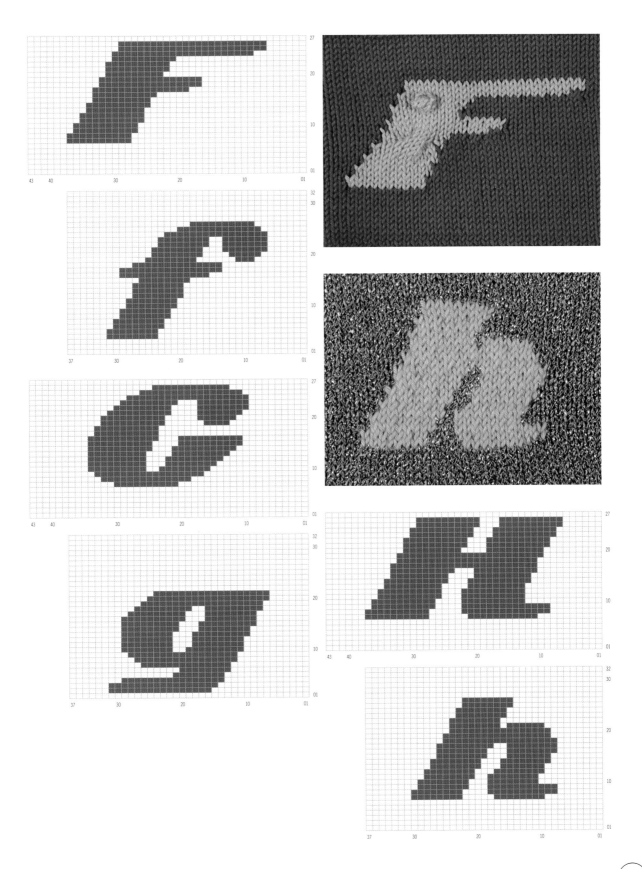

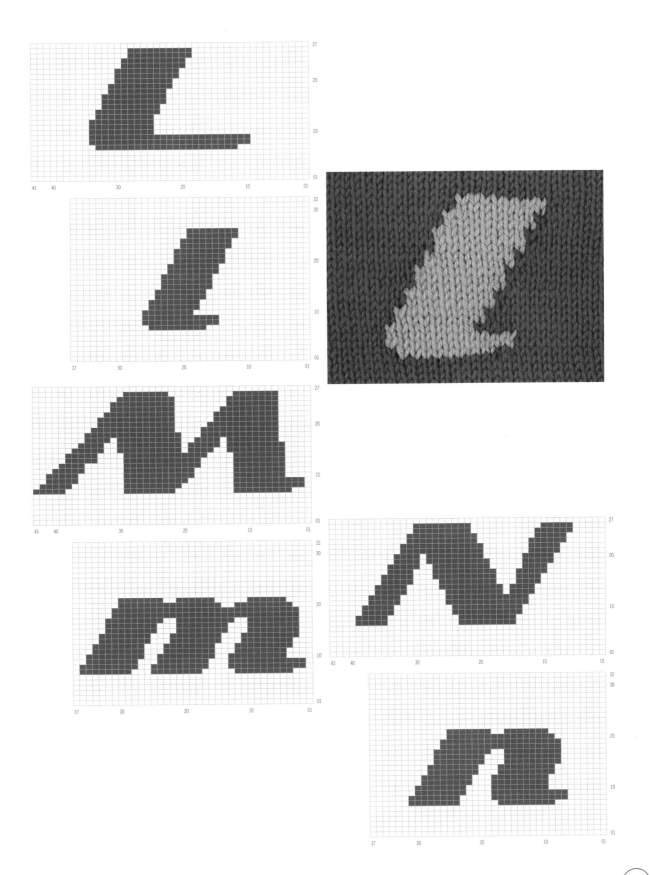

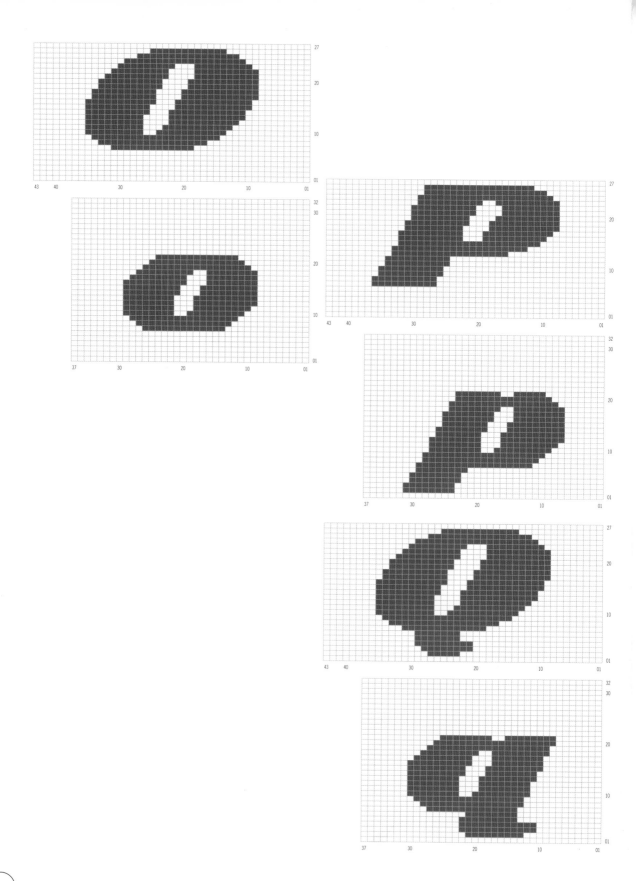

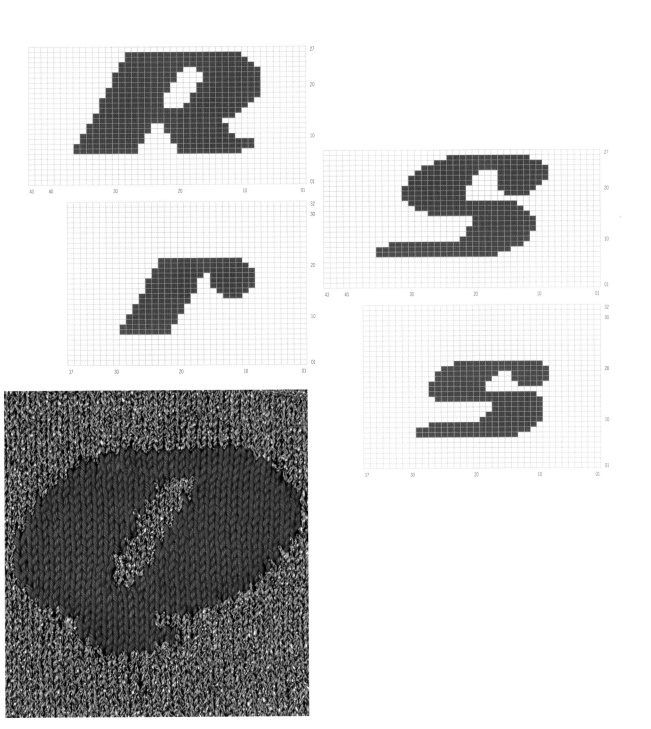

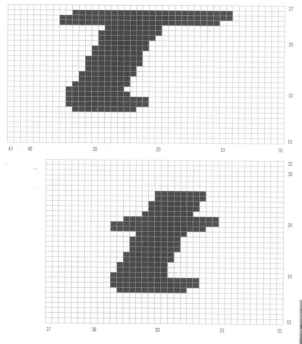

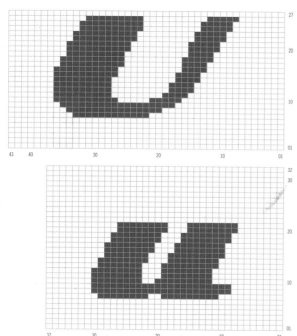

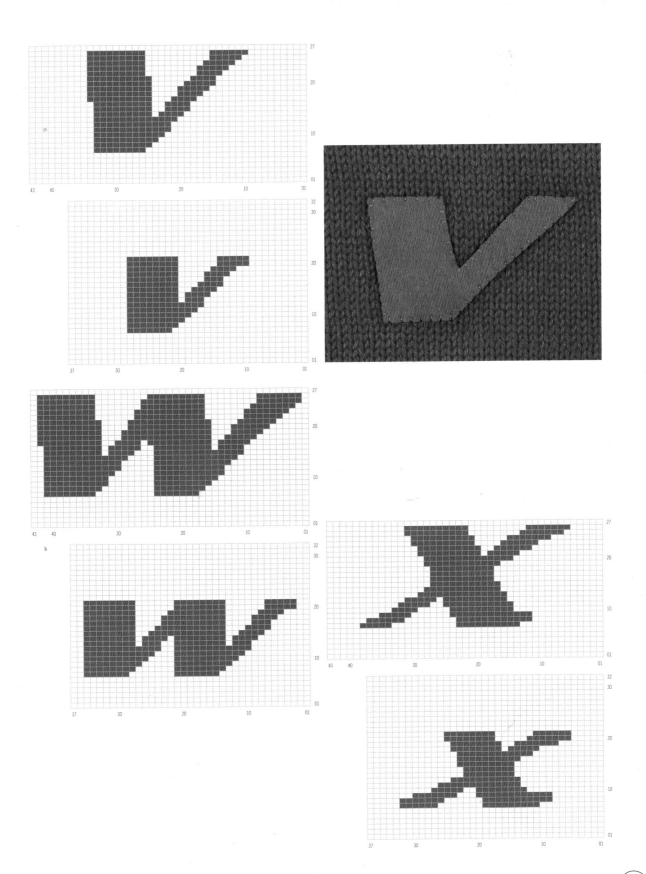

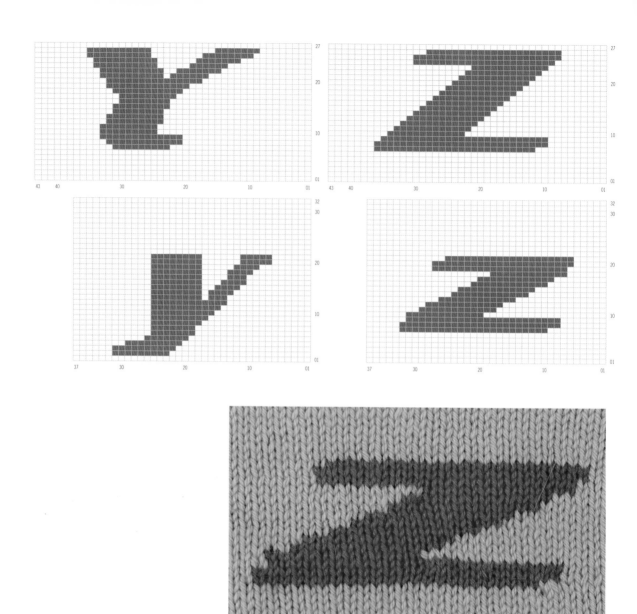

The Knitted Swatches

A Mixing fibers can make any project more visually interesting: here, a metallic yarn is used for the uppercase "A" and a smooth cotton yarn for the background. The smooth sheen of the cotton contrasts well with the sparkle. Remember to check that two yarns have compatible laundering requirements before knitting them together; a lukewarm hand wash in a no-rinse detergent will usually overcome any potential shrinkage issues, but it's worth washing a swatch before starting a sweater that you will never be able to clean.

B Outlining a letter rather than filling in the whole shape can be very successful if the letter shape is bold enough, as this lowercase "B" is, and outlining is best done with duplicate stitch (Swiss darning; see page 252). If you are knitting in some letters of a word and outlining others, be sure to work out the spacing very carefully before you begin, so that there is enough room for your outlined letters once the knitting is complete.

F You can add a cable twist (see page 253) to any letter that has a wide enough stroke; work a front or back cable as required to complement the shape of the letter. This front cable slopes in the same direction as the upright stroke, and is topped with a bobble (see page 252) for jaunty detail.

H Two yarns that are the same basic color can be used together as long as there is enough difference to make the letter readable. Here, the colors are very similar, but the sparkling metallic yarn has such a different surface to the smooth cotton letter that enough contrast is created to make the lowercase "H" clear.

J This letter is knitted in alternating stitches of the background color and letter color, in classic Fair Isle fashion. If you can strand with one yarn in each hand (see page 247), this is a quick and easy effect to work. However, if you have to keeping dropping and picking up yarns (see page 246), it'll be time-consuming.

L This swatch is worked entirely in wool DK yarn. Wool is a naturally slightly elastic fiber, so it's easier to adjust the tension of individual stitches than it is with cotton yarn. Once the knitting is complete, any slightly uneven stitches can be eased out with the tip of a knitter's sewing needle (see page 249), and blocking the knitting will also improve the finish.

Q Looking at it you might think that metallic yarn is scratchy against the skin, but this one is actually very soft. In addition, it has a lovely fluid drape and so would work well as a garment if you like a bit of sparkle. The letter is knitted in cotton 4ply yarn that is a similar weight to the metallic yarn used for the background.

T This letter is beaded using the knitted-in technique (see page 251), where a bead can be added to every stitch on every row. However, as the beads are a little larger than the stitch, they are placed on different "legs" of the stitches on alternate rows. To do this, work the purl rows as normal, then before starting the knit row, slide all the beads along the stitch they are on and over the needle to the back. Then knit the row, placing the beads in the usual way. The beads that were moved will be sitting on the left-hand "leg" and those knitted on the right-hand "leg." This gives each bead a bit more room, and produces the herringbone pattern.

V The charts can be used as templates to create fabric appliqués that are then sewn on to knitted fabric. Be aware that this will prevent the knitting from stretching in the area of the appliqué, but it's a great way of adding a motif or motto if color knitting isn't your thing.

Z Here, the same yarns as letter "L" have been used, but the positions are reversed. Swapping colors like this works very well on an afghan: choose a limited palette and work blocks in all the possible variations to create a finished piece that's colorful, but also restrained. You can choose just a two-color palette and use different fibers to add variety.

PROJECT 5

STRIPED SCARF

This project combines 50s-style lettering, a classic palette, and timeless stripes in a scarf with huge retro appeal. A fabric backing looks good and hides the unattractive back of the color knitting, and making the backing slightly narrower than the knitting gives a lovely rolled edge to the scarf.

Yarns
◎ **Rowan Pure Wool DK**
3 x 1¾ oz (50 g) balls in Shale (002) A,
1 x 1¾ oz (50 g) ball in each of Port (037) B and Tan (054) C
◎ **Rowan Pure Wool 4ply**
2 x 1¾ oz (50 g) balls each of Vintage (449) D and Gerbera
(454) E (both D and E are used double throughout)

Letters
◎ 50s Retro (see page 104)

Tools
◎ Pair of US 6 (4 mm) knitting needles
◎ Knitter's sewing needle
◎ Lightweight cotton fabric for lining, measuring ¾ in (2 cm)
narrower than the knitted scarf, by the length of the knitted
scarf plus 1¼ in (3 cm)
◎ Sewing machine
◎ Sewing thread to match lining

Measurements
◎ Approximately 8¼ in (21 cm) wide by desired length;
this scarf is 88 in (225 cm) long

Gauge (tension)
◎ 22 sts and 30 rows to 4 in (10 cm) over st st
using Rowan Pure Wool DK and US 6 (4 mm) needles

Abbreviations
◎ See page 254.
◎ Note: use the intarsia method
(see page 243) throughout.

KEY

☐ – A

■ – B

▨ – C

▨ – E

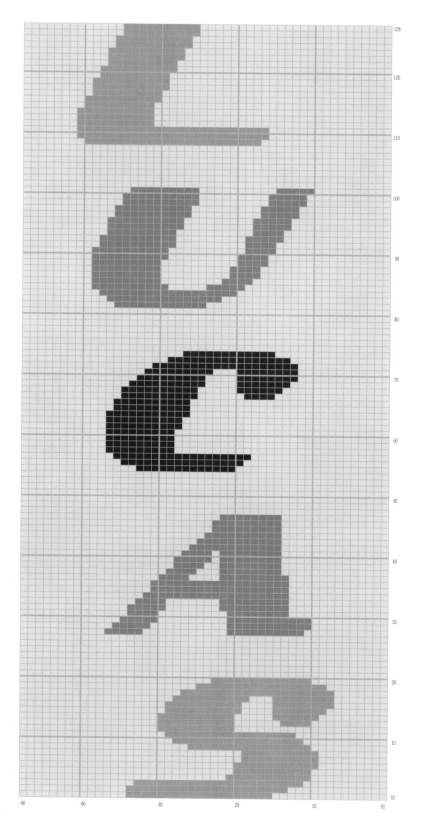

POSITIONING
THE LETTERS

Although the letters of 50s Retro
uppercase are all the same height, they
are slightly different widths, and when
stacked vertically in a straight column,
they look a bit odd; the varying widths
look like a mistake has been made.
Offsetting them into a diagonal vertical
stack both solves that problem, and
complements the slope of the letters.
It will usually be worth photocopying
letters you'd like to use together and
spending time setting them out in
different arrangements—the obvious
choices are not always the best ones.

SCARF

Using yarn B, cast on 48 sts.

Working in st st throughout, work 32 rows in the foll
  stripe patt:

2 rows B.

4 rows A.

4 rows D.

4 rows A.

2 rows C.

4 rows A.

4 rows E.

8 rows A.

PLACE CHART

Work rows 1–128 from chart, joining in separate balls of yarns
  A, B, C, and E as required.

Break yarns B, C, and E.

Work 8 rows A.

STRIPE PATT

4 rows E.

4 rows A.

2 rows C.

4 rows A.

4 rows D.

4 rows A.

2 rows B.

Work stripe patt until scarf is desired length.

Bind (cast) off.

TO MAKE UP

- Weave in loose ends.
- Block knitted piece.
- Press under and sew a double ³⁄₈ in (1 cm) hem at each
  short end of the lining.
- RS together and starting 2 rows up from cast on/bound
  (cast) off edge, pin lining to scarf along each long edge.
- Taking a ¹⁄₄ in (6 mm) seam allowance (about 2 knitted
  stitches), sew pieces together along long edges only.
- Turn scarf RS out through one open end.
- Press scarf, allowing knitting to roll slightly to the back
  along the long edges.

13

SANS SERIF

An utterly classic, simple typeface that will work well on projects with a contemporary, urban style, and those with a naïve, more traditional feel. The letters are quite small and very versatile, and the simple shapes make them easy to knit, even for a color knitting novice. Another benefit of the uncomplicated letters is that you can knit them in almost any yarn or technique, and they will be clear and readable. There are also numbers in this typeface (see page 126). If you are color knitting, work the letters in intarsia (see page 243) overall, stranding (see page 246) both the background yarn and letter yarn within the letter shape, as needed.

Yarns used
◎ Cotton 4ply yarn in dark blue
◎ DK mohair yarn in pale blue and dark blue
◎ Fine mohair yarn in pale blue and dark blue
◎ Fine mohair yarn with integral tiny sequins in pale blue
◎ Metallic yarn in pale blue and dark blue
◎ Tweed yarn in dark blue
◎ Variegated sock yarn in blues
◎ Wool 4ply yarn in pale blue

Other materials
◎ Blue beads
◎ Blue sequins

Techniques used
◎ Intarsia (see page 243)
◎ Stranding (see page 246)
◎ Slip stitch sequins (see page 250)
◎ Embroidery (see page 251)
◎ Knitted-in beading (see page 251)
◎ Duplicate stitching (Swiss darning; see page 252)

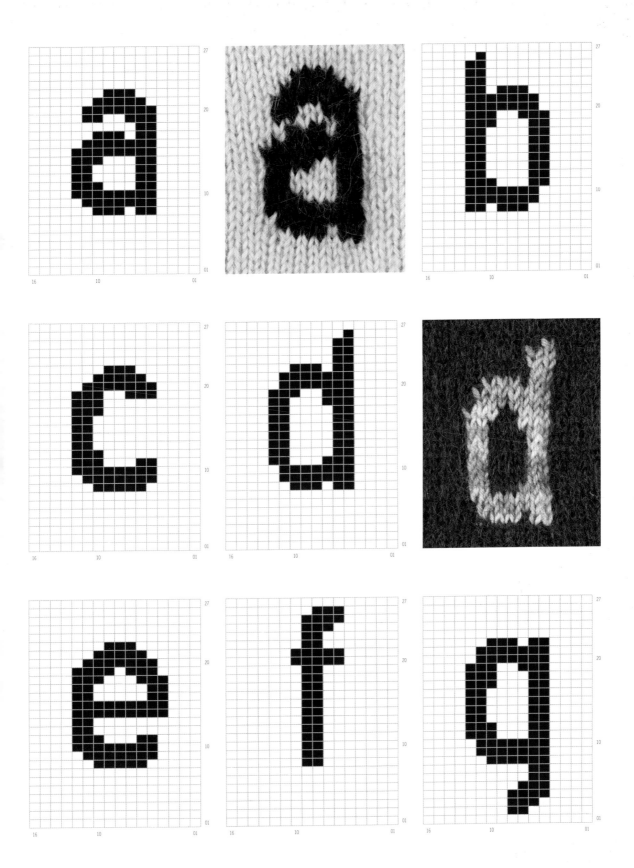

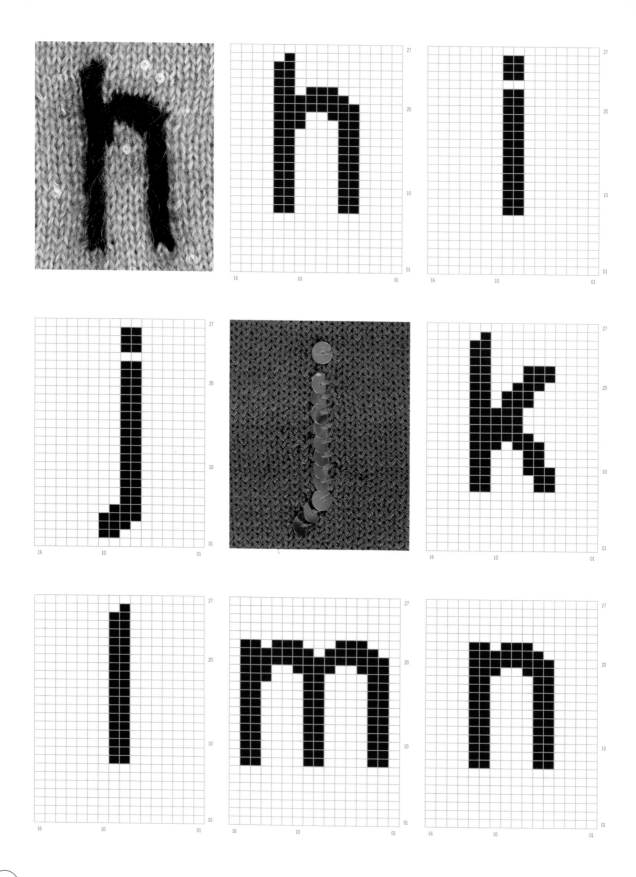

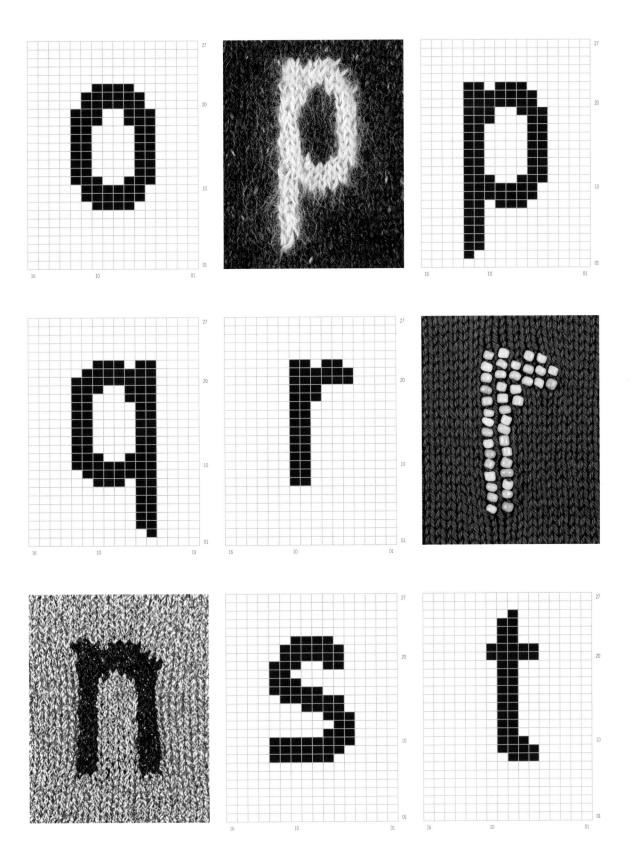

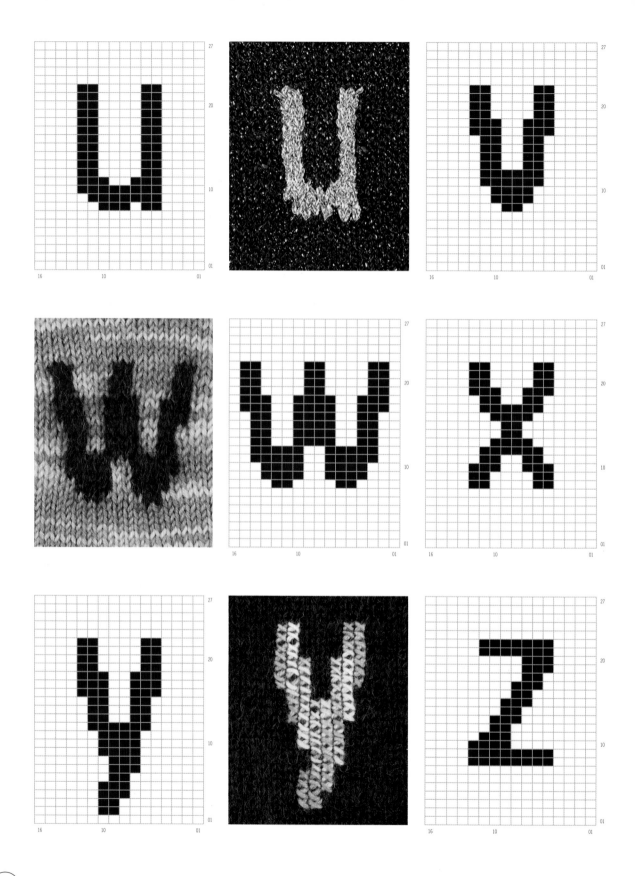

The Knitted Swatches

A } This letter is knitted entirely in a DK-weight mohair yarn, with the letter in dark blue and the background in pale blue. When a letter yarn is much darker than the background yarn, it's best to strand right across the back of gaps in the letters if they are four or fewer stitches, and catch floats in (see page 247)—rather than weaving in (see page 248)—if the gaps are wider.

D } Variegated yarns work great with letters, adding a sprinkle of color for no extra effort on your part. They are usually only available in sock weight, and be careful of those with long color changes as you can end up with a letter that is almost entirely one color. The background of this swatch is a fine mohair used double to make it a similar weight to the variegated sock yarn.

H } Novelty yarns need to be used with some caution when knitting alphabets because heavy texture can blur the letter outline. However, those novelty yarns that are beaded or sequined work well. This is a fine mohair with tiny sequins and it's used double here to make it a similar weight to the DK mohair used to knit the letter. The sequins are actually strung onto a very fine, smooth strand that's twisted with the mohair, so the sequins don't slide around. This is good in that they don't get pushed together by the fingers that you tension the yarn over, but the disadvantage shows in letter "P."

J } This swatch takes advantage of the absolute simplicity of the letter "J" and just indicates the shape with sequins (see page 250). They were placed on the right-hand letter square in the chart and on every knit row only. Bear in mind that sequins can't be ironed—they shrivel and curl from the heat—and often don't launder very well, so it might be best avoided on garments. Work a swatch and launder it as a test before making a sweater with a sequined motto.

N } Glitter on glitter for lots of sparkle. Metallic yarns might look a bit tricky, but they are actually easy to knit with, and the wriggly, sparkly surface is visually very forgiving of any uneven stitches, so this can be an excellent yarn to use if you are a beginner to color knitting.

P } For this swatch, the background yarn of "H" was used for the letter. One potential problem with beaded/sequined yarns is obvious here: only one tiny sequin has appeared in the whole letter. You can sometimes wriggle beads/sequins along a yarn to make them appear on the right side (this would be very time-consuming for a big project), but the construction of this yarn (see letter "H") means that the sequins don't move easily.

R } This letter is beaded using the knitted-in technique (see page 251), where a bead can be added to every stitch on every row. Be aware that a lot of beads can affect gauge (tension), stretch the stitches, and change the drape of the knitting, so while a few beaded letters is probably fine, a whole beaded motto might be too much for the yarn to take.

U } This swatch uses the same yarns as letter "N," but the colors are reversed. Metallic yarns always look rather harsh, as though they might be scratchy against the skin—and some possibly are—but this yarn is beautifully soft and drapes well. If you are choosing an unusual yarn, it's always worth knitting a swatch and safety-pinning it to the inside of your T-shirt for a day to see how it feels against the skin.

W } Here, the same yarn combination as letter "D" has been used, but the positions are reversed. The variegated yarn is shown to full effect when used as the background, and the changing colors distract the eye from any uneven stitches, making this another good yarn choice for beginner color knitters.

Y } This letter is cross-stitched (see page 251) in a variegated yarn onto a background of mohair DK. Each cross-stitch covers just one knitted stitch. The secret here is not to pull the stitches tight, just gently taut so that they sit flat but do not distort the knitting.

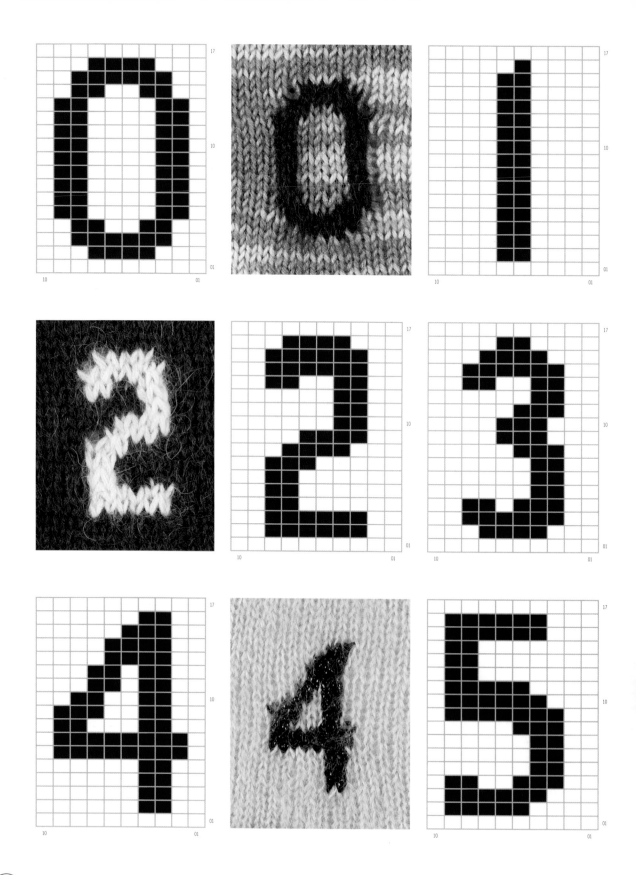

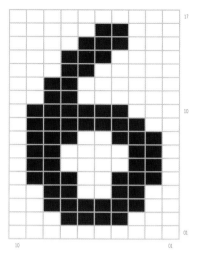

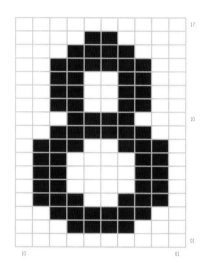

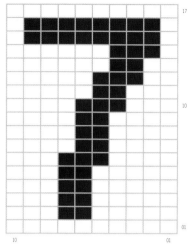

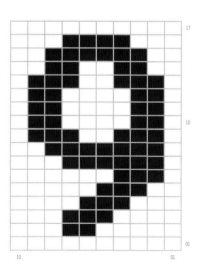

0 This numeral uses the same yarns as letter "W." As the background yarn is stranded across the back of the numeral, the stripes of color—which are short and random—continue on either side of the numeral: if the numeral or letter is worked in intarsia, this doesn't happen (see letter "C" of Graffiti, page 37).

2 Here, the same yarns as letter "A" are used, but the positions of the colors are swapped. Stranding across the back of the numeral will be a test of getting the tension of the floats right (see pages 247–248), but small irregularities in tension can be eased with the tip of a knitter's sewing needle (see page 249) once the knitting is complete.

4 A glitter and texture combination: the background is two strands of fine mohair held together, and the numeral is a single strand of metallic yarn. Used this way, the weights of the two yarns are similar, though the nature of them is entirely different, and you need to be careful to get the tension of the stitches even at the color changes.

7 This numeral is duplicate stitched (Swiss darned; see page 252) in variegated yarn. This embroidery stitch can be worked horizontally or vertically, and obviously the color changes will produce stripes running in the direction you choose. Here, the upright stroke was worked vertically and the top stroke horizontally.

14

QUIRKY HANDWRITING

Letters with an informal handwritten feel add a jaunty touch to a project, especially when the handwriting is a little idiosyncratic, as this is. The letters are quite large and reasonably bold and so not difficult to knit—no awkward single stitches to try to tension perfectly. The fresh, bright color palette of turquoise and lime green boosts the fun feel of this alphabet, though it would also look great in clean contrast colors, such as blue and yellow, or red and white. You can knit these letters in intarsia (see page 243), or strand (see page 246) the background yarn behind them, whichever method you prefer.

Yarns used
◎ Cotton DK yarn in turquoise
◎ Fine mohair yarn in lime green
◎ Metallic yarn in turquoise
◎ Mohair DK yarn in lime green and teal
◎ Multicolored sock yarn in blues
◎ Tweed 4ply yarn in turquoise
◎ Wool/cotton blend 4ply yarn in lime green

Other materials
◎ None

Techniques used
◎ Intarsia (see page 243)
◎ Stranding (see page 246)
◎ Duplicate stitching (Swiss darning; see page 252)

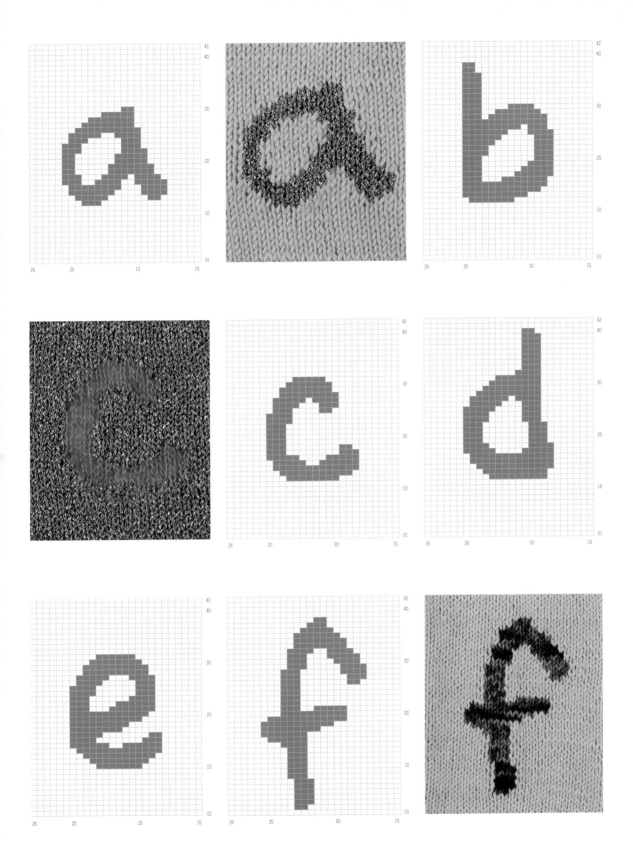

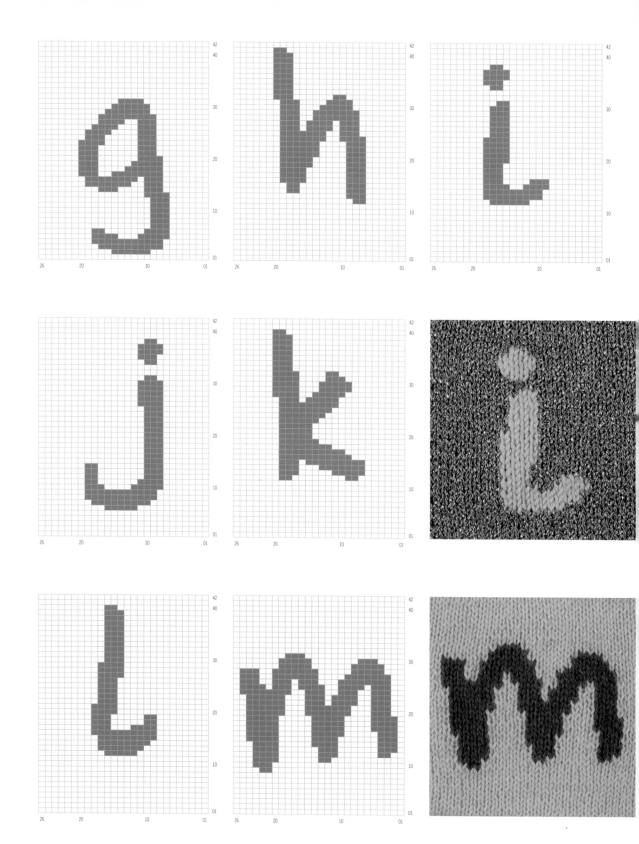

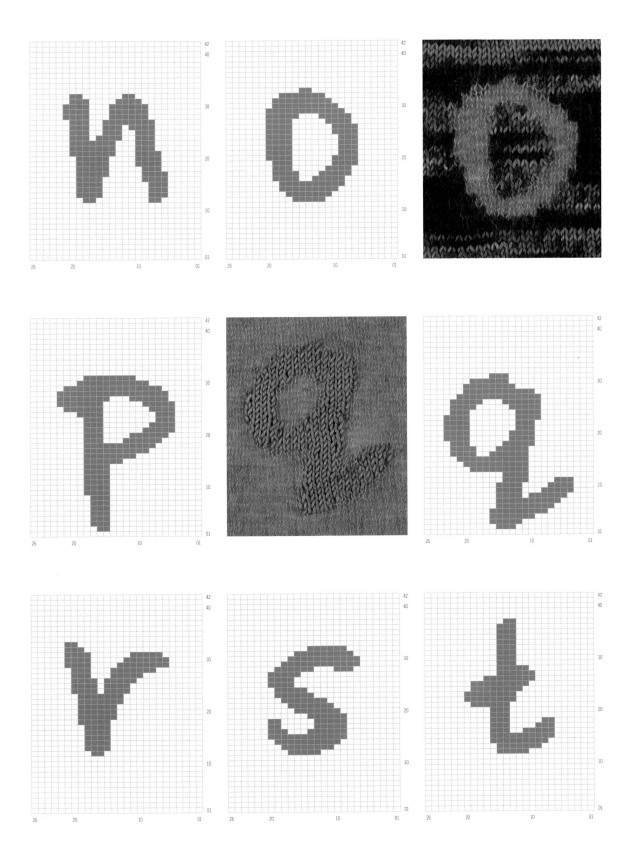

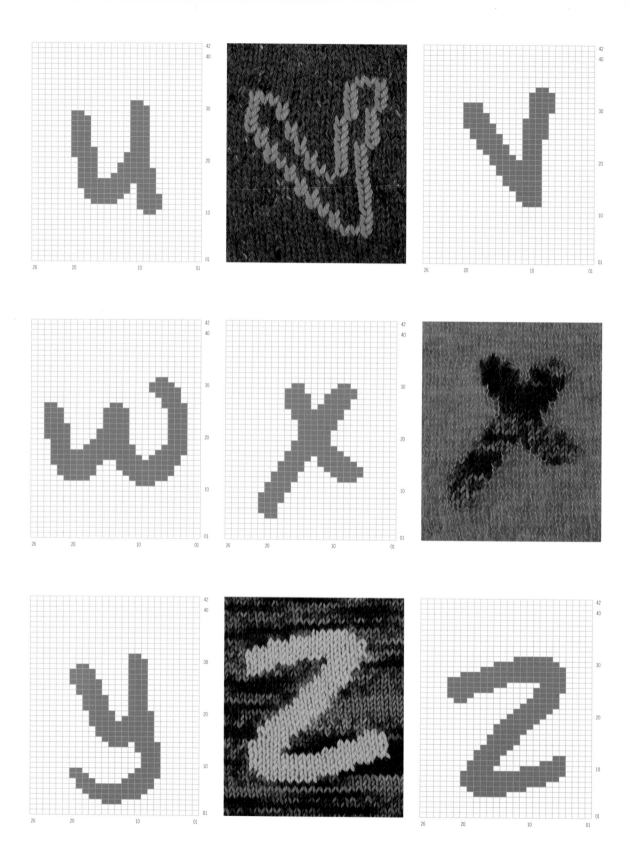

The Knitted Swatches

A} Mixing fibers—here, a metallic yarn and a wool/cotton blend—can make any project more visually interesting, but check that the yarns have compatible laundering requirements before knitting them together. If in doubt, machine wash a swatch. If one fiber shrinks more than the other it will be very visible, and you'll need to hand wash the project.

C} This swatch has a background of metallic yarn and the letter is fine mohair. This combination is quite forgiving of uneven stitches—the fluffy yarn hides them and the wriggly metallic yarn disguises them—so it's one to try if your color knitting is still at the improving stage.

F} Variegated yarns work great with letters, adding a sprinkle of color for no extra effort on your part. They are usually only available in sock weight, and be cautious of those with long color changes (where the color changes only slowly along the yarn's length) as you can end up with a letter that is almost entirely one color, which may not be the effect you had hoped for from a multicolored yarn.

I} Looking at it you might think that metallic yarn is scratchy against the skin, but this one is actually very soft. In addition, it has a lovely fluid drape and so would work well as a garment if you like a bit of sparkle. The letter is knitted in wool/cotton 4ply yarn that is a similar weight to the metallic background.

M} This swatch is knitted entirely in mohair DK yarn. When you are knitting with fuzzy yarns, it's best to work using the intarsia method (see page 243) and not strand either yarn across the back of the other. This is because the fuzz of the stranded color can creep through the stitches and show as a blur on the front.

O} For this swatch, a fine mohair yarn is used to knit a letter on a background of a variegated sock yarn. As this swatch is worked in intarsia, with a separate bobbin (see page 243) of yarn for each side and the middle of the letter, the color differences in the different sections of the background are pronounced.

Q} The background yarn of this swatch is a fine mohair used as a single strand and the letter is a cotton DK yarn. It takes serious color-knitting skills to knit these two very different weights together and achieve such a good-looking result as this. The main issue comes when tensioning the stitches on either side of the intarsia color change (see pages 244–245), and weaving in the ends invisibly (see page 248) will be challenging.

V} You can just outline letters—rather than fill them in with solid color—and they will still be effective, and the best way to outline is to use duplicate stitching (Swiss darning; see page 252). In this swatch, the letter is embroidered with wool/cotton blend yarn on a background of tweed yarn.

X} Variegated color yarn with a short color change (that is, the color changes at short intervals along the yarn's length) can effectively make less of uneven stitches: the shifting tones disguise any slight bagginess. Most variegated yarns are sock weight, so you can easily knit them together with plain 4ply yarns.

Z} Here, the same yarns as letter "F" have been used, but the positions are reversed. Swapping colors like this works very well on an afghan: choose a limited number of colors and work blocks in all the possible variations to create a finished piece that's colorful, but also restrained. Using a variegated sock yarn in one color palette as one of your colors will add extra variety.

15

70s RETRO

The 70s was a decade of bell-bottom trousers, big hair, and fabulous platform shoes. And this groovalicious alphabet—in this perfectly 70s palette of brown, purple, and orange—whisks you back to the decade in an instant. The yarn types are as nostalgic as the colors: glitter and fuzz, with a sprinkle of beads. You could also add sequins (see page 250), as well as the embroidery (see page 251) used to embellish letter "S." The chunky shapes of these letters make them perfect for intarsia knitting (see page 243), though it would be easier to strand (see page 246) the letter color across the backs of the small gaps than introduce another bobbin.

Yarns used
◎ Fine mohair yarn in purple and orange
◎ Metallic yarn in purple and bronze
◎ Mottled sock yarn in purples and in oranges
◎ Wool 4ply yarn in orange and brown
◎ Wool/cotton blend 4ply yarn in purple and brown

Other materials
◎ Brown beads

Techniques used
◎ Intarsia (see page 243)
◎ Stranding (see page 246)
◎ Slip stitch beading (see page 250)
◎ Embroidery (see page 251)
◎ Duplicate stitch (Swiss darning; see page 252)
◎ Bobbles (see page 252)

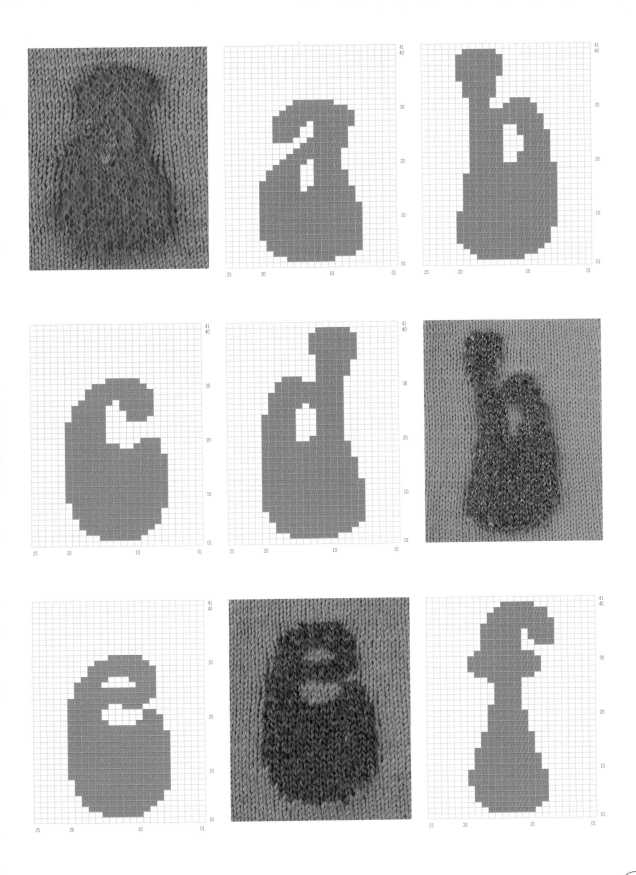

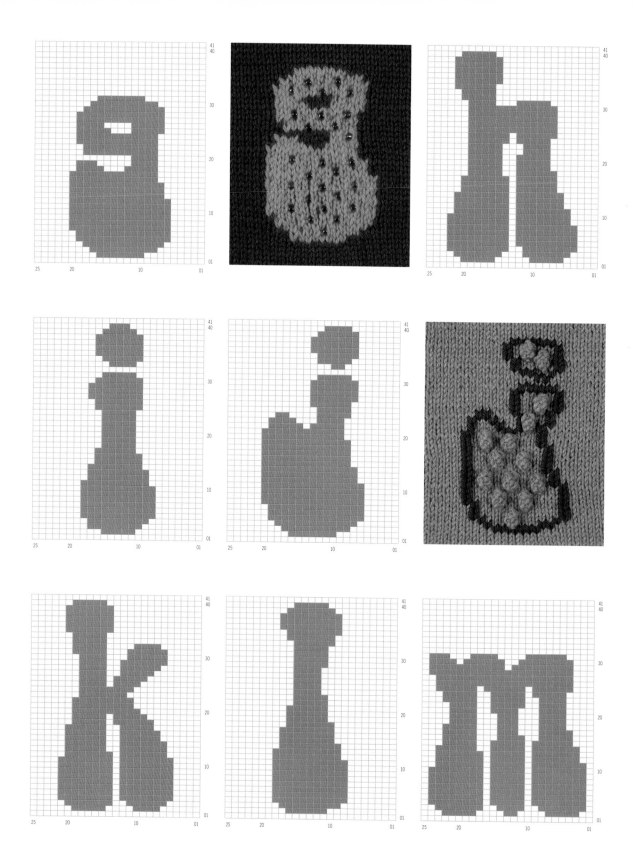

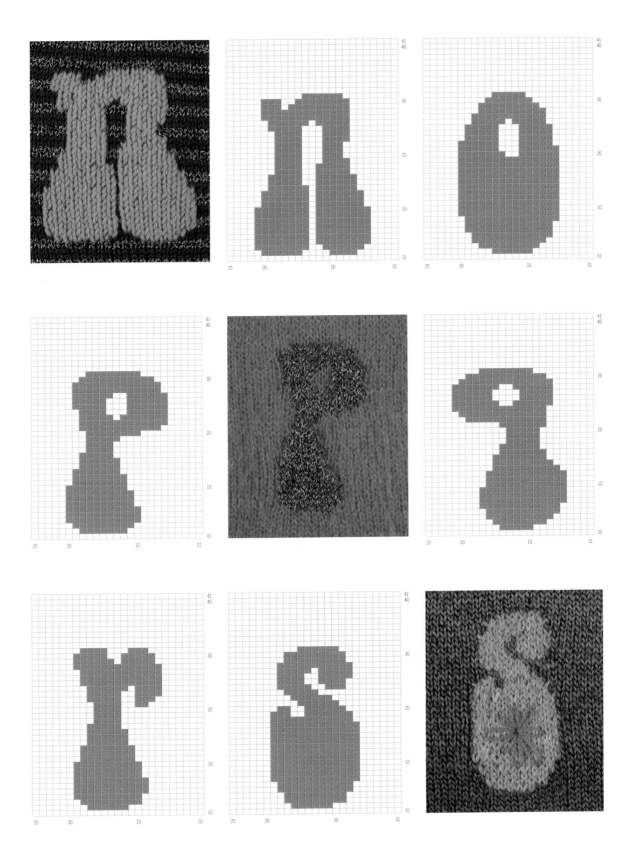

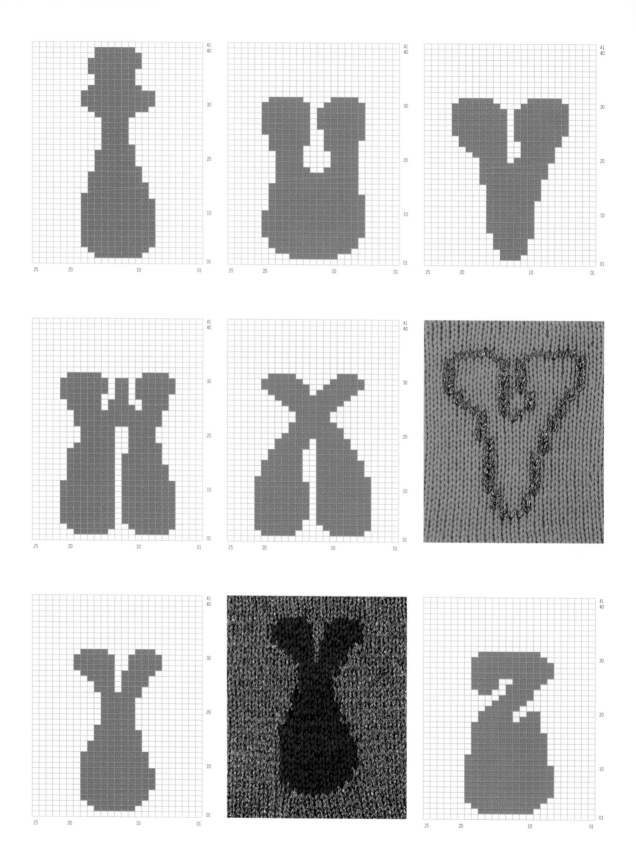

The Knitted Swatches

A Doubling up a fine yarn to make a strand the same weight as a thicker yarn is perfectly viable. Here, the letter is knitted in doubled fine mohair on a background of wool/cotton 4ply. If you are going to use different weight yarns, it's always worth working a swatch first, just to check that you are happy with the result.

B This letter is knitted in one strand of metallic yarn held together with one strand of fine mohair. If you've never knitted with two different yarns held together, don't be alarmed by the idea: they will quickly twist around one another to create a single strand, and the naturally mottled surface means that should you miss one of the yarns for a stitch, it won't show.

E Sock yarns come in a wide variety of colorways, from rainbow self-striping to softly mottled colors, via almost any combination you can think of. They work great with letters, adding an extra sprinkle of color with no extra effort on your part. This letter is worked in a mottled purple sock yarn on a plain wool/cotton background.

G These beads were placed using the slip stitch method (see page 250). When you are planning where to place beads in this way, remember that they lie across the base of the slipped stitch and so sit low on the row of knitting. If you put them on the first row of a new color, they can overlap onto the last row of the previous color.

J These letters are spacious enough for texture to be added, and bobbles (see page 252) seem a suitably 70s addition. The bobbles are plotted on the chart and then the swatch is knitted in one color, working the bobbles as you go. The letter outline is duplicate stitched (Swiss darned; see page 252) onto the knitting once it is complete.

N This letter is duplicate stitched (Swiss darned; see page 252), which allows you to easily include a patterned background in a project. Here, it's a simple stripe pattern, but you can duplicate stitch onto any stockinette (stocking) stitch knitting. Of course, if you are an expert color knitter, then you can knit a patterned background together with letters, but duplicate stitching like this is a great alternative.

P This swatch has a background of fine mohair used double to make it a similar weight to the metallic yarn used for the letter. This is a yarn combination that is quite forgiving of uneven stitches—the fluffy yarn hides them and the wriggly surface of the metallic yarn disguises them—so it's one for beginner color knitters to try.

S You can add color and detail to finished knitting with simple embroidery stitches (see page 251). The secret to successful embroidery on knitting is getting the stitch tension right. If you pull the embroidery stitches tight, as you might on woven fabric, you will distort the knitting, so pull them gently taut and adjust individual stitches as necessary.

V Outlining a letter rather than filling in the whole shape can be very successful if the letter shape is bold enough, and is best done with duplicate stitch (Swiss darning; see page 252). This embroidery stitch can be worked horizontally or vertically, and it's worth experimenting on a swatch of stockinette (stocking) stitch to see if you find one direction easier to work than the other.

Y This letter is knitted in wool 4ply yarn on a metallic background. Metallic yarns might look a bit tricky, but they are actually easy to knit with, and the wriggly, sparkly surface is visually very forgiving of any uneven stitches, so this can be an excellent yarn to use if you are new to color knitting.

PROJECT 6

♥ PILLOW

Using one color palette is a great way to bring together different elements to make a strong design. This pillow has two letters from different alphabets, a big heart and a little heart, but the palette of toning blues prevents it from looking cluttered.

Yarn
◎ **Rowan Creative Focus Worsted**
1 x 3½ oz (100 g) ball in each of Blue Moor Heather (791) A, Blue Smoke (089) B, Marine (660) C, and Delft (321) D

Letters
◎ 70s Retro (see page 134)
◎ Curly (see page 144)

Tools
◎ Pair of US 7 (4.5 mm) knitting needles
◎ Knitter's sewing needle
◎ 16½ x 40 in (41 x 60 cm) of medium-weight cotton fabric for pillow back, plus 16½ x 16½ in (41 x 41 cm) for lining pillow front if required
◎ Sewing machine
◎ Sewing thread to match fabric
◎ 16 x 16 in (40 x 40 cm) pillow pad

Measurements
◎ Approximately 16 x 16 in (40 x 40 cm)

Gauge (tension)
◎ 20 sts and 24 rows to 4 in (10 cm) over st st using Rowan Creative Focus Worsted and US 7 (4.5 mm) needles

Abbreviations
◎ See page 254.
◎ Note: use the intarsia method (see page 243) throughout.

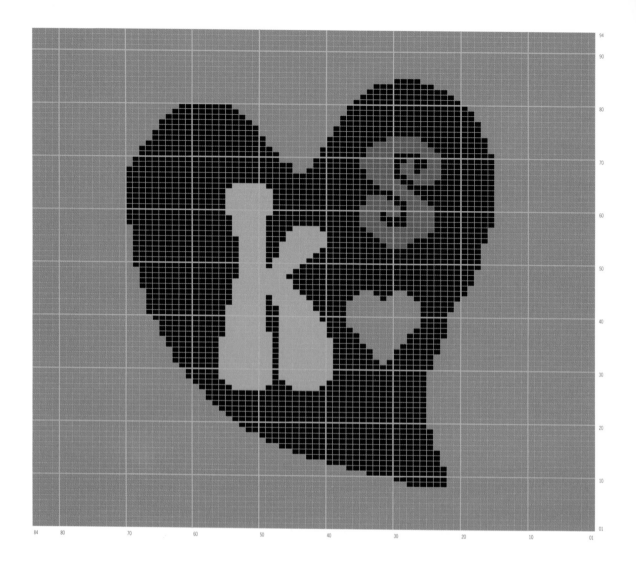

KEY

 – A

 – B

 – C

 – D

POSITIONING THE LETTERS

The large heart motif is generously sized and could contain letters from most of the alphabets in this book. Photocopy the letters you would like to use and the pillow chart to the same scale. Cut out the letters roughly, leaving a border of chart squares around them, and position them on the pillow chart where you want them to be, aligning the letter grids with the pillow grid. If need be, photocopy the small heart separately and cut it out to move it to a new position. Tape all the elements in place to create your own chart.

PILLOW FRONT

Using yarn A, cast on 84 sts.

Working in st st throughout, work chart, joining in separate
balls of yarns A, B, C, and D as required.

Bind (cast) off.

TO MAKE UP

- Weave in loose ends.
- Block knitted piece.
- If you are concerned that the pillow pad will show through
the knitting, then line the knitting with a piece of fabric
that tones in with the yarn: here, the knitting is lined with
the blue cotton used for the cushion back.
- Pin the WS of the knitting to the RS of the lining, then
machine sew all around the edges with a narrow zigzag
stitch to hold the layers together. Then treat this as one
piece. (Lining the knitting will also prevent it from
stretching and increase its durability).
- Cut the piece of backing material in half across the width.
- Press under and sew a double ³/₈ in (1 cm) hem at one long
end of each piece.
- Lay the pillow front flat and RS up.
- Lay one backing piece RS down on top of the pillow front,
with the hemmed end toward the middle and matching all
other raw edges.
- Lay the second piece on the other end of the pillow front in
the same way, so that the hemmed ends overlap in the
middle of the pillow.
- Using straight stitch and taking a ³/₈ in (1 cm) seam
allowance, machine sew right around the edges of
the pillow.
- Turn RS out and insert pillow pad.

16

CURLY

These are quirky, playful letters with a child-friendly feel. They're knitted here in pinks, which makes them look super-girly, but they'd work well in colors more suited to boys, too, or in a grown-up but naïve palette of duck-egg blue and ecru, or Norwegian red and taupe. The shapes are relatively complicated compared to some of the other letters in this book, so you will need to follow the charts carefully to introduce colors at the right places as the strokes of the letters curl back on themselves. As the strokes are thin, you may find it easiest to always strand (see page 246) the background yarn right across the backs of the letters, as was done here.

Yarns used
◎ Cotton 4ply yarn in palest pink
◎ Fine mohair yarn in palest pink
◎ Metallic yarn in bright pink
◎ Variegated fine mohair yarn in pinks
◎ Wool/cotton blend 4ply yarn in dark pink
◎ Wool/cotton blend DK yarn in pale pink and bright pink

Other materials
◎ Bright pink beads
◎ Pale pink beads

Techniques used
◎ Intarsia (see page 243)
◎ Stranding (see page 246)
◎ Knitted-in beading (see page 251)
◎ Duplicate stitching (Swiss darning; see page 252)

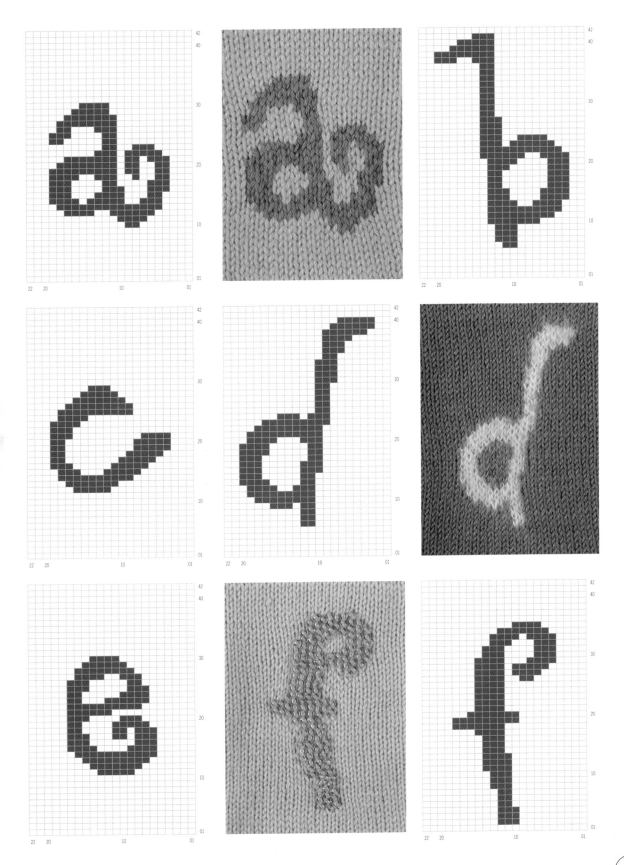

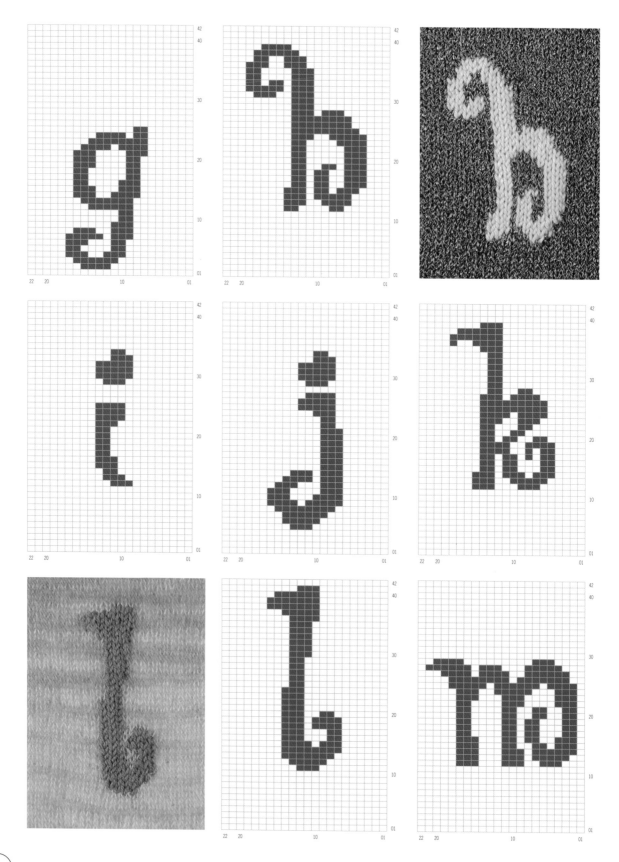

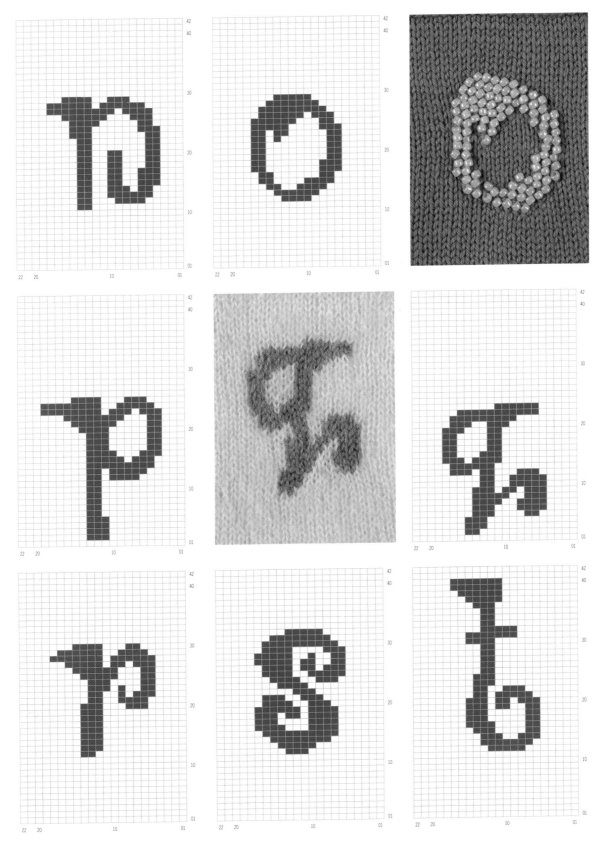

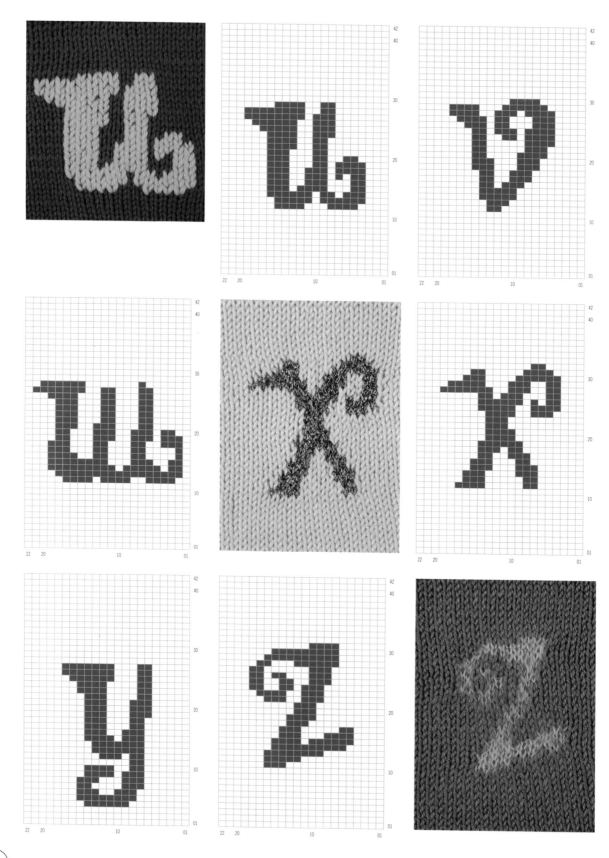

The Knitted Swatches

A This swatch is worked entirely in wool DK yarn. Wool is a naturally slightly elastic fiber, so it's easier to adjust the tension of individual stitches than it is with cotton yarn. Once the knitting is complete, any slightly uneven stitches can be eased out with the tip of a knitter's sewing needle (see page 249), and blocking the knitting will also improve the finish.

D There is one problem you can encounter when using a fluffy yarn and stranding across the back of a smooth yarn; some fluff can creep up through the stitches of the smooth yarn and show on the front. As the gap in this letter is fairly small, and the fluff of the letter is migrating across the surface anyway, it isn't a problem here, but it is something to bear in mind.

F These beads are color-lined; that is, they are made of clear glass and the color is added inside the bead hole. If you are using this type of bead, there are a couple of things to check: first, that the color doesn't flake off onto the yarn as the beads are slipped along it; second, that you can launder the beads without the color vanishing—both these problems can occur with cheaply made color-lined beads.

H You might think that metallic yarns are stiff and unyielding—as the name suggests—but in fact they are usually very fluid and drape well. You can use them with stiffer yarns, such as the cotton 4ply used for the letter here, but you should swatch the two together before starting a project to check that the different knitted fabrics will work together.

L The background of this swatch is a variegated fine mohair, which can't be doubled to match the weight of the wool/cotton 4ply used for the letter without spoiling the stripe pattern. As the background yarn is stranded across the back of the letter, the stripes of color continue either side of the letter: if the letter is worked in intarsia, this doesn't happen (see letter "C" of Graffiti, page 37).

O This letter is beaded using the knitted-in technique (see page 251), where a bead can be added to every stitch on every row. Be aware that a lot of beads can affect gauge (tension), stretch the stitches, and change the drape of the knitting, so while a few beaded letters is probably fine, a whole beaded motto might be too much for the yarn to take.

Q When a letter yarn is much darker than the background, it's best to strand right across the back of gaps in the letters if there are four or fewer stitches, and catch floats in (see page 247)—rather than weaving in (see page 248)—if the gaps are wider. This will prevent flecks of the background yarn from showing through.

U This letter is duplicate stitched (Swiss darned; see page 252) rather than knitted. When working a whole letter in duplicate stitch, be careful to keep the embroidery at a similar tension to the knitting; if you pull the embroidery yarn too tight it won't cover the background neatly and the fabric will be distorted.

X The background of this swatch is cotton 4ply and the letter "A" metallic yarn. Check that two different fibers can be laundered together. If in doubt, machine wash a swatch. If one fiber shrinks more than the other it will be very visible, and you'll need to hand wash the project.

Z Variegated yarns work great with letters, adding a sprinkle of color with no extra effort on your part. However, be careful of those with long color changes (that is, when the color changes only slowly along the yarn's length) as you can end up with a letter almost entirely one color, as here, which may not be the effect you had hoped for from a multicolored yarn.

17

20s RETRO

A combination of delicate and geometric, these letters have a strong Art Deco flavor, which is enhanced by the plum and yellow color palette. These rich, high-contrast colors are a typical 20s combination, though you could choose pastel colors for a Miami Beach feel that would also work well with the letter shapes. The sparkle elements—metallic yarn and sequins—add a luxe touch that's appropriate for both the look and spirit of the period. The thicker lines are best knitted using the intarsia technique (see page 243), while the thin lines can be stranded (see page 246), or duplicate stitched (Swiss darned; see page 252).

Yarns used
◎ Cotton 4ply yarn in yellow
◎ Fine mohair yarn in plum and yellow
◎ Metallic yarn in plum and gold
◎ Tweed DK yarn in plum and yellow
◎ Wool 4ply yarn in yellow
◎ Wool DK yarn in plum and yellow

Other materials
◎ Gold sequins

Techniques used
◎ Intarsia (see page 243)
◎ Stranding (see page 246)
◎ Slip stitch sequins (see page 250)
◎ Duplicate stitching
(Swiss darning; see page 252)

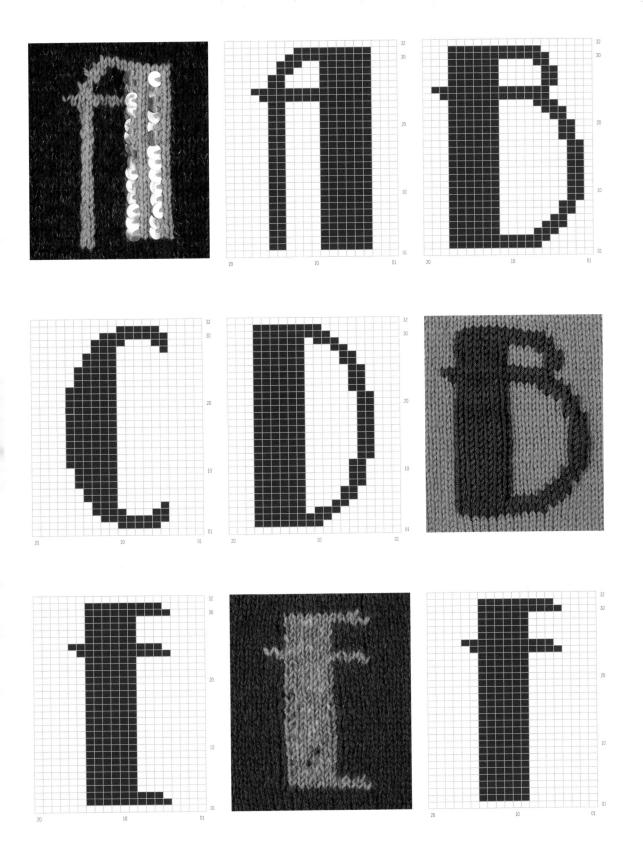

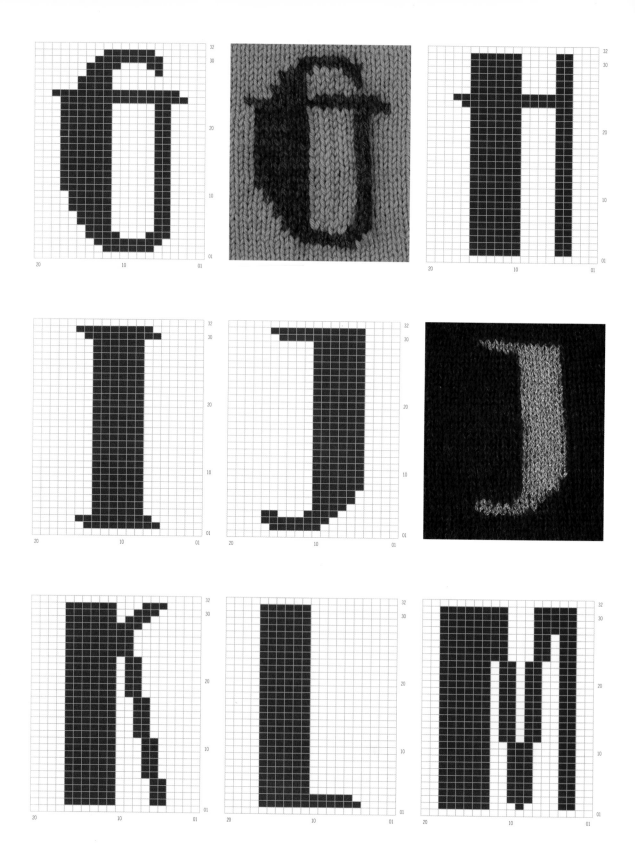

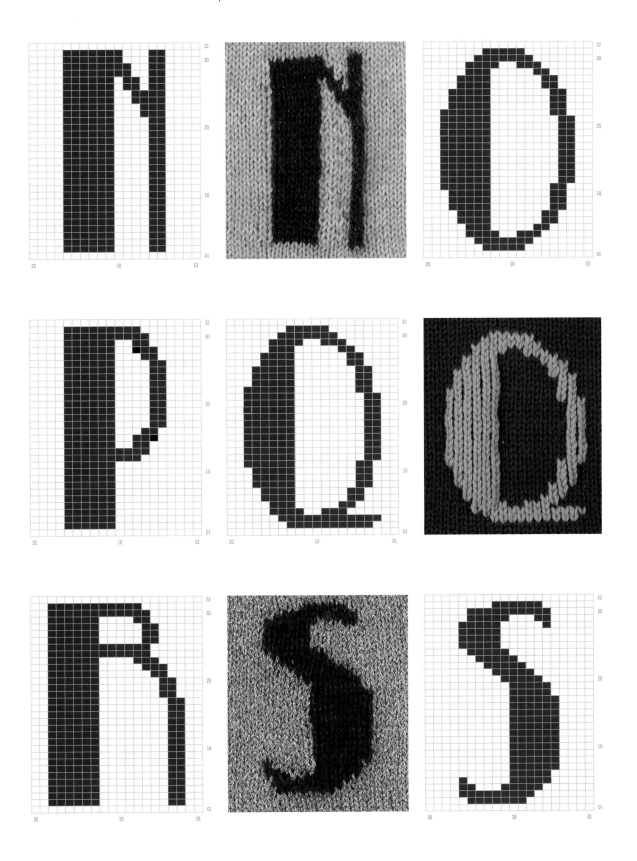

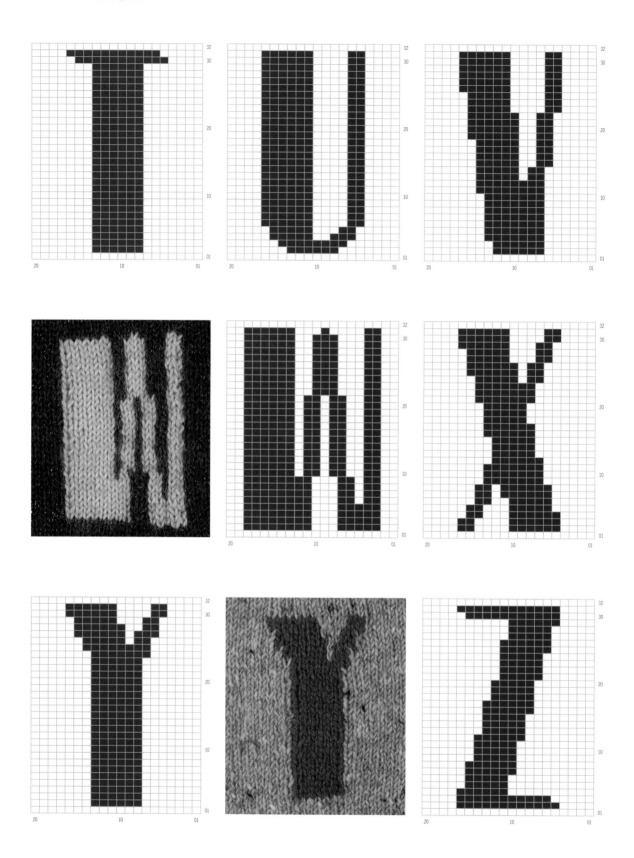

The Knitted Swatches

A Here, the background is one strand of tweed and one of mohair held together to create a textural fabric that is also softly mottled. The letter is worked in wool 4ply used doubled, with sequins added using the slip stitch technique (see page 250) on the second and fifth stitches of the right-hand vertical stroke.

B This letter is worked in wool yarns: the background is 4ply and the letter is duplicate stitched (Swiss darned; see page 252) with DK. Using a heavier yarn for the duplicate stitch gives the letter an embossed feel, and helps prevent the background fabric from showing between the surface stitches, which can happen with duplicate stitch (see letter "Q"). Be careful to get the tension of the stitches right or the fabric can be distorted.

E The background of this letter is wool DK with the letter knitted in tweed. A knitter's tip: tweed yarns are forgiving if you are new to color knitting, as the flecked colors help to hide any uneven stitches. This tweed is very vibrantly colored (see letter "Y"); such bright yarns can be a bit overwhelming in large areas, but work great for small accents.

G For this swatch the background is wool DK, and the letter is one strand of wool DK and one strand of mohair held together. The fine mohair adds soft texture, but only a little extra bulk, so used over a small area the overall gauge (tension) and drape of the fabric shouldn't be affected.

J A glitter and texture combination: the background is two strands of mohair held together and the letter is a single strand of metallic yarn. Used this way the weights of the two yarns are similar, though the nature of them is entirely different and you need to take a bit of care to get the tension of the stitches even at the color changes.

N For this swatch, both the background and letter are worked with two yarns held together. The background is one strand of cotton 4ply and one strand of mohair, and the letter is one strand of metallic yarn and one strand of mohair (see also letter "W"). If you've never knitted with two different yarns together, don't be alarmed by the idea: they will quickly twist around one another to create a single strand, and the naturally mottled surface means that should you miss one of the yarns for a stitch, it won't show.

Q This letter is duplicate stitched (Swiss darned; see page 252) in the same weight yarn as was used to knit the background: both are wool DK. You can see the background color between the surface stitches, though the vertical lines rather suit the elongated letter shape and so the effect is generally good.

S This swatch uses the same yarns as letter "J," but the positions are reversed: the background is metallic yarn and the letter two strands of mohair. Although the metallic yarn is not as stable as the two strands of mohair, it's much easier to knit with than it might seem, and the glittering surface is very forgiving of any uneven stitches.

W Here, the same yarn combination as letter "N" has been used, but the positions are reversed. The glitter of the metallic yarn is softened by the fuzz of the mohair and the resulting fabric has a lovely drape, soft but not too fluid. The cotton 4ply/mohair blend of the letter is a little stiffer, but the two combinations are perfectly viable together. Remember to check that the two yarns have compatible laundering requirements before knitting them together.

Y For this letter, the same yarns as letter "E" have been used, but with the tweed as the background. The full effect of the flecked tweed yarn comes to the fore here, and the two yarns are similar enough in weight to be knitted together without having to double up either one.

EMOTICONS, DINGBATS, AND PUNCTUATION

Textspeak can hop from your phone to your knitting with the help of the various symbols charted here. There is a good selection of punctuation marks and digits that you can use to compose your own emoticons, plus a few useful dingbats. You can, of course, also use the punctuation as it was originally intended… If the charts here are not the right size for the alphabet you want to use, then treat them as a template and scale the symbols up to suit your chosen letters. As the elements are small, you may find it easiest to strand (see page 246) the background yarn right across the backs of the symbols, as was done here.

Yarns used
◎ Cotton 4ply yarn in orange
◎ Fine mohair yarn in orange
◎ Metallic yarn in blue
◎ Wool 4ply yarn in blue and orange

Other materials
◎ Blue beads

Techniques used
◎ Intarsia (see page 243)
◎ Stranding (see page 246)
◎ Knitted-in beading (see page 251)
◎ Duplicate stitch (Swiss darning; see page 252)

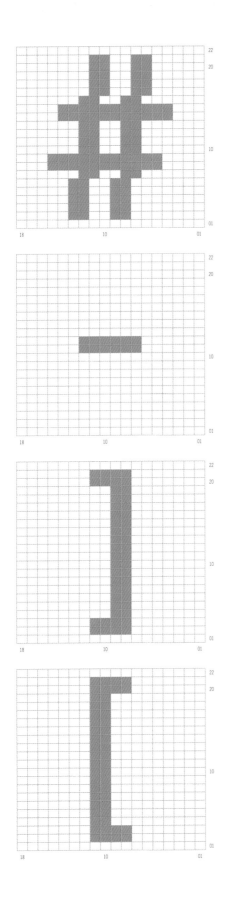

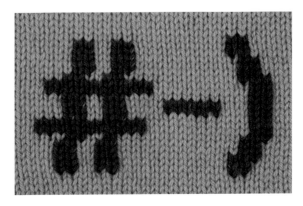

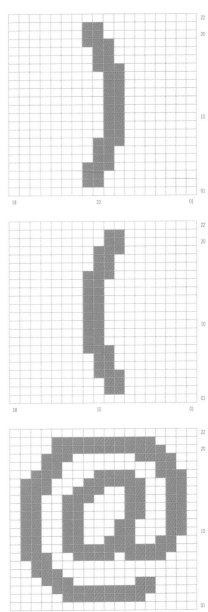

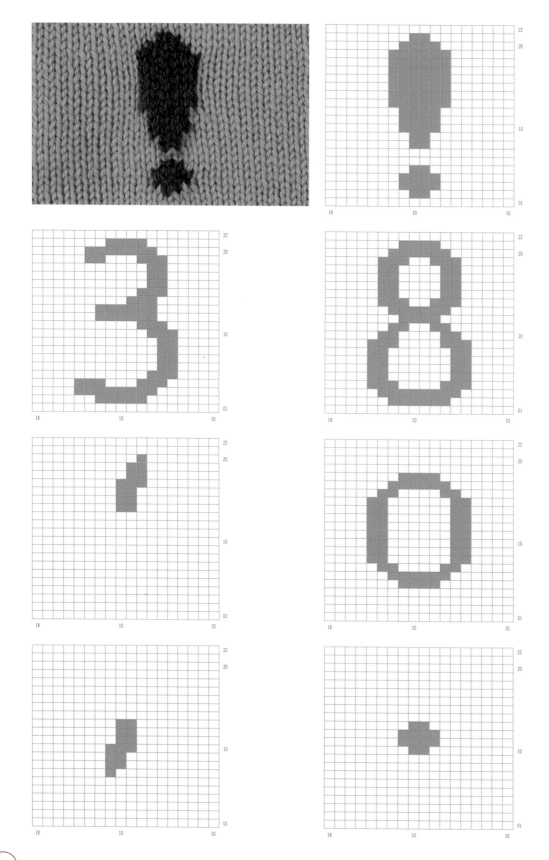

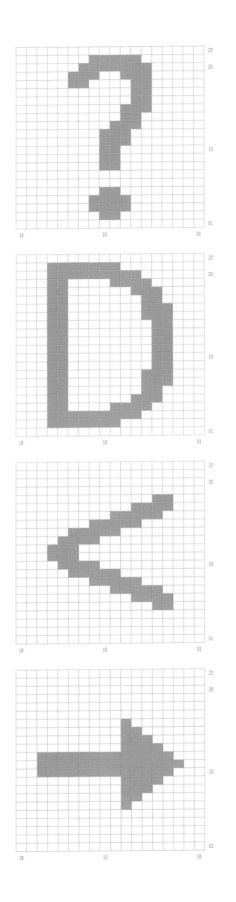

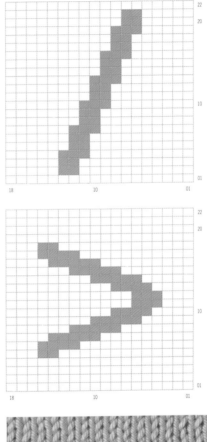

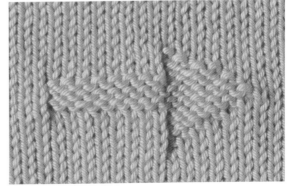

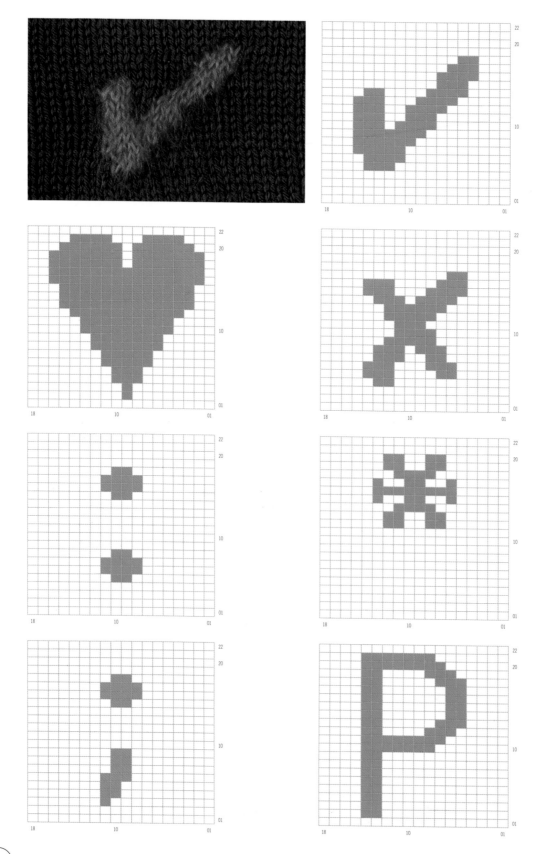

The Knitted Swatches

#-) This emoticon is duplicate stitched (Swiss darned; see page 252) in the same weight yarn as was used to knit the background: both are wool 4ply yarn. When working duplicate stitch, be careful to keep the embroidery at a similar tension to the knitting; if you pull the embroidery yarn too tight, it won't cover the background neatly and the fabric will be distorted.

! This swatch is worked entirely in wool 4ply yarn. Wool is a naturally slightly elastic fiber, so it's easier to adjust the tension of individual stitches than it is with cotton yarn. Once the knitting is complete, any slightly uneven stitches can be eased out with the tip of a knitter's sewing needle (see page 249), and blocking the knitting will also improve the finish.

? This symbol is beaded using the knitted-in technique (see page 251), where a bead can be added to every stitch on every row. However, as the beads are a little larger than the stitch, the knit stitches are twisted to make the beads lie at a different angle and so give each bead a bit more room. To do this, simply work the technique in the usual way on the purl rows, but on the knit rows, work the beaded stitches through the back loop: this produces the herringbone pattern of beads.

→ You can also work digits or symbols in texture, though it might take a bit of planning: simpler textures and bolder shapes will usually work best. This symbol is knitted in reverse stockinette (stocking) stitch, and the smooth cotton yarn makes the most of the changing stitch patterns.

✔ The dingbat on this swatch is knitted in a fine mohair and it's been used double to make it a similar weight to the wool yarn of the background. If you have never worked with doubled yarn, don't be put off: the strands twist around one another as you work, making it easy to treat them as a single strand, and with fluffy yarn such as this, it won't show if you miss one strand in a stitch.

;P This swatch has a background of fine mohair used double to make it a similar weight to the metallic yarn used for the emoticon. This combination is quite forgiving of uneven stitches—the fluffy yarn hides them and the wriggly metallic yarn disguises them—so it's one to try if you are fairly new to color knitting.

PROJECT 7

EMOTICON CUFFS

Here are some easy-to-knit wrist-warmer cuffs with cute emoticons that say just how you feel. Use the happy and mad charts given on page 164, or create your own emoticons from the selection of symbols, numbers, letters, and dingbats we have charted for you.

Yarns
◎ **Rowan Siena 4ply**
1 x 1¾ oz (50 g) ball in Alpine (671) A and Cream (652) B

Letters
◎ Emoticons, Dingbats, and Punctuation (see page 156)

Tools
◎ Pair of US 2 (2.75 mm) knitting needles
◎ Knitter's sewing needle

Measurements
◎ Approximately 3½ in (9 cm) wide by 7 in (18 cm) around

Gauge (tension)
◎ 28 sts and 38 rows to 4 in (10 cm) over st st
using US 2 (2.75 mm) needles

Abbreviations
◎ See page 254.
◎ Note: strand (see page 246) the background
yarn behind the emoticons.

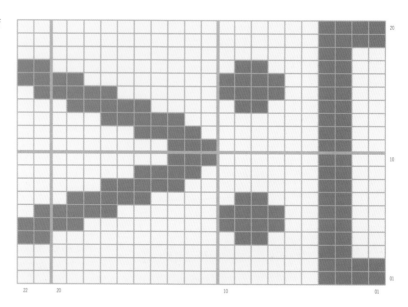

Happy Cuff

Mad Cuff

POSITIONING THE SYMBOLS

As the emoticons are so small and simple, it's easy to position symbols you want to use by eye. Photocopy them, then cut them out roughly, allowing a border of chart squares all around. Lay the symbols out and slide them into the best positions, aligning the rows of the border squares as desired. Tape them together to make your chart.

HAPPY CUFF

Using yarn A, cast on 52 sts.

Row 1 (RS): [K1, p1] to end of row.

Row 2: [P1, k1] to end of row.

Rep rows 1–2 once more.

Starting with a k row, work 4 rows st st.

PLACE CHART

Row 9: K15, place row 1 of chart over next 22 sts, joining in separate balls of yarn B as required, k15.

Row 10: P15, place row 2 of chart over next 22 sts, p15.

Cont in patt as set until row 20 of chart is complete.

Break yarn B and cont in yarn A.

Starting with a k row, work 4 rows st st.

Row 33: [K1, p1] to end of row.

Row 34: [P1, k1] to end of row.

Rep rows 33–34 once more.

Bind (cast) off.

MAD CUFF

Using yarn B, cast on 52 sts.

Row 1 (RS): [K1, p1] to end of row.

Row 2: [P1, k1] to end of row.

Rep rows 1–2 once more.

Starting with a k row, work 4 rows st st.

PLACE CHART

Row 9: K15, place row 1 of chart over next 22 sts, joining in separate balls of yarn A as required, k15.

Row 10: P15, place row 2 of chart over next 22 sts, p15.

Cont in patt as set until row 20 of chart is complete.

Break yarn A and cont in yarn B.

Starting with a k row, work 4 rows st st.

Row 33: [K1, p1] to end of row.

Row 34: [P1, k1] to end of row.

Rep rows 33–34 once more.

Bind (cast) off.

TO MAKE UP

- Weave in loose ends.
- Block knitted pieces.
- Join back seam with mattress stitch or backstitch as preferred.

18

STENCIL

I was so pleased to find that you can still buy plastic rulers with these letters cut into them, ready to decorate and label anything that will stay still long enough to be stenciled on. To make the breaks in the letters workable in knitted stitches, this is quite a large-scale alphabet. It's ideal for blankets, bags, sweaters, scarves—it would make a great alternative typeface for the Striped Scarf (see page 116). You can knit these letters in intarsia (see page 243), or strand (see page 246) the background yarn behind them, whichever method you prefer; here, they are stranded.

Yarns used
◎ Fine mohair yarn in pale blue and red
◎ Metallic yarn in red
◎ Mohair DK yarn in pale blue, bright blue, and red
◎ Tweed 4ply yarn in pale blue and red
◎ Wool 4ply yarn in white

Other materials
◎ Blue beads
◎ Blue sequins
◎ White beads

Techniques used
◎ Intarsia (see page 243)
◎ Stranding (see page 246)
◎ Slip stitch beading (see page 250)
◎ Slip stitch sequins (see page 250)
◎ Knitted-in beading (see page 251)
◎ Duplicate stitch (Swiss darning; see page 252)

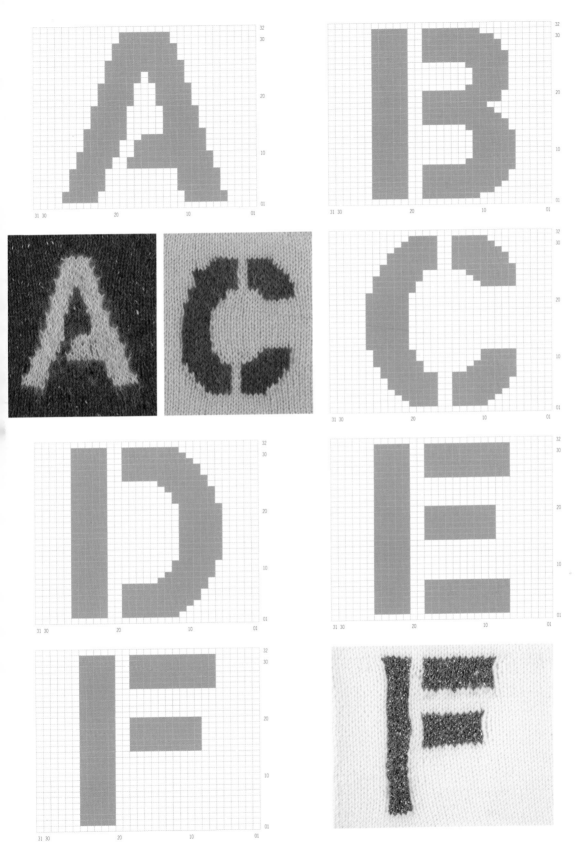

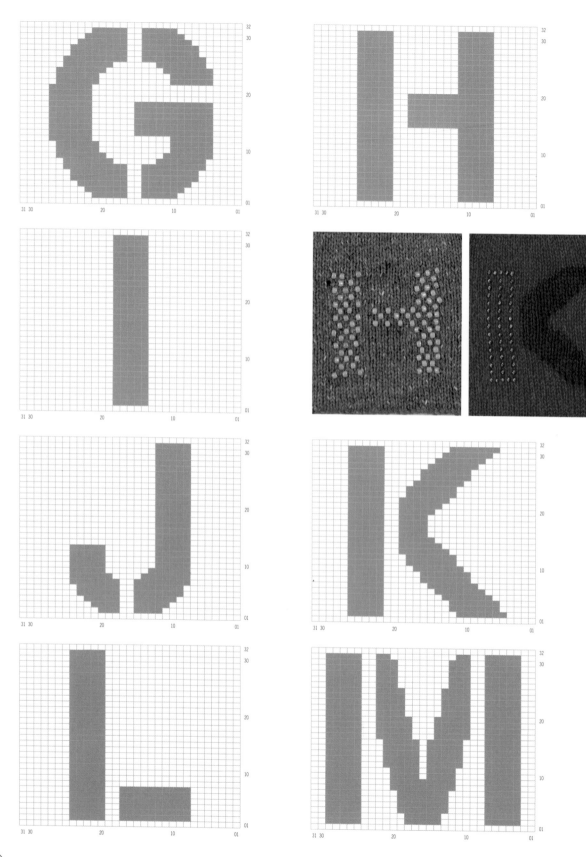

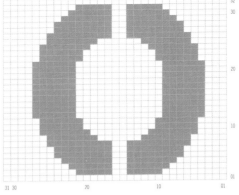

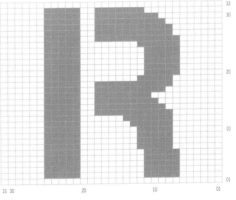

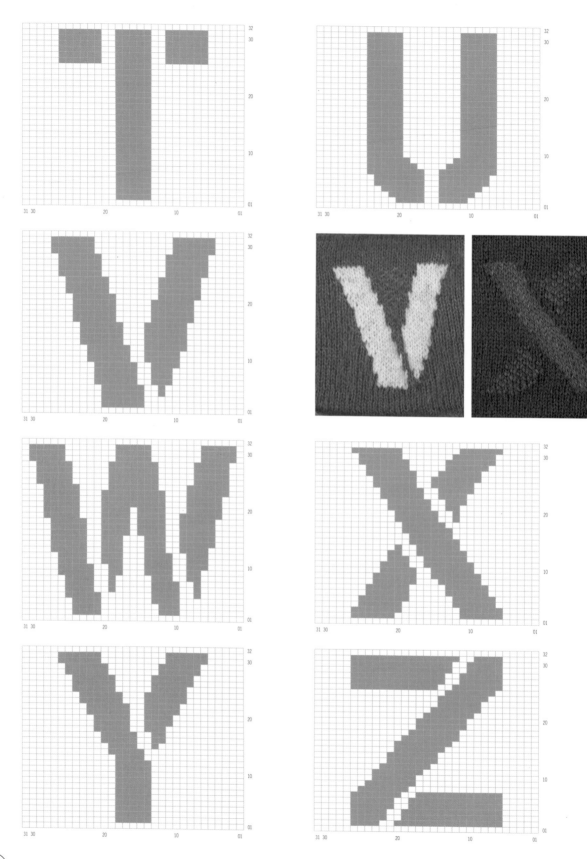

The Knitted Swatches

A The background yarn of this swatch is a fine mohair and it's been used double to make it a similar weight to the tweed 4ply yarn that the letter is knitted in. If you have never worked with doubled yarn, don't be put off: the strands twist around one another as you work, making it easy to treat them as a single strand, and with fluffy yarn such as this, it won't show if you miss one strand in a stitch.

C Double-knitting weight yarns are probably the most commonly available weight and there are many, many fiber and textural variations: this yarn is a lambswool and mohair blend, so it's both soft and fluffy. Using two yarns of the same weight does make it relatively easy to tension the stitches evenly at the color changes and so work neat color knitting, especially when the yarn has a little elasticity, as this wool yarn does.

F This swatch has a background of wool 4ply with the letter knitted in a metallic yarn. Metallic yarns might look a bit tricky, but they are actually easy to knit with, and the wriggly, sparkly surface is visually very forgiving of any uneven stitches, so this can be an excellent yarn to use if you are a beginner to color knitting.

H If you hate color knitting, then there are other ways of creating letters; this letter is made from just beads placed using the slip stitch method (see page 250). When you are planning where to place beads in this way, remember that they lie across the base of the slipped stitch and so sit low on the row of knitting.

K Letters can be made using more than one technique: the upright stroke of this letter is beaded using the knitted-in technique (see page 251), where the beads sit at a slight angle on one "leg" of the stitch. The sloping strokes are duplicate stitched (Swiss darned; see page 252) in the same mohair DK yarn that the swatch is knitted in.

O This swatch takes advantage of the absolute simplicity of the letter "O" and just indicates the shape with sequins (see page 250). They were placed on the squares on the outside edge of the letter and on every knit row only. Bear in mind that sequins can't be ironed—they shrivel and curl from the heat—and often don't launder very well, so might be best avoided on garments.

R This letter is duplicate stitched (Swiss darned; see page 252), which allows you to easily experiment with working on a patterned background. Here, it's a simple stripe pattern and the letter is worked in the lighter of the two stripe colors, so only the darker stripes actually need to be embroidered.

S Duplicate stitch (Swiss darning; see page 252) is excellent for adding small details to a motif that you'd find tricky to color knit, or for correcting a mistake in a color-knitted motif. Here, the letter "S" was knitted as a solid, complete shape, then the breaks were duplicate stitched in the background yarn.

V This letter is knitted in wool 4ply yarn on a background of fine mohair used double. It clearly shows one problem you can encounter when using a fluffy yarn and stranding across the back of a smooth yarn; some fluff can creep up through the stitches of the smooth yarn and show on the front. Here, it's a blur of color over the whole letter, so you can always argue that it's a deliberate effect.

X One stroke of this letter is solid and the other knitted in alternating stitches of the background color and letter color, in classic Fair Isle fashion. If you can strand with one yarn in each hand (see page 247), this is a quick and easy effect to work, but if you keep dropping and picking up yarns (see page 246), it'll be time-consuming.

19

HEARTS

When I was younger we used to buy candy hearts—pastel-colored discs with an embossed heart and a motto in it: "Be mine," "True love," "Kiss me." These letters are inspired by those sweets. This is one of the more complicated alphabets to knit, as you have to follow the rows carefully to work the heart and letter at the same time. As the strokes of the letters and the outline heart are thin, you may find it easiest to strand (see page 246) both the background yarn right across the backs of the letters and heart, and the heart/letter yarn across the back of the area of background within the heart, as was done here.

Yarns used
◎ Cotton 4ply yarn in red and lilac
◎ Fine mohair yarn in red and lilac
◎ Metallic yarn in red and pink
◎ Mohair DK yarn in red and pale blue
◎ Tweed DK yarn in red
◎ Wool 4ply yarn in yellow
◎ Wool/cotton blend 4ply yarn in pale green
◎ Wool/cotton blend DK yarn in red and pale pink
◎ Wool DK yarn in red, pale mint, pale blue, and yellow

Other materials
◎ Red beads

Techniques used
◎ Intarsia (see page 243)
◎ Stranding (see page 246)
◎ Slip stitch beading (see page 250)
◎ Duplicate stitch (Swiss darning; see page 252)

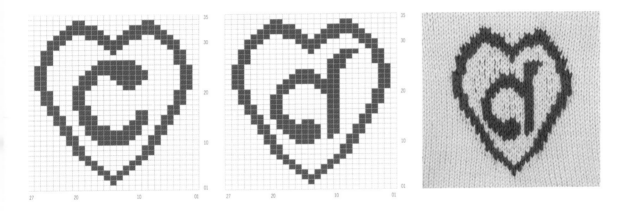

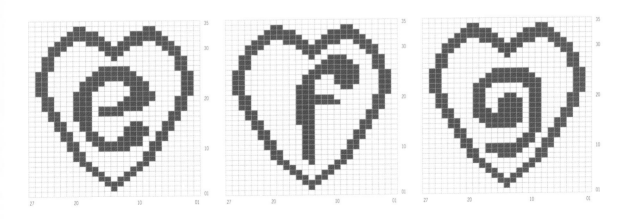

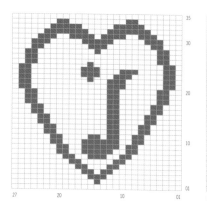

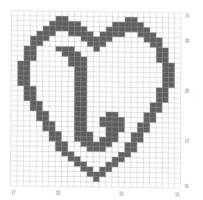

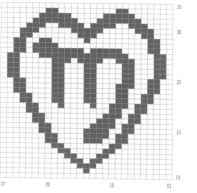

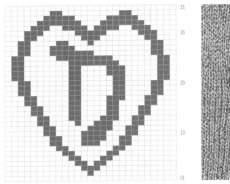

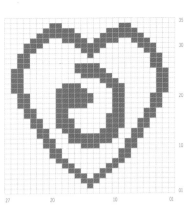

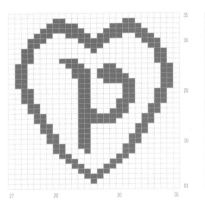

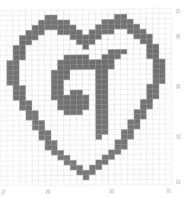

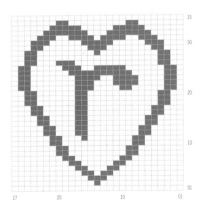

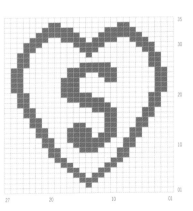

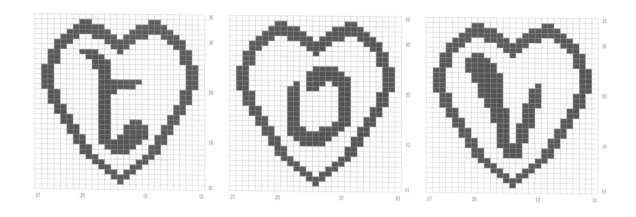

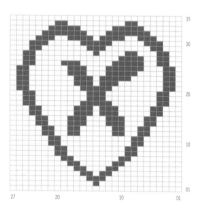

The Knitted Swatches

A This swatch is worked entirely in wool/cotton blend yarn. Wool is a naturally slightly elastic fiber, so it's easier to adjust the tension of individual stitches than it is with 100 percent cotton yarn. Once the knitting is complete, any slightly uneven stitches can be eased out with the tip of a knitter's sewing needle (see page 249), and blocking the knitting will also improve the finish.

D Double-knitting weight yarns are probably the most commonly available weight and there are many, many fiber and textural variations: here, both yarns are pure wool DK yarn. Using two yarns of the same weight does make it relatively easy to tension the stitches evenly at the color changes, and so work neat color knitting, especially when the yarn has a little elasticity, as these wool yarns do.

H This letter and heart are duplicate stitched (Swiss darned; see page 252), but the lines are not completely filled in. The letter has alternate stitches embroidered on each row, giving a look that resembles traditional Fair Isle patterns. The heart also has alternate stitches embroidered, but stacked to create stripes rather than checks.

I For this swatch, the fabric is worked in seed (moss) stitch and that is used to define the outline of the heart, which itself is worked in stockinette (stocking) stitch. Working intricate letters in texture isn't usually successful, but shapes around a letter, and chunky letters, can be worked in simple textured stitch patterns.

L This letter is beaded using the slip stitch method (see page 250). With this technique you can only place a bead on every alternate stitch and row, but the shape of the letter is simple enough for it to be clear even though it isn't completely filled in.

N Mixing fibers can make any project more visually interesting: here, a smooth cotton yarn is used for the letter and a metallic for the background. The smooth sheen of the cotton contrasts well with the sparkle, and as both yarns are a similar weight they knit up easily together. When making a large project with different fibers, always buy just a ball of each yarn first and knit a swatch to check that the combination works.

Q You might think that metallic yarns are stiff and unyielding—as the name suggests—but in fact they are usually very fluid and drape well. You can use them with stiffer yarns, such as the cotton 4ply used for the background here, but you should swatch the two together before starting a project to check that the different knitted fabrics will work together.

S Tweed yarns, such as the red tweed used to knit the letter in this swatch, are usually one dominant color with flecks of other, sometimes quite bright, contrasting colors. You can use these flecks to pick up colors used in another part of a project, or in an accessory worn with a knitted tweed piece.

W The background of this swatch is knitted in a fine mohair and it's been used double to make it a similar weight to the wool DK yarn of the letter and heart. If you have never worked with doubled yarn, don't be put off: the strands twist around one another as you work, making it easy to treat them as a single strand, and with fluffy yarn such as this, it won't show if you miss one strand in a stitch.

Y Working the long, thin, looping strokes of these letters will be a test of getting the tension of the floats right in stranded knitting (see pages 247–248), but small irregularities in tension can be eased with the tip of a knitter's sewing needle (see page 249) once the knitting is complete.

20

TALL AND THIN

This is, as the name suggests, a slim and elegant alphabet, though the slightly idiosyncratic shapes of some of its letters prevent it from being too formal or conventional. A palette of just one color—purple, in this instance—can work well for a letter project, as long as there is enough contrast to make the letters readable. Knit a swatch to check, since what looks effective in two balls held together may not work as well when one yarn is used in a much smaller quantity. As the strokes of the letters are thin, you may find it easiest to strand (see page 246) the background yarn right across the backs of the letters, as was done here.

Yarns used
◎ Cotton 4ply yarn in pale lilac and purple
◎ Cotton/linen blend yarn in pale lilac and purple
◎ Fine mohair yarn in pale lilac
◎ Metallic yarn in purple
◎ Tweed 4ply yarn in mauve and purple
◎ Variegated sock yarn in purple/green
◎ Wool 4ply yarn in pale lilac and purple

Other materials
◎ Purple beads

Techniques used
◎ Intarsia (see page 243)
◎ Stranding (see page 246)
◎ Slip stitch beading (see page 250)
◎ Duplicate stitch (Swiss darning; see page 252)

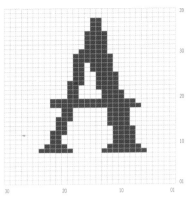

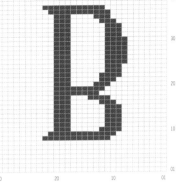

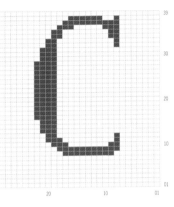

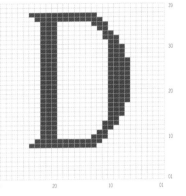

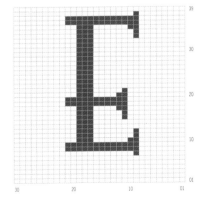

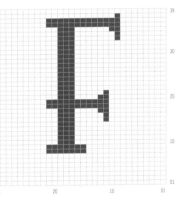

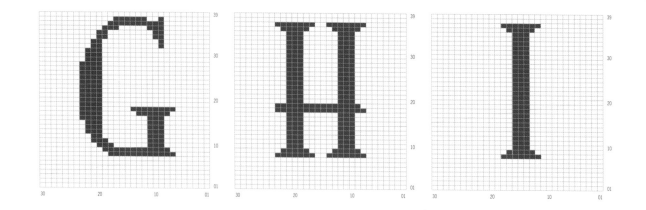

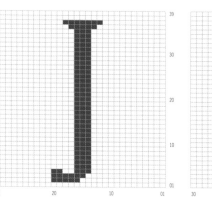

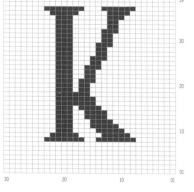

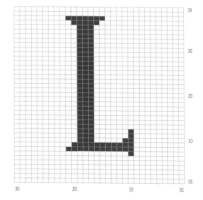

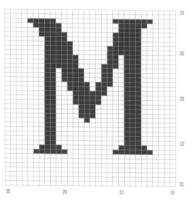

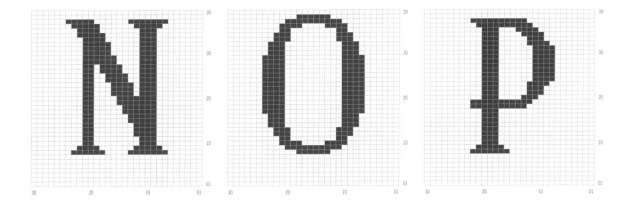

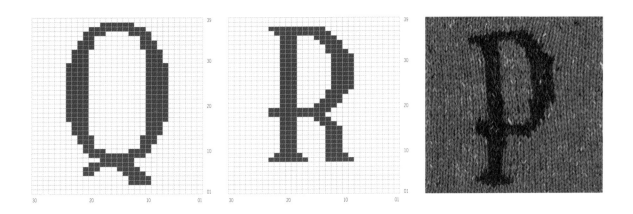

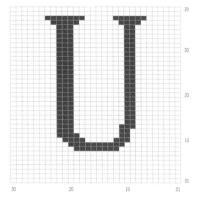

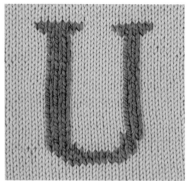

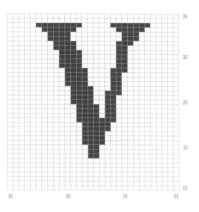

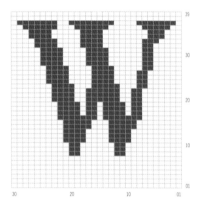

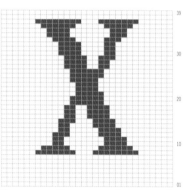

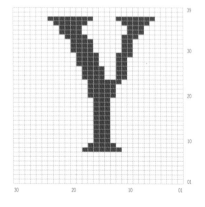

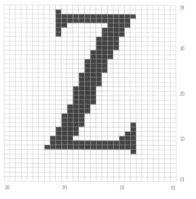

The Knitted Swatches

A } This swatch is knitted in a cotton/linen blend yarn that produces a slightly irregular surface when knitted up. This makes it forgiving for knitters whose color-work skills are still improving, but it does make the letter look slightly askew.

C } This swatch has a background of fine mohair used double to make it a similar weight to the tweed yarn used for the letter. This is a combination that is quite forgiving of uneven stitches—the fluffy yarn hides them and the flecked tweed yarn disguises them—so it's one to try if you are new to color knitting.

F } Double-knitting weight yarns are probably the most commonly available weight and there are many, many fiber and textural variations: here, wool tweed DK is used. Using two yarns of the same weight does make it relatively easy to tension the stitches evenly at the color changes, and so work neat color knitting, especially when the yarn has a little elasticity, as wool yarns usually do.

J } Working the long, thin stroke of this letter "J" is a test of getting the tension of the floats right in stranded knitting (see pages 247–248), but small irregularities in tension can be eased with the tip of a knitter's sewing needle (see page 249) once the knitting is complete.

M } This swatch uses wool for the background and sparkly purple metallic yarn for the letter. If you find metallic yarns a little gaudy in quantities, try them as smaller accents in a project; just one or two letters in a name or word, with the other letters knitted in a non-metallic yarn of the same color.

P } Here, the same yarns as letter "F" have been used, but the positions are reversed. Swapping colors like this works very well on an afghan: choose a limited palette and work blocks in all the possible variations to create a finished piece that's colorful, but also restrained. You can choose just a two-color palette and use different fibers to add variety.

R } This letter is duplicate stitched (Swiss darned; see page 252) in the same weight yarn as was used to knit the background: both are wool 4ply. When working a whole letter in duplicate stitch, be careful to keep the embroidery at a similar tension to the knitting; if you pull the embroidery yarn too tight, it won't cover the background neatly and the fabric will be distorted.

U } This letter is duplicate stitched (Swiss darned; see page 252) in a variegated color yarn. One great advantage of this technique is that it can be added once the knitting is complete, so if you have finished your project and it looks somewhat plainer than you hoped, you can easily add detail and color.

X } Here, the same yarns as for letter "C" are used, but the positions are swapped. Today, many yarns are treated to be machine washable, but check that two different fibers can be laundered together. If in doubt, machine wash a swatch. If one fiber shrinks more than the other it will be very visible, and you'll need to hand wash the project.

Z } For this swatch, a wool 4ply is used to knit a letter on a background of a variegated sock yarn, one that has a very long color change (the color changes very slowly along the length of the yarn). This works well as a background, but in a letter—such as letter "U"—you don't get the effect.

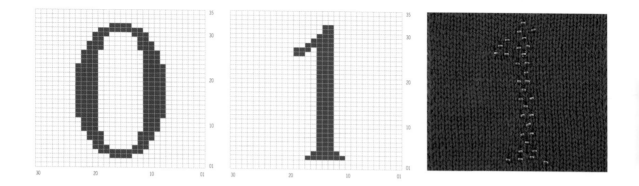

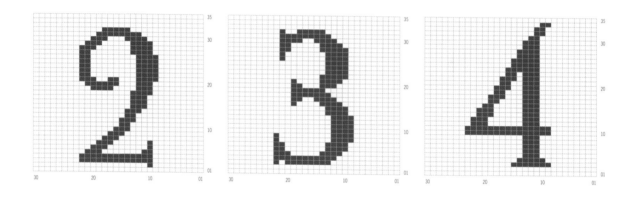

Numerals

The numerals are charted to be a suitable scale for the alphabet they accompany, and when positioning them in your own chart, note that they all sit on the same line: the tail of the "9" does not hang lower than the base of the "8."

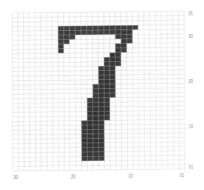

1 } This numeral is beaded using the slip stitch method (see page 250). With this technique, you can only place a bead on every alternate stitch and row, but the shape of the numeral is simple enough for it to be clear even though it isn't completely filled in.

4 } This swatch uses the same yarns as letter "R," but reversed, and the results look very different. Here, the dark letter recedes into the pale background instead of a pale letter floating on the dark background. Color and shade relationships can be subtle and complex, and it's always worth swatching two colors together before starting a project, just to check that the results are as you anticipated.

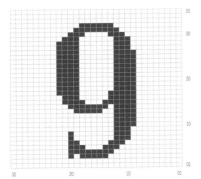

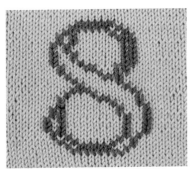

6 } Tweed yarns are usually one dominant color with flecks of other, sometimes quite bright, contrasting colors. You can use these flecks to pick up colors used in another part of a project, or in another garment or accessory worn with a tweed piece.

8 } Outlining a numeral rather than filling in the whole shape can be very successful if the shape is bold enough, and is best done with duplicate stitch (Swiss darning; see page 252). Here, the swirling lines give the numeral a three-dimensional effect.

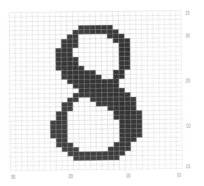

PROJECT 8

ANKLE SOCKS

These little ankle socks are knitted on two needles and seamed so that the letters can be worked using the intarsia technique (see page 243). If you want longer socks, just increase the number of rib rows for the cuff.

Yarns
◎ **Regia 4-fadig Monaco Color**
2 x 1¾ oz (50 g) balls in 01835, A
◎ **Rowan Wool Cotton 4ply**
1 x 1¾ oz (50 g) ball in Inky (497) B

Letters
◎ Tall and Thin (see page 178)

Tools
◎ Pair each of US 1 (2 mm) and US 2 (2.75 mm)
knitting needles
◎ Knitter's sewing needle

Measurements
◎ To fit average female foot

Gauge (tension)
◎ 30 sts and 42 rows to 4 in (10 cm) using US 2 (2.75 mm)
needles and measured over st st

Abbreviations
◎ See page 254.
◎ Note: strand (see page 246) the background
yarn behind the letters.

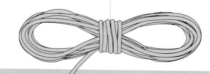

NOTE

The charts show the letters upside down and back to front in order for them to come out the right way up and around on the finished socks.

KEY

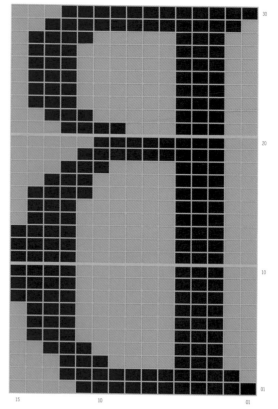

- A

- B

POSITIONING THE LETTERS

Positioning a letter a stitch off-center if it is an odd number of stitches across (as the letter "B" is here), won't show on the finished sock. As the "N" is wider than the "B," and an even number of stitches across, it needs to be positioned slightly differently. Whichever letters you choose, you have a space of approximately 20 stitches by 40 rows on the top of the foot that you can place the letter in. It's worth sitting down with some graph paper and plotting out the letter position to make sure it will all be visible.

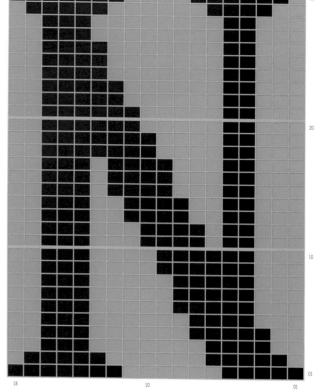

SOCK B

*Using US 1 (2 mm) needles and yarn A, cast on 54 sts.

CUFF

Row 1 (RS): [K1, p1] to end of row.

Rep row 1, 11 times more.

Change to US 2 (2.75 mm) needles.

Starting with a k row, work 12 rows st st.

HEEL: FIRST SIDE

Row 1 (RS): K15, turn.

Row 2 and every alt row: Purl.

Row 3: K14, turn.

Row 5: K13, turn.

Cont in patt as set, working one less st on every k row before turning until you have worked the row, "K7 and turn."

Next row: Purl all 7 sts.

Row 19: K8, turn.

Row 21: K9, turn.

Cont in patt as set, working one more st on every k row before turning until you have worked the row, "K15 and turn."

Next row: Purl.

Row 35: Knit across all 54 sts.

HEEL: SECOND SIDE

Row 1 (WS): P15, turn.

Row 2 and every alt row: Knit.

Row 3: P14, turn.

Row 5: P13, turn.

Cont in patt as set, working one less st on every p row before turning until you have worked the row, "P7 and turn."

Next row: Knit all 7 sts.

Row 19: P8, turn.

Row 21: P9, turn.

Cont in patt as set, working one more st on every p row before turning until you have worked the row, "P15 and turn."

Next row: Knit.

Row 35: Purl across all 54 sts.

FOOT

Starting with a k row, work 12 rows st st.*

PLACE CHART

Join in yarn B.

Next row: K19, place row 1 of chart over next 15 sts, joining in yarn B as required, k20.

Next row: P20, place row 2 of chart over next 15 sts, p19.

Cont in patt as set until row 30 of chart is complete.

Break yarn B and cont in yarn A.

Starting with a k row, work 10 rows st st.

**TOE

Row 1(RS): K11, k2tog, k2, k2togtbl, k20, k2tog, k2, k2togtbl, k11. (50 sts)

Row 2 and every alt row: Purl.

Row 3: K10, k2tog, k2, k2togtbl, k18, k2tog, k2, k2togtbl, k10. (46 sts)

Row 5: K9, k2tog, k2, k2togtbl, k16, k2tog, k2, k2togtbl, k9. (42 sts)

Row 7: K8, k2tog, k2, k2togtbl, k14, k2tog, k2, k2togtbl, k8. (38 sts)

Row 9: K7, k2tog, k2, k2togtbl, k12, k2tog, k2, k2togtbl, k7. (34 sts)

Row 11: K6, k2tog, k2, k2togtbl, k10, k2tog, k2, k2togtbl, k6. (30 sts)

Row 13: K5, k2tog, k2, k2togtbl, k8, k2tog, k2, k2togtbl, k5. (26 sts)

Row 15: K4, k2tog, k2, k2togtbl, k6, k2tog, k2, k2togtbl, k4. (22 sts)

Row 17: K3, k2tog, k2, k2togtbl, k4, k2tog, k2, k2togtbl, k3. (18 sts)

Row 18: Purl.

Bind (cast) off.**

SOCK N

Work as for Sock B from * to *.

PLACE CHART

Join in yarn B.

Next row: K18, place row 1 of chart over next 18 sts, joining in yarn B as required, k18.

Next row: P18, place row 2 of chart over next 18 sts, p18.

Cont in patt as set until row 30 of chart is complete.

Break yarn B and cont in yarn A.

Starting with a k row, work 10 rows st st.

Work as for Sock B from ** to **.

TO MAKE UP

- Weave in loose ends.
- Block knitted pieces.
- With RS of work facing, fold sock in half and join back seam then toe seam using mattress st.

21

BRUSHSCRIPT

These eccentric, looping letters are wonderfully exuberant. The letters with ascenders or descenders are quite large, so the typeface is ideal for projects, such as blankets and big pillows, where a statement is needed. The strokes of the letters vary in width, but some are quite thin and it can be a challenge to knit them beautifully; try duplicate stitching (Swiss darning; see page 252) them instead. However, the varying widths and inherent irregularity of the letters does mean that uneven stitches are less noticeable than they can be on very uniform typefaces. If you are color knitting, work the letters in intarsia (see page 243) overall, stranding (see page 246) both the background yarn and letter yarn within the letter shape, as needed.

Yarns used
◎ Bouclé yarn in cream
◎ Cotton/linen blend yarn in cream
◎ Fine mohair yarn in dark brown
◎ Metallic yarn in bronze
◎ Wool 4ply yarn in cream and dark brown
◎ Wool/alpaca worsted yarn in tan and dark brown
◎ Wool DK yarn in dark brown

Other materials
◎ Bronze beads

Techniques used
◎ Intarsia (see page 243)
◎ Stranding (see page 246)
◎ Knitted-in beading (see page 251)
◎ Duplicate stitch (Swiss darning; see page 252)

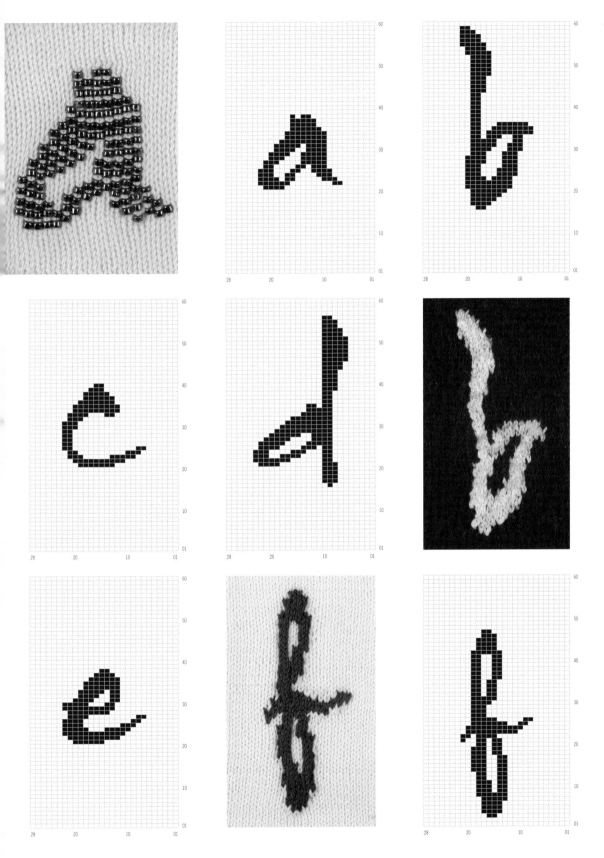

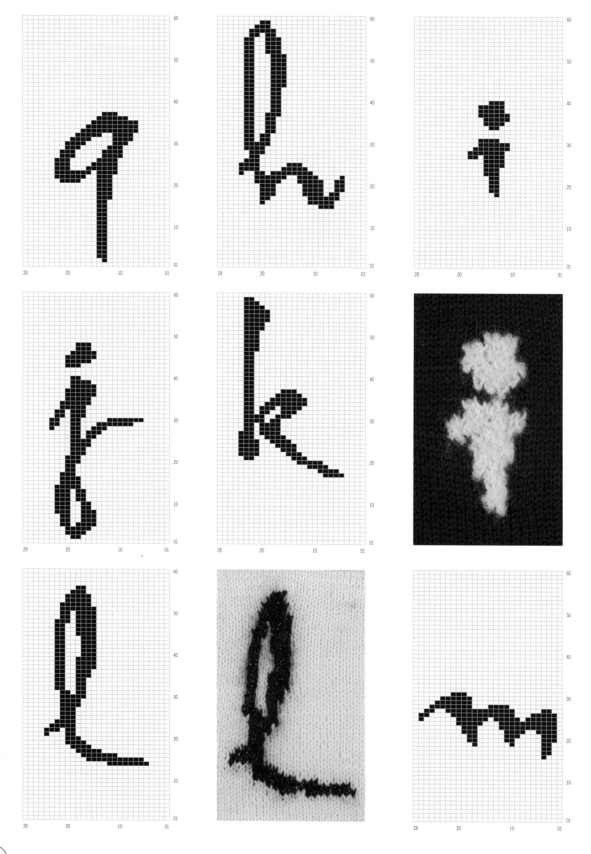

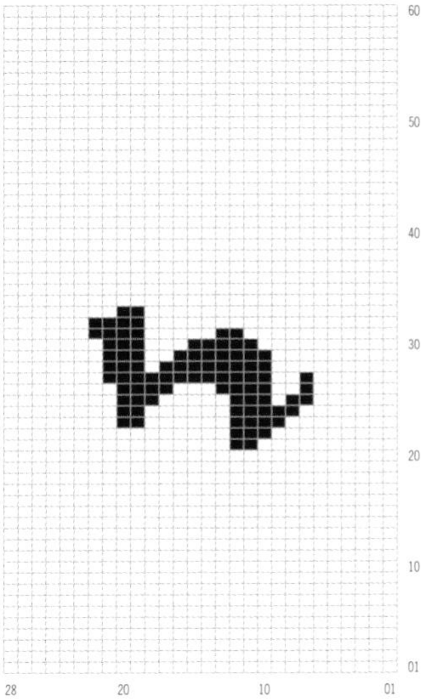
60
50
40
30
20
10
01
28
20
10
01

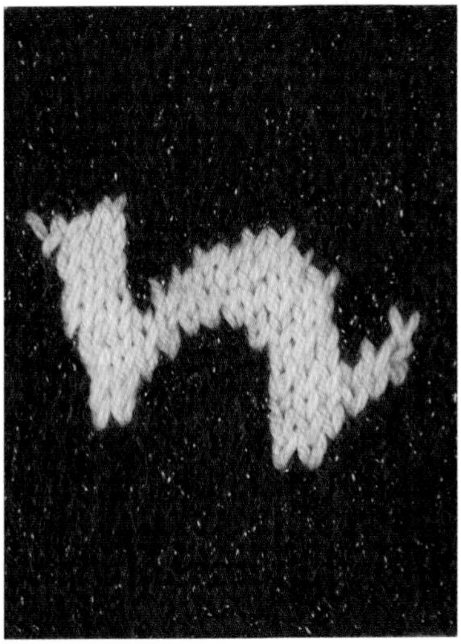

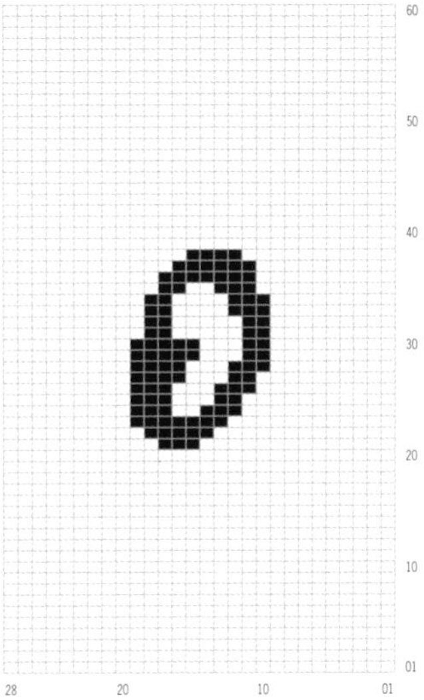
60
50
40
30
20
10
01
28
20
10
01

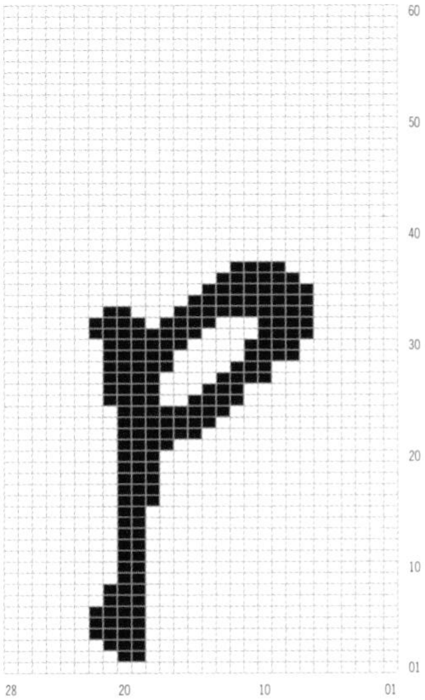
60
50
40
30
20
10
01
28
20
10
01

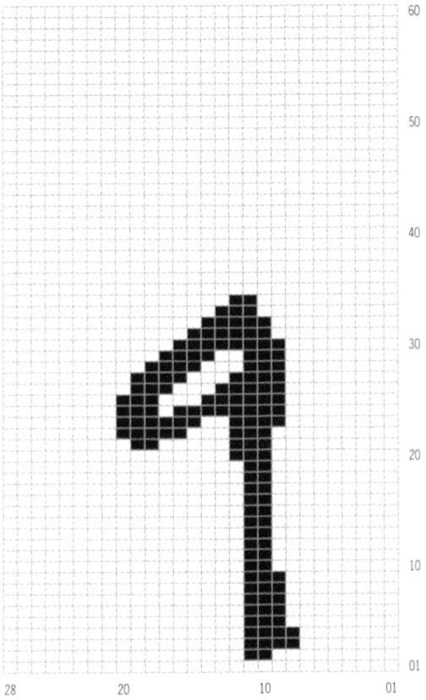
60
50
40
30
20
10
01
28
20
10
01

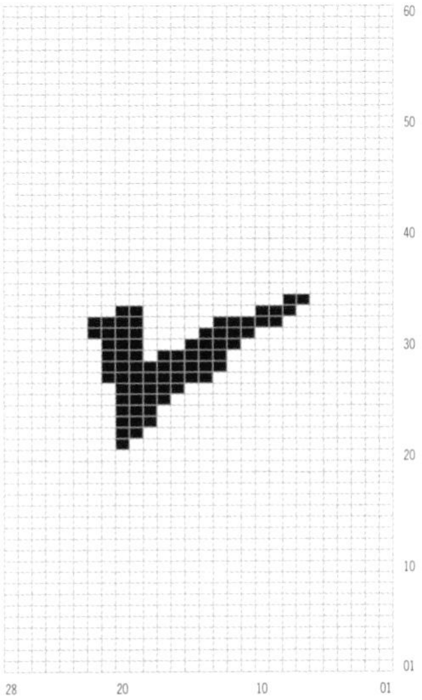
60
50
40
30
20
10
01
28
20
10
01

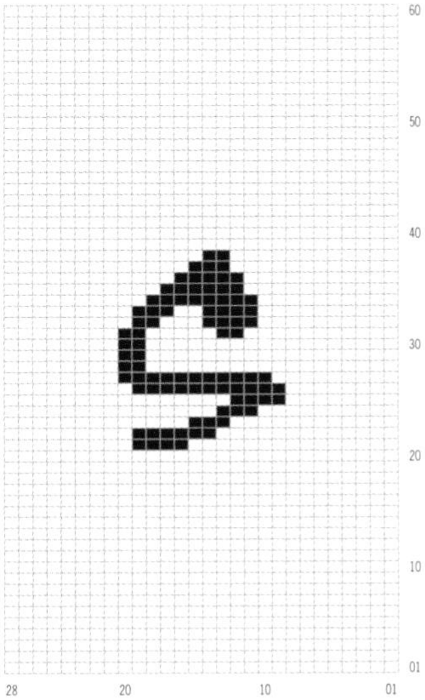
60
50
40
30
20
10
01
28
20
10
01

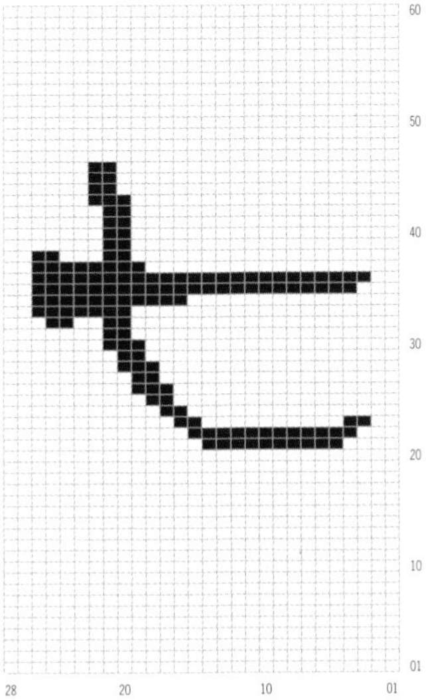
60
50
40
30
20
10
01
28
20
10
01

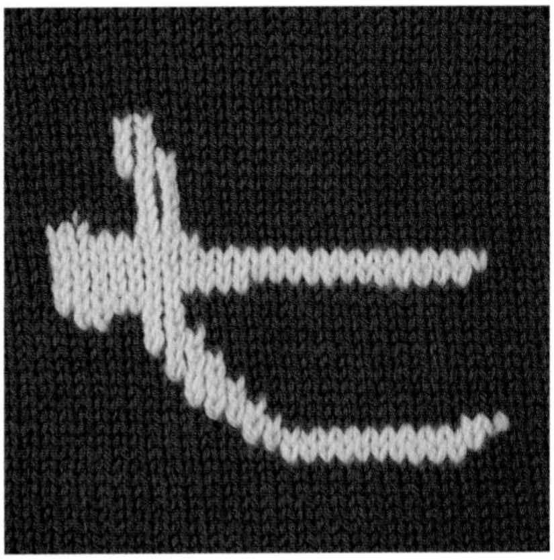

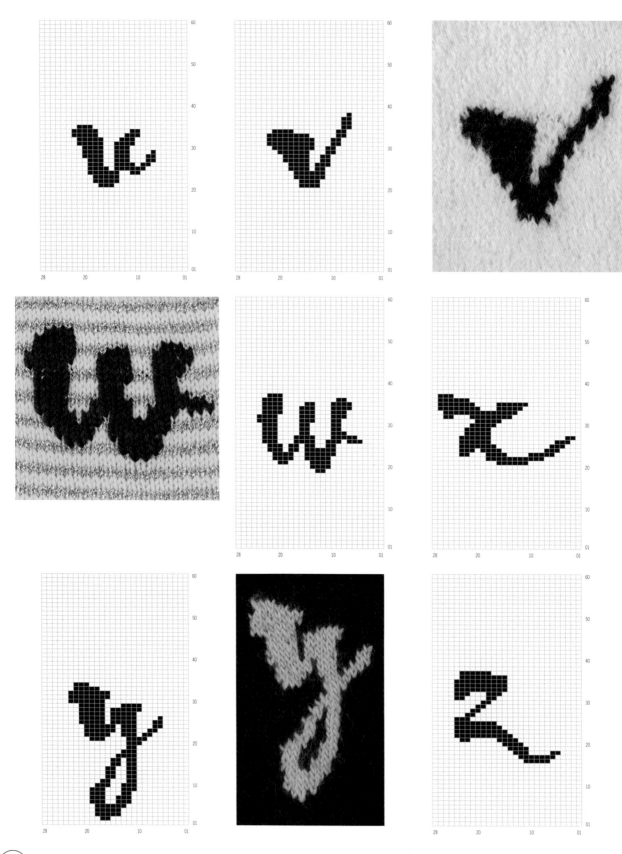

The Knitted Swatches

A This letter is beaded using the knitted-in technique (see page 251), where a bead can be added to every stitch on every row. Working only a few letters in this technique on a reasonably firm yarn should be fine, but a lot of beads can affect gauge (tension), stretch the stitches, and change the drape of the knitting, all of which are not usually good.

B Two very different yarns are used in this swatch. The letter is in a cotton/linen blend that has a sheen that creates a rather uneven-looking fabric as it reflects the light. The background is a fine mohair used double to make it a similar weight to the cotton/linen. Both yarns are quite forgiving of uneven stitches as the fluffy yarn hides them and the cotton/linen incorporates them into its natural irregularity, so this is a combination a novice color knitter might try.

F This is classic color knitting in two colors of 4ply wool yarn. Working the long, thin, looping strokes of this letter "F" will be a test of getting the tension of the floats right in stranded knitting (see pages 247–248), but small irregularities in tension can be eased out with the tip of a knitter's sewing needle (see page 249) once the knitting is complete.

I Bouclé yarns work best on quite bold, chunky letters as the heavy texture can blur or overwhelm finer lines: the boldness and large dot of this letter "I" are ideal. The background is a smooth DK wool to provide maximum contrast to the bouclé. Although heavily textured yarns can disguise slightly uneven stitches, they aren't always very easy to knit with, so try to work a swatch before embarking on a project to make sure that you like using the yarn.

L This letter is worked in two different yarns held together; a strand of fine mohair and a strand of metallic yarn. The combination is a little thicker than the single strand of 4ply used to knit the background, giving the letter a slightly embossed feel. Slightly different yarn weights can often be used together with no problems, but always work a swatch first to check.

N Here, the same yarn combination as letter "L" has been used, but the positions are reversed. If you use different fiber yarns together (here, there are three), bear laundering in mind. A lukewarm hand wash in a no-rinse detergent will usually overcome any potential shrinkage issues, but it's worth washing a swatch before starting a sweater that you may never be able to clean.

T This swatch uses the same yarns as letter "F," but the colors are reversed and the letter is duplicate stitched (Swiss darned; see page 252) rather than knitted. This embroidery stitch can be worked horizontally or vertically, and it's worth experimenting on a swatch of stockinette (stocking) stitch to see if you find one direction easier to work than the other.

V These are the same yarns used in letter "I," but here the bouclé is the background. It has been woven in (see page 248) across the back of the smooth DK yarn, giving the latter an uneven surface that complements the bouclé. This is one of those happy accidents that comes about through experimentation, so try crazy ideas as swatches, just to make sure they aren't actually great ideas.

W This letter is duplicate stitched (Swiss darned; see page 252), which allows you to easily experiment with working on a patterned background. Here, it's a simple stripe pattern, but you can duplicate stitch onto any stockinette (stocking) stitch knitting. Of course, if you are an expert color knitter, then you can knit a patterned background together with letters, but this is a great alternative.

Y This letter is knitted entirely in a wool/alpaca worsted yarn in two colors. Heavier yarns are often best reserved for larger letters; the fewer stitches a small letter needs can start to look a bit crude if blown up in scale by a thick yarn.

22

DIGITAL DISPLAY

Based on the typeface used in LED signs, these letters are entirely contemporary and have a pleasingly geeky feel. An industrial-looking red and gray color palette suits the letters' machine-made nature, though some fluff and glitter make them visually— and literally—a little softer. Other color palettes that would work well with these letters are bright yellow and black, vivid orange and white, and neon blue and very pale gray. You can knit these letters in intarsia (see page 243), or strand (see page 246) the background yarn behind them, whichever method you prefer.

Yarns used
◎ Cotton 4ply yarn in red and pale gray
◎ Fine mohair yarn in gray
◎ Metallic yarn in red and pewter
◎ Wool DK yarn in red and gray

Other materials
◎ None

Techniques used
◎ Intarsia (see page 243)
◎ Stranding (see page 246)
◎ Duplicate stitch (Swiss darning; see page 252)

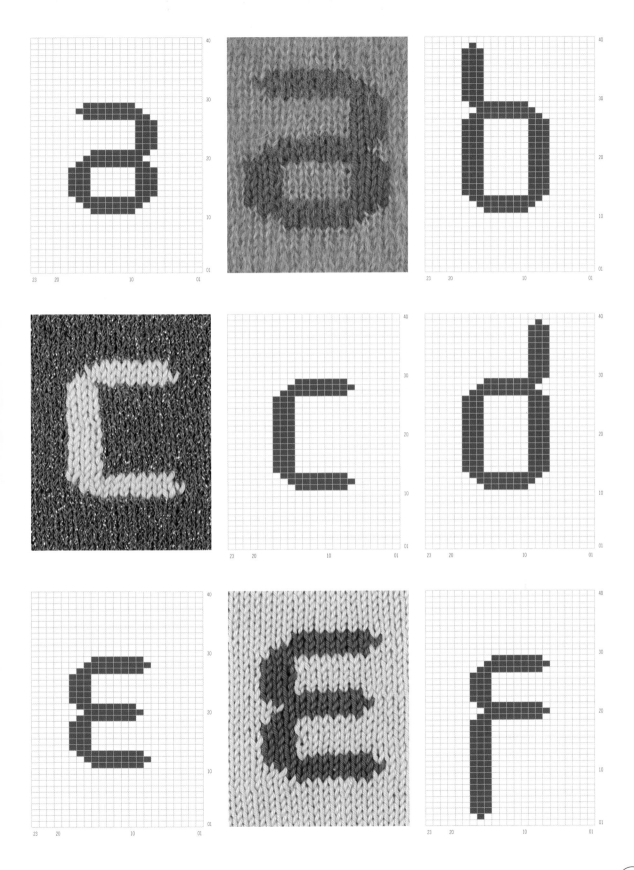

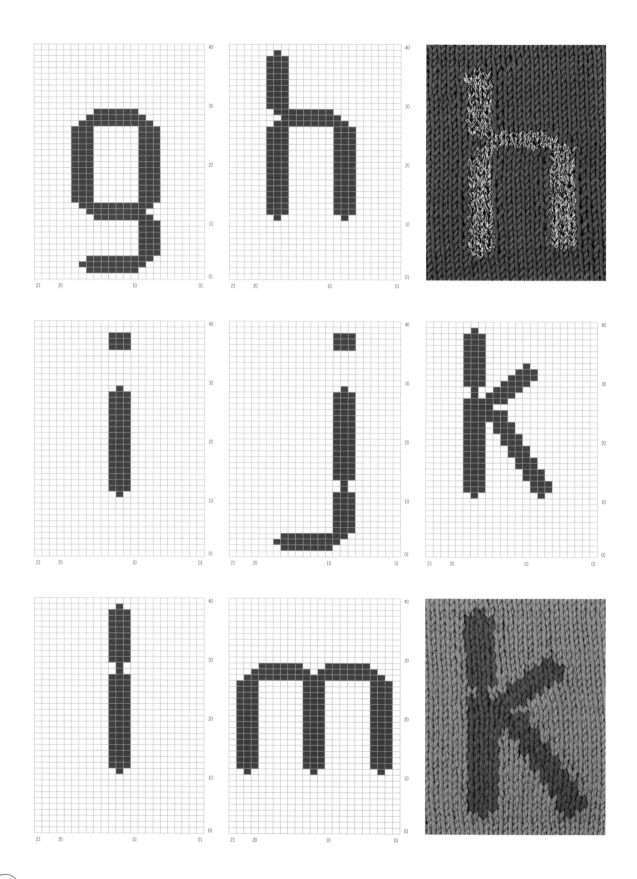

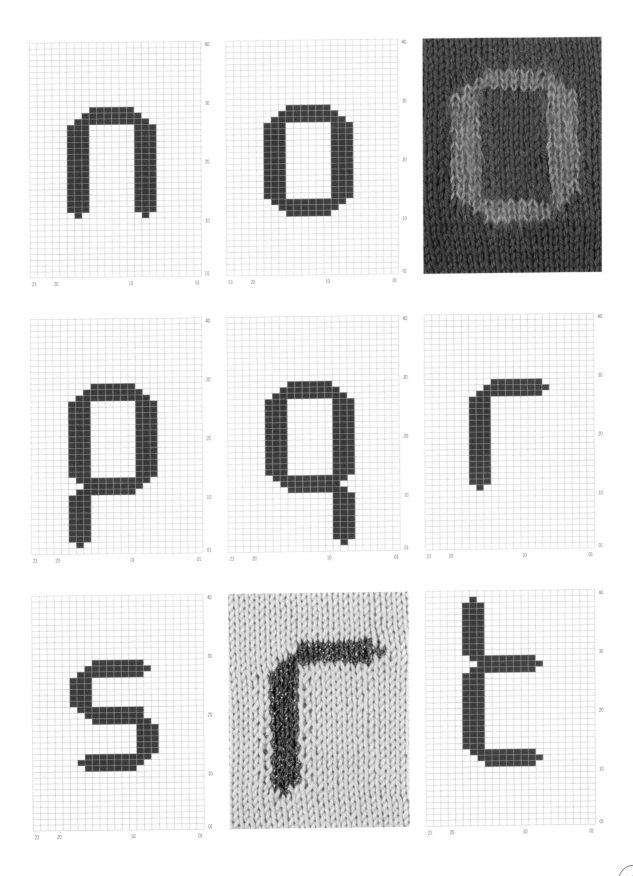

The Knitted Swatches

A Doubling up a finer yarn to make a strand the same weight as a thicker yarn is perfectly viable, and here the letter is knitted in wool DK yarn on a background of doubled fine mohair. If you have never worked with doubled yarn, don't be put off: the strands twist around one another as you work, making it easy to treat them as a single strand.

C Mixing fibers can make any project more visually interesting: here, a smooth cotton yarn is used for the letter and a metallic for the background. The smooth sheen of the cotton contrasts well with the sparkle, and as both yarns are a similar weight they knit up easily together. When making a large project with different fibers, always buy just a ball of each yarn first and knit a swatch to check that the combination works.

E This swatch is knitted entirely in cotton yarn, which is often used for working textured stitch patterns as its crispness and sheen shows up the individual stitches really well. However, this benefit can become a disadvantage in that the yarn also shows up unintentionally uneven stitches equally well, so only use cotton if you are an expert color knitter.

H If you find full-on metallic yarns a bit much used in quantities, try them as smaller accents in a project; just one or two letters in a name or word, with the other letters knitted in a non-metallic yarn of the same color.

K This swatch is worked entirely in wool DK yarn. Wool is a naturally slightly elastic fiber, so it's easier to adjust the tension of individual stitches than it is with cotton yarn. Once the knitting is complete, any slightly uneven stitches can be eased out with the tip of a knitter's sewing needle (see page 249), and blocking the knitting will also improve the finish.

O This swatch uses the same yarns as letter "A," but the positions are swapped. When using a fluffy yarn and stranding across the back of a smooth yarn, some fluff can creep up through the stitches of the smooth yarn and show on the front, so it's best to use the intarsia method (see page 243) with this combination.

R For this swatch the same yarns as letter "C" are used, with the positions swapped. The two yarns are similar enough in weight to be knitted together without having to double up either one, but you have to be careful to tension them both neatly at the color changes to avoid the stitches distorting.

V Here, the same yarns as letter "E" have been used, but the positions are reversed and the letter is outlined, rather than filled in with solid color. The best way to outline is to use duplicate stitch (Swiss darning; see page 252), being careful to keep the stitch tension even and not too tight or the embroidered stitches can slip under the knitted stitches and almost completely disappear.

W You might think that metallic yarns are stiff and unyielding—as the name suggests—but in fact they are usually very fluid and drape well. You can use them with stiffer yarns, such as the cotton 4ply used for the letter here, but you should swatch the two together before starting a project to check that the different knitted fabrics will work together.

Z When a background yarn is a very different color from the letter yarn, it's best to strand right across the back of gaps in the letters if they are four or fewer stitches, and catch floats in (see page 247)—rather than weaving in (see page 248)—if the gaps are wider. This will prevent flecks of the background yarn showing through where they aren't wanted.

23

60s RETRO

It's been said that if you can remember the 60s, then you weren't really there. Maybe the coolest decade ever, certainly one of the most influential—in music, design, and fashion—the 60s can be wild, woolly, and psychedelic, or sleekly stylish and super sharp: think Janis Joplin or Twiggy. This alphabet has the best of both, with simple, well-cut shapes, and a vivid green and purple palette that gives a nod to letting it all hang out. It is best knitted in intarsia (see page 243); use short cut lengths of yarn for the openings in letters (see page 243 for how to judge the amount of yarn needed) and bobbins for the letters.

Yarns used
◎ Cotton 4ply yarn in purple
◎ Fine mohair yarn in green
◎ Metallic yarn in purple
◎ Wool 4ply yarn in green
◎ Wool/cotton blend DK yarn in
  purple and green

Other materials
◎ Green beads
◎ Purple beads

Techniques used
◎ Intarsia (see page 243)
◎ Stranding (see page 246)
◎ Knitted-in beading (see page 251)
◎ Embroidery (see page 251)
◎ Duplicate stitch (Swiss darning;
  see page 252)

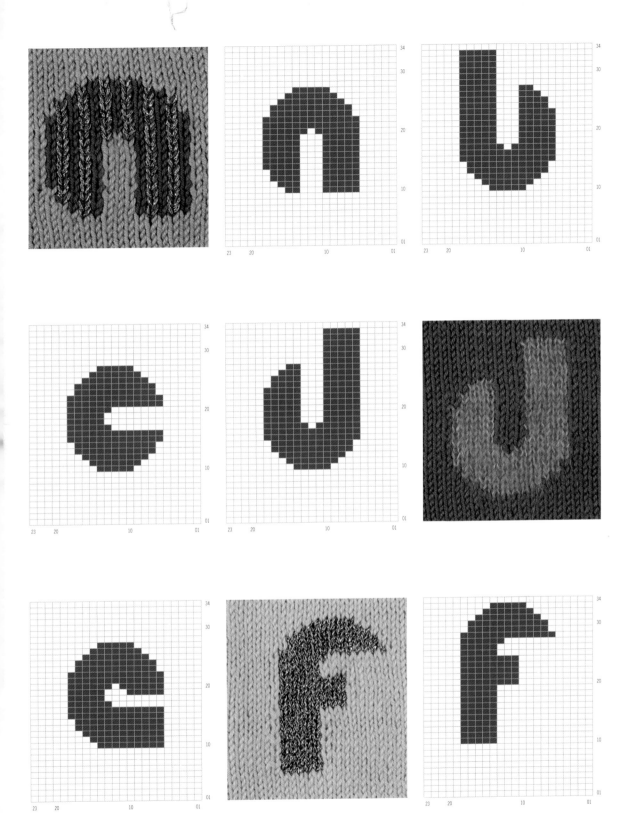

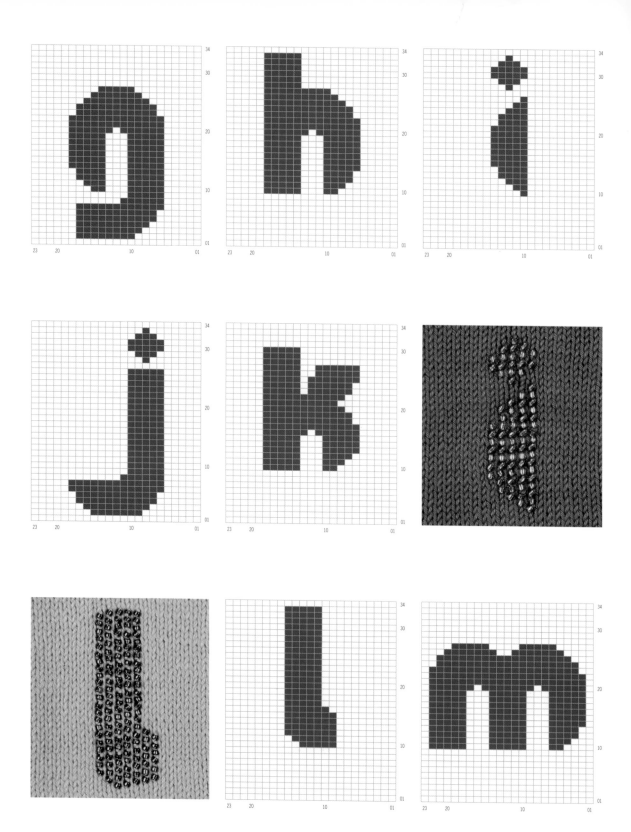

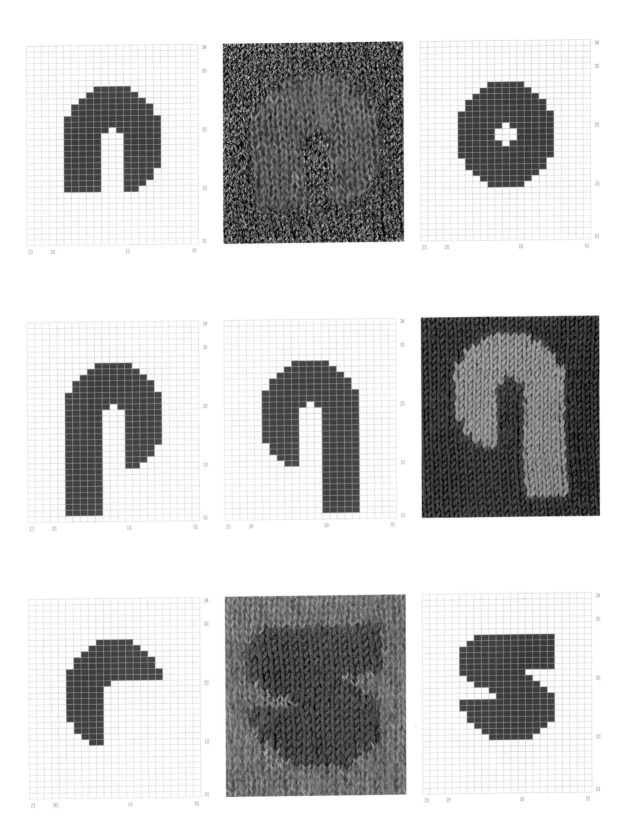

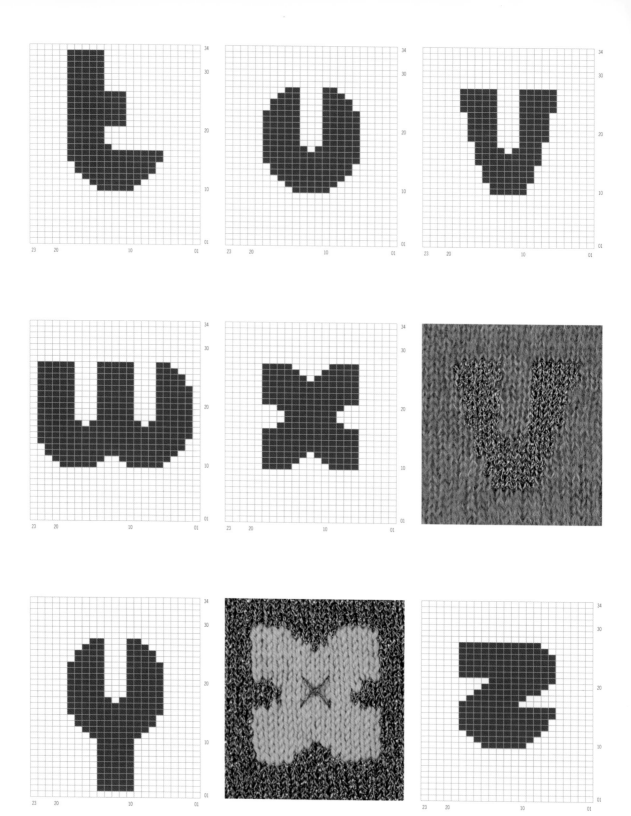

The Knitted Swatches

A This letter is worked in wool/cotton blend yarn, and the stripes are duplicate stitched (Swiss darned; see page 252) in a metallic yarn. One great advantage of this technique is that it can be added once the knitting is complete, so if you have finished your project and it looks plainer than you hoped, you can easily add detail and color.

D This letter is knitted in a fine mohair used doubled and the background is a wool/cotton blend DK yarn. A lukewarm hand wash in a no-rinse detergent will usually overcome any potential shrinkage issues, but it's worth washing a swatch before starting a sweater that you may never be able to clean.

F If you find metallic yarns a bit gaudy in quantities, try them as smaller accents in a project; just one or two letters in a name or word, with the other letters knitted in a non-metallic yarn of the same color.

I This letter is beaded using the knitted-in technique (see page 251), where a bead can be added to every stitch on every row as needed. With this technique the beads sit at a slight angle on one "leg" of the stitch, so the columns of beads look a bit wriggly, but that's the nature of this style of beading.

L Here, the beads were a bit too large for the size of the knitted stitch, so the 4ply yarn was used doubled on thicker needles to make the stitches larger. The beads are threaded onto the doubled yarn, which is then just treated as a single strand.

N This is a glitter and texture combination: the letter is two strands of mohair held together and the background is a single strand of metallic yarn. Used this way, the weights of the two yarns are similar, though the nature of them is entirely different, and you need to take care to get the tension of the stitches even at the color changes.

Q Here, the same yarns as letter "A" have been used, but reversed. Swapping colors like this works very well on an afghan: choose a limited palette and add embroidery details, as in letter "A," to increase the number of possible color combinations.

S The background yarn of this swatch is a fine mohair and it's been used double to make it a similar weight to the wool/cotton 4ply yarn that the letter is knitted in. The light texture of the mohair contrasts well with the smooth matte surface of the wool/cotton, and the chunkiness of the letter shape isn't blurred by the fuzz.

V Metallic yarns might look a bit tricky, but they are actually easy to knit with, and the wriggly, sparkly surface is visually very forgiving of any uneven stitches, so this can be an excellent yarn to use if you are a beginner to color knitting.

X You can add color and detail to finished knitting with simple embroidery stitches (see page 251); here, just one large central cross-stitch echoes the shape of the letter. The secret to successful embroidery on knitting is getting the stitch tension right. If you pull the embroidery stitches tight, as you might on woven fabric, you will distort the knitting, so pull them gently taut and adjust individual stitches as necessary.

PROJECT 9

FLOWER BOLSTER

Dress up your bed or sofa with an easy-to-knit bolster that just requires a little simple hand sewing to put the velvet end pieces in. Add as many, or as few, flowers and pretty buttons as you wish to your own version.

Yarns
◎ **Rowan Kid Classic**
2 x 1¾ oz (50 g) balls in Bitter Sweet (866) A
◎ **Rowan Pure Wool DK**
1 x 1¾ oz (50 g) ball in each of Dahlia (042) B and Tea Rose (025) C

Letters
◎ 60s Retro (see page 202)

Tools
◎ Pair of US 2 (3 mm) knitting needles
◎ Buttons
◎ Pins
◎ Knitter's sewing needle
◎ Two 7 in (18 cm) diameter circles of pink velvet
◎ Sewing needle and thread
◎ Bolster pad 16½ in (42 cm) long and 23 in (59 cm) around

Measurements
◎ Approximately 16½ in (42 cm) long and 23 in (59 cm) around

Gauge (tension)
◎ 22 sts and 30 rows to 4 in (10 cm) over st st using Rowan Kid Classic and US 2 (3 mm) needles

Abbreviations
◎ See page 254.
◎ Note: use the intarsia method (see page 243) throughout.

POSITIONING
THE LETTERS

These letters work perfectly well simply spaced equal distances apart. With lowercase letters that have ascenders and descenders, you can refer to the original charts to see how they sit on a baseline in relation to one another.

KEY

 – A

– B

– C

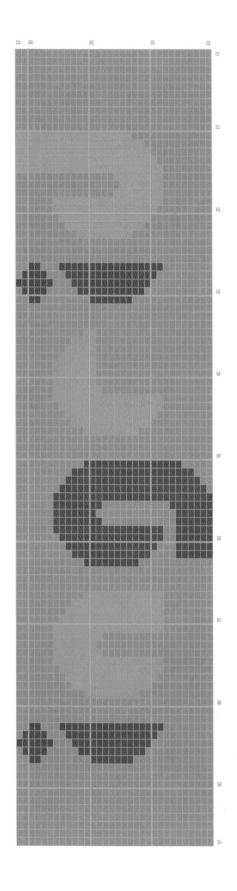

MAIN SECTION

Using yarn A, cast on 97 sts.

Starting with a k row, work 60 rows st st.

Join in yarn B.

Rows 61–62: Knit in yarn B.

Break yarn B and join in yarn C.

Rows 63–64: Knit in yarn C.

Break yarn C.

Work 8 rows st st in yarn A.

PLACE CHART

Work rows 1–32 from chart, joining in separate balls of yarns B and C as required.

Break yarns B and C.

Work 8 rows st st in yarn A.

Join in yarn C.

Rows 113–114: Knit in yarn C.

Break yarn C and join in yarn B.

Rows 115–116: Knit in yarn B.

Break yarn B.

Work 60 rows st st in yarn A.

Bind (cast) off.

FLOWERS

LARGE: MAKE 1

Using yarn B, cast on 80 sts.

Row 1 (WS): Knit.

Row 2: *K1, bind (cast) off next 14 sts (one st on RH needle after bind (cast) off), rep from * 4 more times.

Break yarn, leaving tail long enough to pass through rem 10 sts. Pull up and fasten off securely.

SMALL: MAKE 2

Using yarn C, cast on 50 sts.

Row 1 (WS): Knit.

Row 2: *K1, bind (cast) off next 8 sts (one st on RH needle after bind (cast) off), rep from * 4 more times.

Break yarn, leaving tail long enough to pass through rem 10 sts. Pull up and fasten off securely.

TO MAKE UP

- Weave in loose ends.
- Block main knitted piece.
- Using photograph as a guide, sew flowers and buttons to main piece using yarns B and C.
- Pin the cast on and bound (cast) off rows of the main section together, then sew up 3 in (8 cm) at each end of the seam. Turn WS out.
- Taking a $^3/_8$ in (1 cm) seam allowance on the velvet and 2 rows of the knitting, pin a circle of velvet to each end of the main section. Using sewing thread and backstitch, sew the circles in place.
- Turn the bolster cover RS out, insert pad, and sew gap in seam closed.

24

CLASSIC SERIF

A truly traditional set of letters in the copperplate font tradition, these are a little tricky to knit as there are single stitches to tension neatly to form the serifs. However, these can be added with duplicate stitch (Swiss darning; see page 252) once the knitting is complete (see letter "E"). A palette of rich coppery oranges and intense blacks matches the formality of these letters, though you could use a much more muted palette, such as brown and ecru for a more relaxed, but still grown-up, feel. As the strokes of the letters are thin, you may find it easiest to strand (see page 246) the background yarn right across the backs of the letters, as was done here.

Yarns used

◎ Fine mohair yarn with integral tiny sequins in black
◎ Metallic yarn in copper
◎ Mohair DK yarn in black and rust
◎ Tweed 4ply yarn in black and rust
◎ Variegated yarn in rusts
◎ Wool 4ply yarn in black and orange

Other materials

◎ Black beads
◎ Orange beads

Techniques used

◎ Intarsia (see page 243)
◎ Stranding (see page 246)
◎ Slip stitch beading (see page 250)
◎ Duplicate stitch (Swiss darning; see page 252)

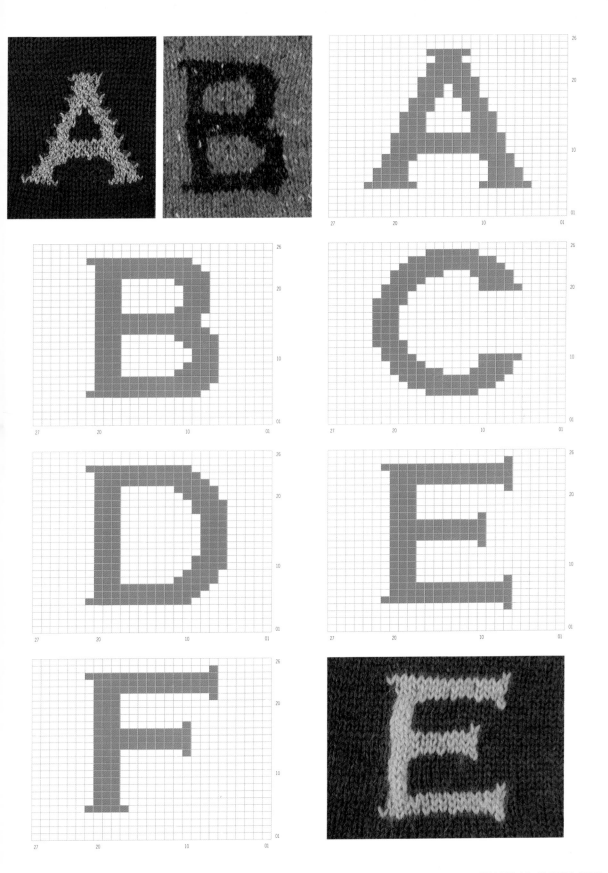

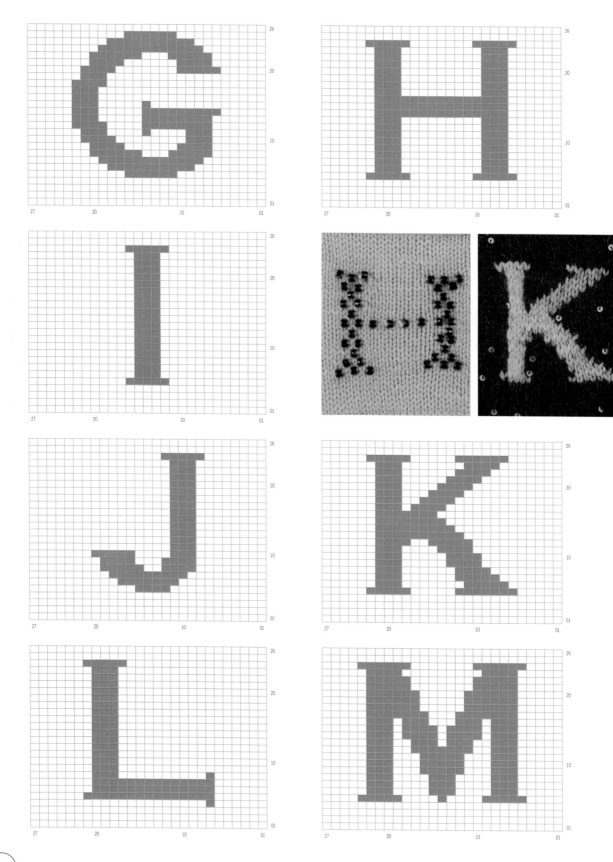

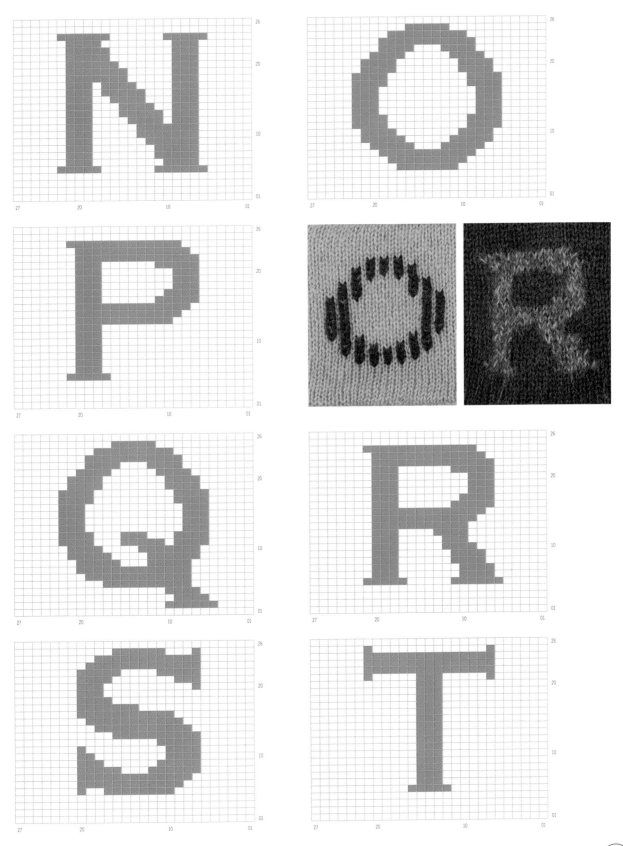

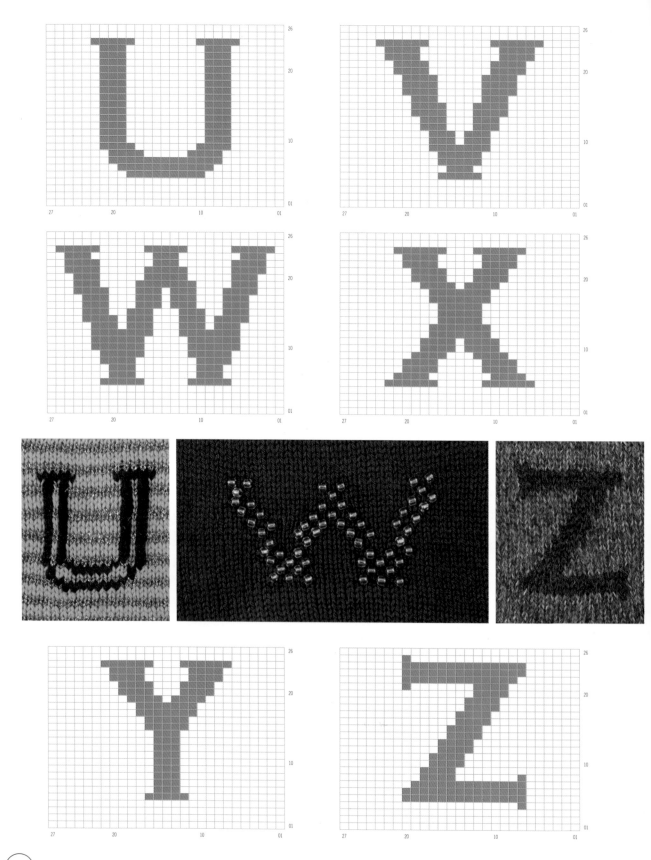

The Knitted Swatches

A Looking at it, you might think that metallic yarn is scratchy against the skin, but this one is actually very soft. In addition, it has a lovely fluid drape and so would work well as a garment if you like a bit of sparkle. The background is knitted in wool 4ply yarn that is a similar weight to the metallic yarn.

B Tweed yarns are usually one dominant color with flecks of other, sometimes quite bright, contrasting colors. You can use these flecks to pick up colors used in another part of a project, or in an accessory worn with a knitted tweed piece.

E Double-knitting weight yarns are probably the most commonly available weight and there are many, many fiber and textural variations: this yarn is a lambswool and mohair blend, so it's both soft and fluffy. Using two yarns of the same weight does make it relatively easy to tension the stitches evenly at the color changes and so work neat color knitting, especially when the yarn has a little elasticity, as this wool yarn does.

H This letter is beaded using the slip stitch method (see page 250). With this technique, you can only place a bead on every alternate stitch and row, so the letter has a sketched feel, drawn in with light lines rather than filled in with solid colors.

K This background is a fine mohair with tiny sequins and it's used double here to make it a similar weight to the wool 4ply used to knit the letter. The sequins are actually strung onto a very fine, smooth strand that's twisted with the mohair, so the sequins don't slide around. This is good in that they don't get pushed together by the fingers that you tension the yarn over.

O This letter is duplicate stitched (Swiss darned; see page 252) in the same weight yarn as was used to knit the background. Just alternate columns of stitches are embroidered, but it's enough to make the shape of the letter clear.

R Variegated yarns work great with letters, adding an extra sprinkle of color for no extra effort on your part. Be cautious of those with long color changes (where the colors change at long intervals along the yarn) as you can end up with a letter that is almost entirely one color, which may not be the effect you had hoped for from a multicolored yarn.

U This letter is duplicate stitched (Swiss darned; see page 252), which allows you to easily experiment with working on a patterned background. Here, it's a simple stripe pattern, but you can duplicate stitch onto any stockinette (stocking) stitch knitting. Of course, if you are an expert color knitter, then you can knit a patterned background together with letters, but duplicate stitching like this is a great alternative.

W This letter is beaded using the slip stitch method (see page 250). With this method, you can use larger beads than with the knitted-in method, as you don't have to pull each bead through a stitch loop. However, the beads should not be longer than a stitch is wide.

Z This swatch uses a variegated yarn as the background for a mohair DK letter. As the background yarn is stranded across the back of the letter, the stripes of color—which are short and random—continue on either side of the letter: if the letter is worked in intarsia, this doesn't happen (see letter "C" of Graffiti, page 37).

25

CHALKED

This is a casual alphabet, reminiscent of chalk letters written on a schoolroom blackboard. The simple letter shapes are modern, without being aggressively urban, so they will work for both contemporary and vintage-inspired projects. It's also a super-versatile alphabet as it comes with uppercase and lowercase letters, and a set of numbers, so you can knit any message to anyone. Plus, it's a convenient size for all sorts of projects, from sweaters to afghans to bags. As the strokes of the letters are thin, you may find it easiest to strand (see page 246) the background yarn right across the backs of the letters, as was done here.

Yarns used
◎ Fine mohair yarn in lime green
◎ Fine mohair yarn with integral tiny sequins in gray
◎ Marled sock yarn in greens and gray
◎ Mohair DK yarn in green and black
◎ Tweed DK yarn in green and dark gray
◎ Wool 4ply yarn in green and black
◎ Wool/cotton blend DK yarn in lime green and gray
◎ Wool DK yarn in pale gray

Other materials
◎ Gray beads
◎ Gray wool sewing thread
◎ Wool felt

Techniques used
◎ Intarsia (see page 243)
◎ Stranding (see page 246)
◎ Slip stitch beading (see page 250)
◎ Embroidery (see page 251)
◎ Chain stitch (see page 252)
◎ Duplicate stitch (Swiss darning; see page 252)

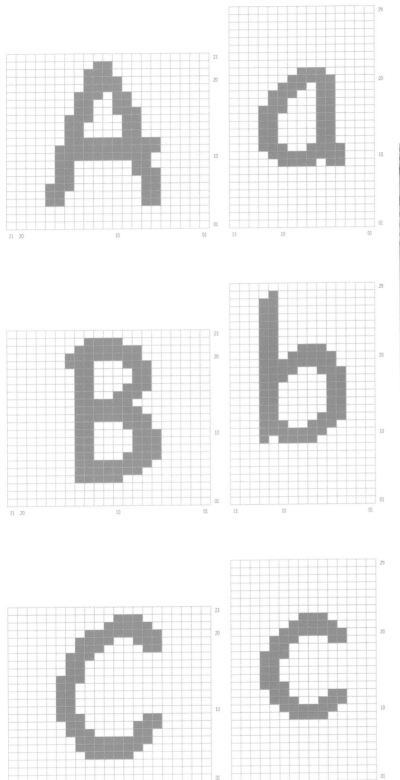

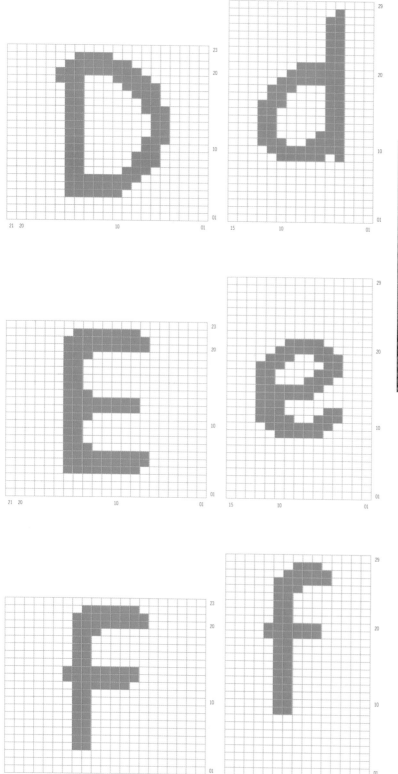

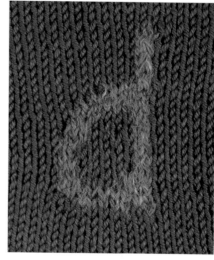

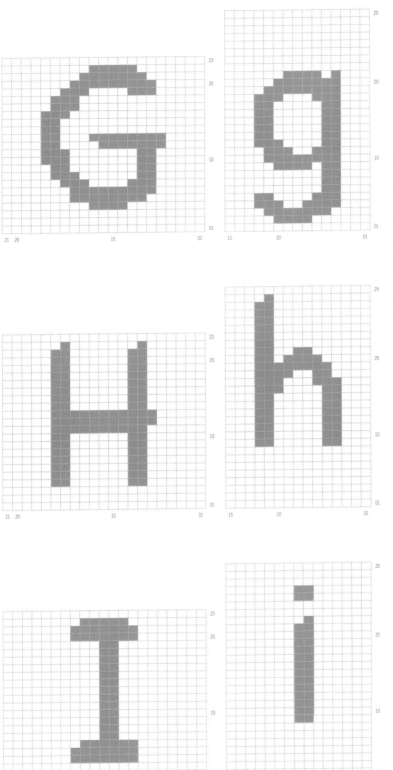

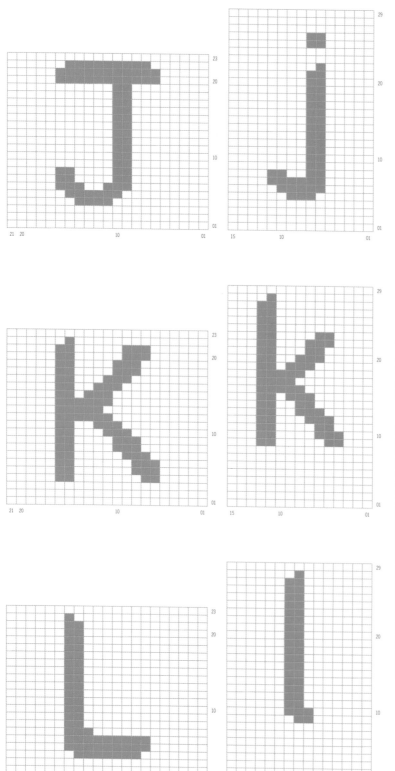

THE KNITTED ALPHABET

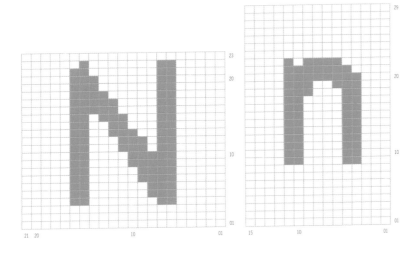

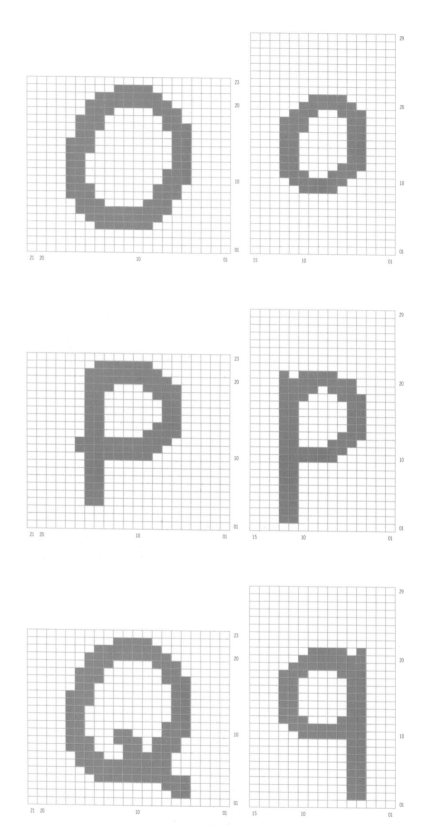

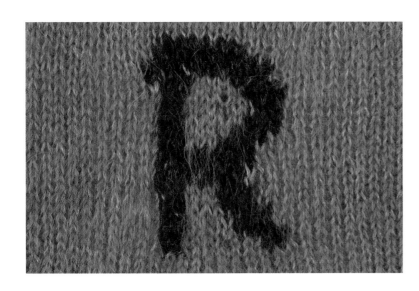

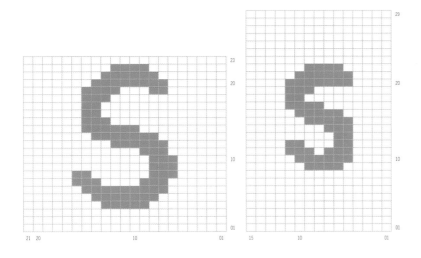

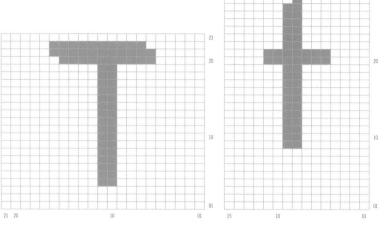

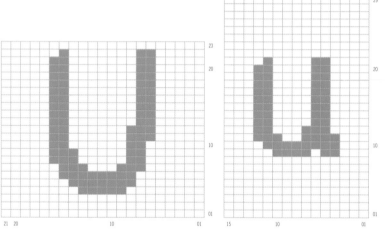

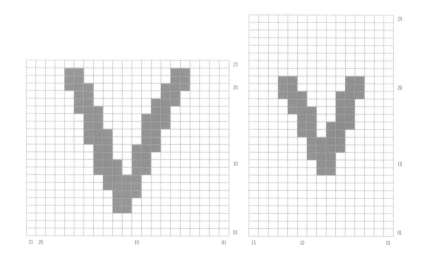

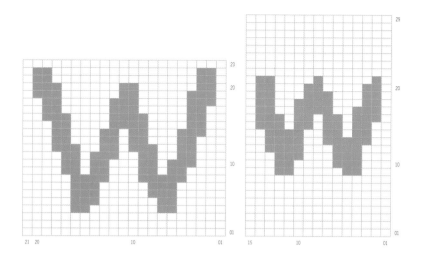

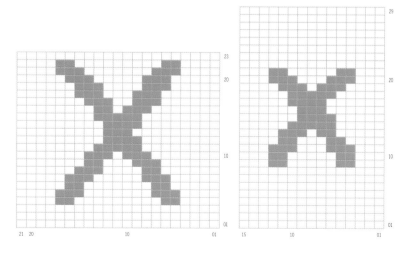

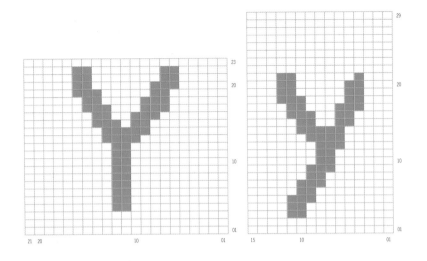

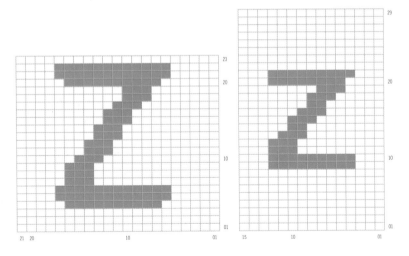

The Knitted Swatches

A The "A" is knitted in a yarn with tiny sequins strung on it. One potential problem with this type of yarn is obvious here: only a very few sequins have appeared on the right side. You can sometimes wriggle beads/sequins along a yarn to make them appear on the right side, but the construction of this yarn (see letter "N") means that the sequins don't move easily.

D For this swatch, the letter is knitted in wool tweed yarn and the background in a wool/cotton blend. Today, many yarns are treated to be machine washable, but always check that two different fibers can be laundered together. If in doubt, machine wash a swatch. If one fiber shrinks more than the other it will be very visible, and you'll need to hand wash the project.

G The background yarn of this swatch is marled; that is, the yarn is made up of two strands of different colors—green and a very thin black strand—and the green strand also changes tone slowly along its length.

J Simple letter shapes can be described with simple stitches: here, large cross-stitches (see page 251) span the knitted stitches that would have been worked in contrast color if the letter was color knitted.

L These beads are placed using the slip stitch method (see page 250). With this technique, you can only place a bead on every alternate stitch and row, but the shape of the letter is simple enough for it to be clear even though it isn't completely filled in.

N The background is a fine mohair with tiny sequins and it's used double here to make it a similar weight to the DK mohair used to knit the letter. The sequins are actually strung onto a very fine, smooth strand that's twisted with the mohair, so the sequins don't slide around. This is good in that they don't get pushed together by the fingers that you tension the yarn over.

R The background of this swatch is knitted in a fine mohair and it's been used double to make it a similar weight to the tweed yarn of the letter. If you have never worked with doubled yarn, don't be put off: the strands twist around one another as you work, making it easy to treat them as a single strand, and with fluffy yarn such as this, it won't show if you miss one strand in a stitch.

T This letter is duplicate stitched (Swiss darned; see page 252) in a marled color yarn. One great advantage of this technique is that it can be added once the knitting is complete, so if you have finished your project and it looks plainer than you hoped, you can easily add detail and color—and marled yarn offers extra color for no extra effort.

W This swatch is worked entirely in wool tweed DK yarn. Wool is a naturally slightly elastic fiber, so it's easier to adjust the tension of individual stitches than it is with cotton yarn. Once the knitting is complete, any slightly uneven stitches can be eased out with the tip of a knitter's sewing needle (see page 249), and blocking the knitting will also improve the finish.

Y Double-knitting weight yarns are probably the most commonly available weight and there are many, many fiber and textural variations: here, both yarns used are a wool/cotton blend. Using two yarns of the same type does make it relatively easy to tension the stitches evenly at the color changes, and so work neat color knitting.

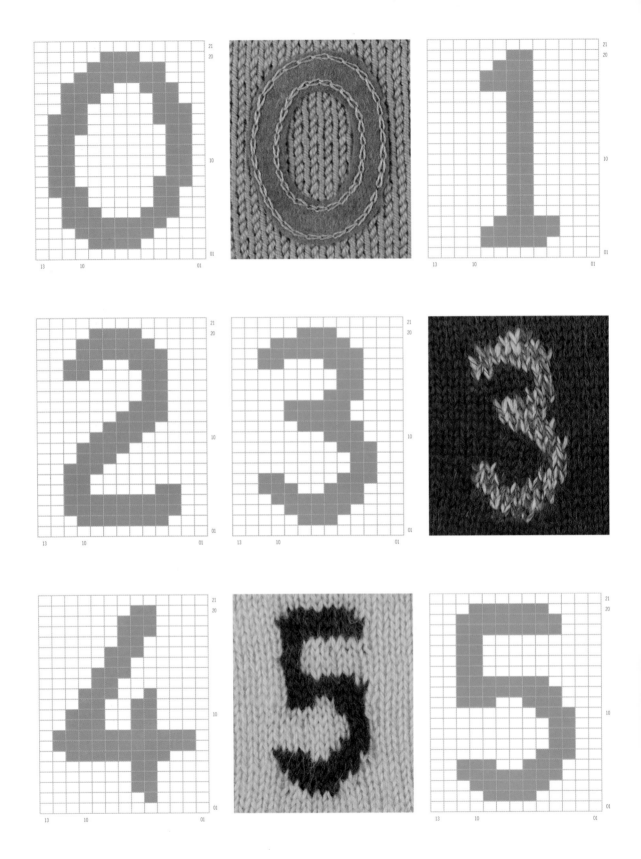

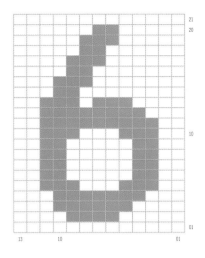

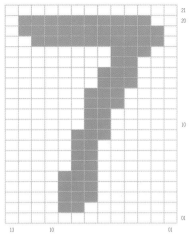

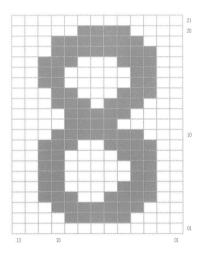

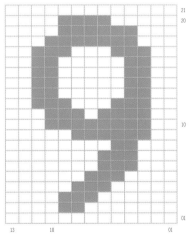

0 The charts can be used as templates to create fabric appliqués that are then sewn onto knitted fabric: here, the numeral is sewn on with chain stitch (see page 252) for an extra decorative touch. Be aware that appliqués will stop the knitting stretching in the area they are sewn to, but it's a great way of adding a motif or motto if color knitting isn't your thing.

3 This swatch has a background of mohair DK and the numeral is knitted in tweed DK. This combination is quite forgiving of uneven stitches—the fluffy yarn hides them and the flecked tweed yarn disguises them—so it's one to try if your color knitting is still at the improving stage.

5 Here, the same yarns as letter "J" have been used, but the positions are reversed and the numeral is knitted, not embroidered. Swapping colors like this works very well on an afghan: choose a limited palette and work blocks in all the possible variations to create a finished piece that's colorful, but also restrained. You can choose just a two-color palette and use different techniques to help ring the changes.

9 When a background yarn is much darker than the numeral yarn, it's best to strand right across the back of the numeral if there are four or fewer stitches, and catch floats in (see page 247)—rather than weaving in (see page 248)—if it is wider. This will prevent flecks of the background yarn showing through where they aren't wanted.

Numbers

Although these numbers have been charted to suit the style and scale of the Chalked letters on pages 218–229, they will also work well with the Quirky Handwriting alphabet (see pages 128–133).

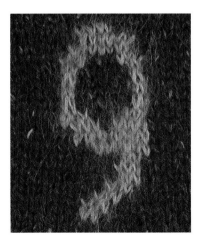

(26)

POSTER

Each letter in this alphabet is 57 rows high, making it perfect either for a single initial on a project—such as the album cover on page 238—or for whole words on big afghans and blankets. Based on the letters traditionally used on circus and fair signs, it's bold and straightforward to knit, though the sheer size means it's not the quickest. The letters are also great candidates for embellishment, as there are lots of stitches and rows to work with. This alphabet is best knitted in intarsia (see page 243); use short, cut lengths of yarn for the openings in letters (see page 243 for how to judge the amount of yarn needed), and bobbins for the letters. The charts have been scaled down in order to fit them in the book; you may wish to enlarge them on a photocopier.

Yarns used
- Fine mohair yarn in orange
- Mohair DK yarn in teal and orange
- Tweed DK yarn in teal and orange
- Wool/cotton blend DK yarn in teal and orange

Other materials
- Crewel wool
- Teal sequins

Techniques used
- Intarsia (see page 243)
- Slip stitch sequins (see page 250)
- Embroidery (see page 251)
- Chain stitch (see page 252)
- Cable (see page 253)

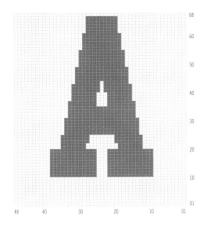
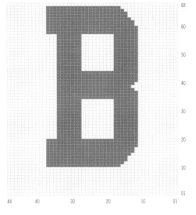
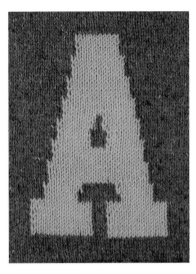

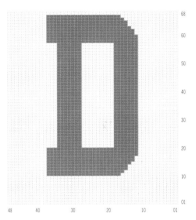

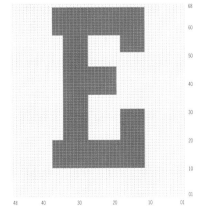
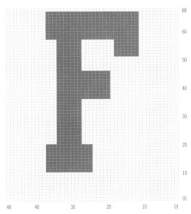
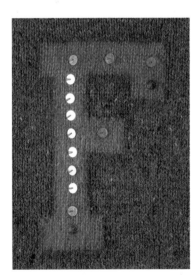

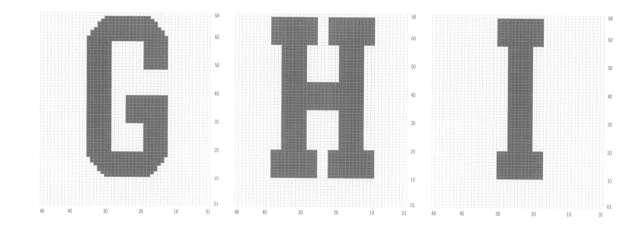

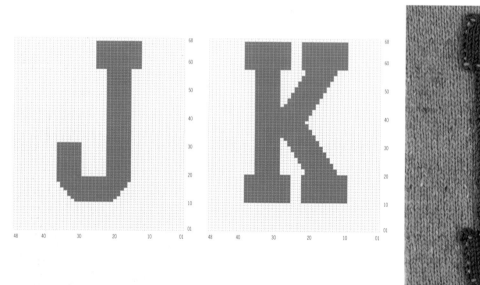

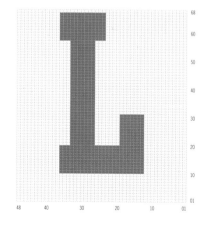

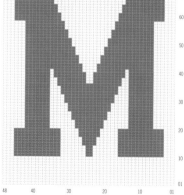

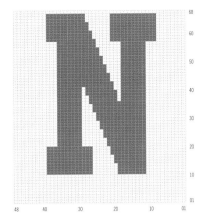

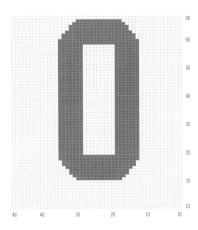

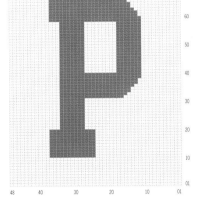

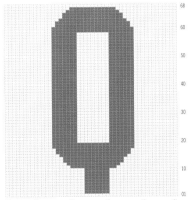

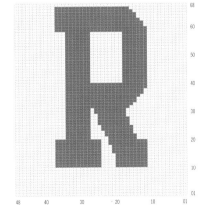

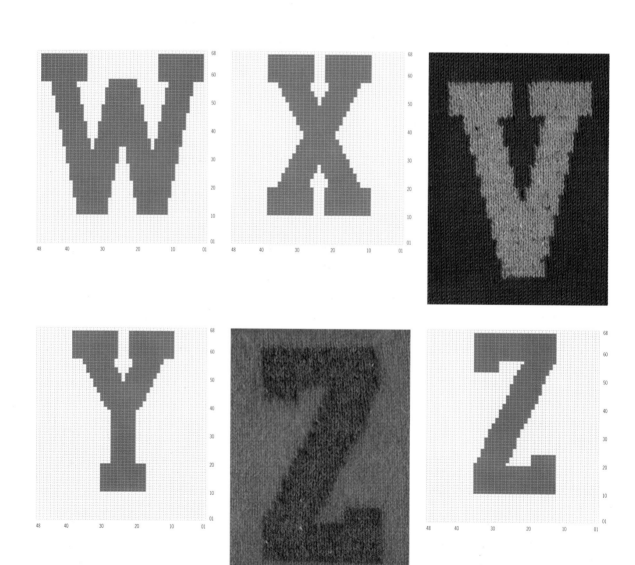

The Knitted Swatches

A This letter is knitted in a wool/cotton blend yarn and the background in wool tweed. The two yarns are similar enough in weight to be knitted together, though it's always worth working a swatch first, just to check. A knitter's tip: tweed yarns are forgiving if you are new to color knitting as the flecked colors help to hide any uneven stitches.

C Double-knitting weight yarns are probably the most commonly available weight and there are many, many fiber and textural variations: this yarn is a lambswool and mohair blend, so it's both soft and fluffy. Using two yarns of the same weight does make it relatively easy to tension the stitches evenly at the color changes and so work neat color knitting, especially when the yarn has a little elasticity, as this wool yarn does.

F This swatch has a background of tweed DK yarn and the letter is in fine mohair used doubled to make it a suitable weight to combine with the tweed. The sequins are placed using the slip stitch method (see page 250) on the middle stitch of the seven stitches making up the vertical stroke of the "F."

I Bold and fairly simple letters, such as this "I," can easily be knitted as shapes to create appliqué motifs. And indeed, all the letters in this alphabet would work this way, though you would need to spend some time reviewing charts first and deciding where to bind (cast) off and where to hold then pick up stitches for the neatest results.

K The large scale and wide strokes of these letters make them perfect for cables. Here, six-stitch cables are used in the middle of the "K" and at the serifs on the angled strokes, while four-stitch ones are at the serifs on the straight strokes. The cables twist left or right to complement the shape of the letter. Mark the cables onto the letter charts before you begin.

N This swatch uses the same yarns as letter "A," but the positions are swapped. Today, many yarns are treated to be machine washable, but always check that two different fibers can be laundered together. If in doubt, machine wash a swatch. If one fiber shrinks more than the other it will be very visible, and you'll need to hand wash the project.

Q Here, the same yarns as letter "C" have been used, but the positions are reversed. Swapping colors like this works very well on an afghan: choose a limited palette and work blocks in all the possible variations to create a finished piece that's colorful, but also restrained. You can choose just a two-color palette and use different fibers to help ring the changes.

S This letter is embellished with bands of chain stitch (see page 252) worked in crewel wool. Designed for traditional crewel embroidery, this is a 100 percent wool thread and is available in a huge range of colors from a multitude of suppliers. The secret to successful embroidery on knitting is getting the stitch tension right. If you pull the embroidery stitches tight, as you might on woven fabric, you will distort the knitting, so pull them gently taut and adjust individual stitches as necessary.

V Color-effect yarns, such as this tweed, can be a bit overpowering used in large quantities—especially when the color is as strong as this orange—but they work well as accents in a project. Putting them with a plain yarn shows off the flecks and shifting colors well, often making more of them than when the tweed is used alone.

Z The background yarn of this swatch is a fine mohair and it's been used double to make it a similar weight to the tweed yarn that the letter is knitted in. If you have never worked with doubled yarn, don't be put off: the strands twist around one another as you work, making it easy to treat them as a single strand, and with fluffy yarn such as this, it won't show if you miss one strand in a stitch.

PROJECT 10

ALBUM COVER

Customize and personalize a photo album or journal with a very easy-to-knit
cover featuring just one huge letter. You can crochet the edging, as here,
or sew it together if you prefer.

Yarns

◎ **Rowan Siena 4ply**

3 x 1¾ oz (50 g) balls in Sloe (670) A and 1 x 1¾ oz (50 g)
ball in Sorbet (683) B (for crochet edging)

◎ **Anchor Artiste Metallic**

1 x 1 oz (25 g) ball in 314 C

◎ **Rowan Kidsilk Haze**

1 x 1 oz (25 g) ball in Brick (649) D

◎ Note: yarns C and D are used held together
as one strand throughout.

Letters

◎ Poster (see page 232)

Tools

◎ Pair of US 2 (2.75 mm) knitting needles
◎ Knitter's sewing needle
◎ Pins
◎ C/2 (2.75 mm) crochet hook

Measurements

◎ To fit an album measuring 11½ in (29 cm) wide and
10¼ in (26 cm) high. For advice on altering the pattern
to fit a different-size album, turn to Positioning the
Letters (see page 240).

Gauge (tension)

◎ 28 sts and 38 rows to 4 in (10 cm) over st st
using Siena 4ply and US 2 (2.75 mm) needles

Abbreviations

◎ See page 254.
◎ Note: use the intarsia method
(see page 243) throughout.

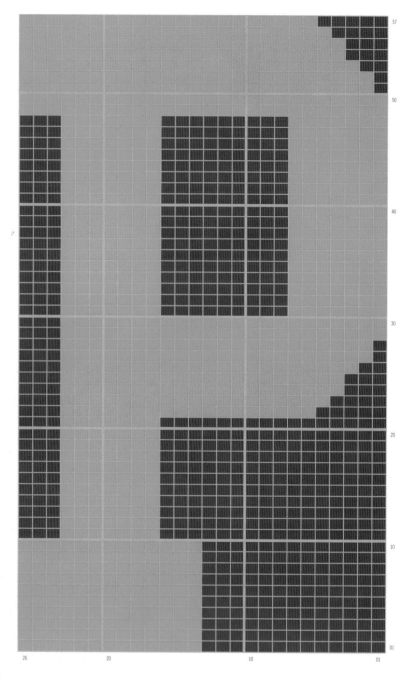

POSITIONING THE LETTERS

You can place the letter wherever you like on the cover; you just need to do the math. First, use a cloth tape measure to measure from the edge of the front cover of your album right around the spine to the edge of the back cover. Add half that measurement again to allow for flaps that will fold over to the inside of the front and back of the album. Measure the height of the album. Using the gauge (tension) given on page 238, work out how many stitches to cast on to get the required measurement, and how many rows to knit. Draw out the size of the knitting on graph paper (or at least, the size of the front panel) and decide where to place your letter.

ALBUM COVER

Using yarn A, cast on 245 sts.

Starting with a k row, work 18 rows st st.

PLACE CHART

Join in yarns C and D and use them held together as
one strand.

Row 19 (RS): K84, place row 1 of chart over next 26 sts,
joining in yarns C and D, held together as one strand, as
required, k to end of row.

Row 20: P135, place row 2 of over next 26 sts, p to end
of row.

Cont in patt as set until row 57 of chart is complete.

Break yarns C and D and cont in yarn A.

Work 18 rows st st.

Bind (cast) off.

TO MAKE UP

- Weave in loose ends.
- Block knitted piece.
- Wrap knitting around album, folding excess over front and
  back covers to create flaps (see Positioning the Letters,
  page 240).
- Put in pins along front edges of covers to mark positions
  of flaps then take knitting off album. Refold flaps and pin
  in place.
- Using a C/2 (2.75 mm) crochet hook and yarn B, pick up
  and work a row of single (double) crochet along the top
  edge of the knitted cover, starting at the front fold and
  working through both layers with each stitch to hold flap
  in place. Hold back flap in place in same way as you work
  along the edge of the knitting. Fasten off and weave in
  ends. Repeat along bottom edge of cover.
- If you prefer, make the knitting two rows deeper and
  mattress seam the flaps in place.

TECHNIQUES

You need to be able to work both intarsia and stranded color knitting in order to knit letters from this book into your own projects, so if you are a color-knitting novice, then here are all the techniques you need to master. Color knitting is simpler than you might think, but it is worth practicing these techniques on sample swatches before you embark on a project. Also included here are techniques for beading, embroidery, cables, and bobbles, all of which are used in some of the knitted swatches and projects in this book.

WORKING FROM A CHART

Knitting charts are often shown on squared graph paper, and the shape of a knitted stitch is rectangular—it's wider than it is deep—so a square-grid chart is deceptive as the actual knitted motif will be wider and shorter than shown. So that you can tell exactly how the letters, numbers, punctuation, emoticons, and dingbats in this book will look knitted in to your own projects, all the charts are given on knitter's graph paper, with rectangular boxes that reflect the shape of a knitted stitch.

The charts are given with at least one blank square around the letter to make it easier for you to count and mark off rows as you knit them. The rows and stitches of the whole chart are numbered, so count off any blank squares to establish exactly how many stitches and rows are in an individual letter.

Decide whether the first row of the charted letter will be a right-side or wrong-side row. If it is a right-side row, then follow along it from right to left, changing yarn colors as the colored squares dictate. The next row will be a wrong-side row, and you'll follow the chart along that row from left to right. Continue in this way, working all right-side rows from right to left across the chart and vice versa for all wrong-side rows. You will probably find it easiest to mark off the rows as you knit: if you are marking the book, then use a pencil so that you can erase the marks when you have finished and not confuse yourself if you knit the letter again. Alternatively, use a sticky note to underline the row you are knitting, unpeeling and moving it up at the start of each new row. You can work charts in the round, but only using the stranded

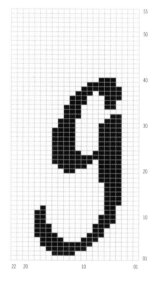

knitting method, because the yarn will always be at the wrong edge of the motif if you try to use intarsia. To work a chart in the round, knit every row from right to left, because every row is now a right-side row.

INTARSIA

This is the method of color knitting that you will mainly use for knitting letters. Some of the chunkier letters—such as 70s Retro (see page 134) and Graffiti (see page 36)—can be knitted entirely in this technique, while letters with thinner strokes will combine intarsia with stranding (see page 246). The most important part of the intarsia technique to get right is the way the yarns link at the color changes to prevent holes from appearing in your knitting, and while the principle of doing this is always the same, it does vary in its detail depending on the outline shape you are knitting. So if you are an intarsia novice, practice the variations carefully on a swatch to get the best results.

YARN BOBBINS

If you are knitting several letters, you need to have a separate yarn supply for each one, so you will need to make up little bobbins of yarn. You can buy plastic bobbins to wind yarn around, or make these yarn butterfly bobbins.

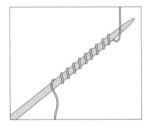

1 To establish how much yarn you need for a letter, count roughly how many stitches it contains: let's say there are 70. Loosely wind the yarn around a knitting needle ten times, then measure out seven times the wound length. Add a bit extra for safety and for sewing in the ends (see page 248), and that's your bobbin quantity.

2 Lay the tail end of the yarn in the middle of your palm, then wrap the length of yarn in a figure eight around your thumb and little finger.

3 Take the butterfly bobbin off your fingers and wind the tail that was in the middle of your palm tightly around the middle and tuck the end under the wraps. Pull gently on the loose end to pull out the yarn from the center of the bobbin.

JOINING IN A NEW COLOR YARN

This is the method for joining in a new color in the middle of a row. Twisting the yarns in this way will help to tension the first new color stitch correctly and prevent it from twisting.

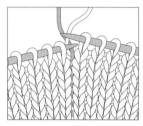

1 At the change in color on a knit row, lay the new color yarn over the old color yarn, as shown.

2 Twist the new color under the old color, bringing it around into the right position to knit with.

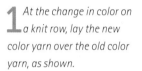

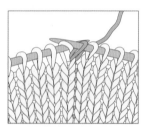

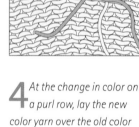

3 Knit the first stitch in the new color. At the end of the row, pull gently on the tail of yarn to tighten the first stitch. When the knitting is complete, weave in the loose tails (see page 248).

4 At the change in color on a purl row, lay the new color yarn over the old color yarn and make one complete twist, as shown.

5 Purl the first stitch in the new color. Tighten stitches and weave in ends as for a knit row.

CHANGING COLOR IN A STRAIGHT VERTICAL LINE

Try to work in an even gauge (tension) across the color change, rather than pulling the first stitch in the new color as tight as possible. Doing that will just distort the last stitch in that color on the previous row. You can adjust baggy stitches once the knitting is complete (see page 249).

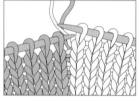

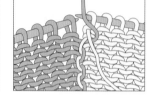

1 At the change in color on a knit row, bring the new color under the old color and up into position to knit with. Drop the old color and knit with the new color.

2 On a purl row, bring the new color under and around the old color from left to right, as shown. Drop the old color and purl with the new color.

CHANGING COLOR ON A RIGHT-SLOPING DIAGONAL

Because the colour change is moving on each row, the yarns are linked in a slightly different way to a straight line color change (see above). Note that the diagonal will slope to the left on the wrong side of the knitting.

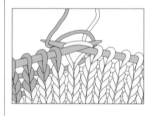

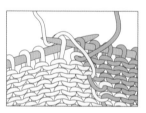

1 At the change in color on a knit row, bring the new color under the old color and up, ready to knit with. Drop the old color and knit with the new color.

2 On a purl row, bring the new color across and purl with it: you are not actually interlinking the yarns, but as the colors are moving across by one stitch, a hole won't form.

CHANGING COLOR ON A LEFT-SLOPING DIAGONAL

Note that the diagonal will slope to the right on the wrong side of the knitting.

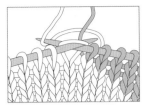 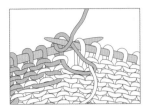

1 *At the change in color on a knit row, bring the new color under the old color and up ready to knit with. Drop the old color and knit with the new color.*

2 *On a purl row, bring the new color under the old color and around ready to purl with. Drop the old color and purl with the new color.*

CARRYING A COLOR ACROSS THE BACK OF THE KNITTING

Here is how to carry a color farther along a row from where it was last used, so that it is in the right position on the next row. Alternatively, you can strand (see page 246) the yarn to the right position on the previous row.

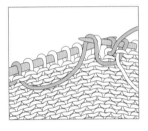

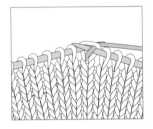 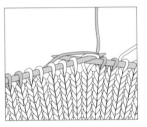 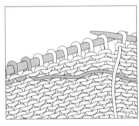

1 *On a knit row, bring the new color yarn across the back of the knitting to where it is needed. Keep the strand of yarn quite loose. Knit the first stitch needed in the new color.*

2 *You need to catch in the loose strand as you knit across the row: This is done the same way on a purl row and you may find those illustrations clearer (see steps 3–5). Put the tip of the right-hand needle knitwise into the next stitch and then under the loose strand. Knit with the new color, but do not let the loose strand come through with the new stitch. Repeat on every alternate stitch to catch all of the strand against the back of the knitting.*

3 *On a purl row, bring the new color across to where it is needed. Keep the strand of yarn quite loose and take it under the old color, then purl the first stitch needed in the new color.*

4 *To catch in the loose strand, put the tip of the right-hand needle purlwise into the next stitch and then under the loose strand.*

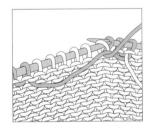

5 *Purl with the new color, not allowing the strand to come through with the new stitch. Repeat on every alternate stitch to catch all of the strand against the back of the knitting.*

STRANDING

You may be familiar with the term "Fair Isle" for this method of color knitting, but strictly speaking Fair Isle is a type of stranded knitting. The two most popular ways to work this type of knitting involve either working with one yarn at a time and dropping the yarn not in use, or working holding a yarn in each hand. Once mastered, the latter is the quickest and can produce very even results. Both techniques are shown here, so experiment to see which suits you best.

A very important thing to get right is the tension on the floats—the strands of yarn lying across the back of the knitting. If they are too tight, then the knitting will be puckered, too loose, and the stitches will be baggy. If you spread out the stitches on the right-hand needle before you change color, then bring the new color across the back and work the first stitch with it, the tension should be right. As you become more familiar with the technique, you'll get better at judging this tension. As with intarsia knitting (see page 243), try to work in an even gauge (tension) across the color change, rather than pulling the first stitch in the new color as tight as possible. You can adjust baggy stitches once the knitting is complete (see page 249).

WORKING WITH ONE YARN AT A TIME

This is the simplest way of stranding and one to try if you are a beginner to color knitting, but it is the slowest method.

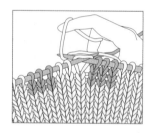 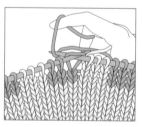 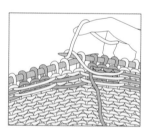 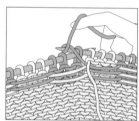

1 At the color change on a knit row, drop the old color and pick up the new color, bringing it across the back and over the old color. Knit with the new color.

2 At the next color change, repeat the process, but bring the new color across and under the old color. Taking the yarns over and under one another in this systematic way will make them interlace neatly on the back.

3 The principle is the same on a purl row. At one color change, bring the new yarn over the old yarn.

4 At the next color change, bring the new yarn under the old yarn.

WORKING WITH ONE YARN IN EACH HAND

Most people have one dominant hand and will find it difficult to control the yarn with the other hand, but practice will help. Hold the yarn that appears more often—or first—in your dominant hand and that which appears less often—or second—in your other hand.

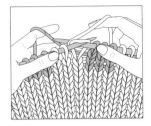 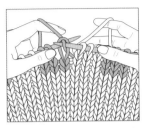 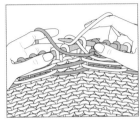 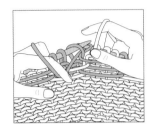

1 *On a knit row, knit the stitches in the first color.*

2 *When the second color yarn is needed, work with the other hand. Holding the yarns like this means that the colors will automatically interlace neatly on the back.*

3 *The principle is exactly the same on a purl row, though you may have to adjust the position of your fingers to catch the yarn with the needle. Purl the first color, controlling the yarn with one hand.*

4 *Purl the second color with the other hand.*

CATCHING IN FLOATS

If there are five or more stitches between different colors, then you need to trap the floats against the back of the knitting to prevent long floats catching and to help tension the stitches neatly. The simple way of doing this is to use the working yarn to trap the float against the back of every second or third stitch.

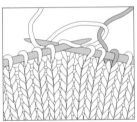 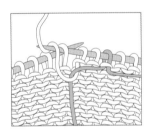

1 *On a knit row, insert the right-hand needle into the stitch. Lay the yarn to be trapped over the working yarn, then knit the stitch. Make sure the trapped yarn does not appear through the stitch, it should just be held firmly against the back of it.*

2 *On a purl row, insert the right-hand needle into the stitch. Lay the yarn to be trapped in over the working yarn, then purl the stitch.*

WEAVING IN FLOATS

If you hold yarns in both hands for stranded knitting, hold them the same way to weave the floats into the back. This is a good idea on garments and blankets, because fingers can snag loosely caught floats. If you are weaving in across the same stitches for several rows, don't weave in to the back of the same stitch each time as this will create a ridge that shows on the front. Hold the yarn you are knitting with in your dominant hand and the yarn to be woven in with the other.

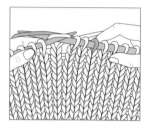 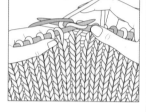

1 On a knit row, insert the right-hand needle into the stitch. Lay the yarn to be woven in over the needle's tip.

2 Wrap the working yarn around the tip of the needle ready to knit it.

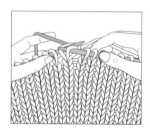 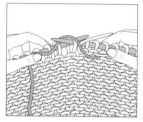

3 Bring the working yarn through the stitch on the left-hand needle, making sure the woven yarn doesn't come through at the same time. Knitting the next stitch will lock the float in place.

4 On a purl row, insert the right-hand needle into the stitch. Lay the yarn to be woven in over the tip of the needle.

5 Wrap the working yarn around the tip of the needle and purl it, making sure the woven yarn doesn't come through at the same time. Purling the next stitch will lock the float in place.

FINISHING

When you have completed your knitting, there are a few tidying-up procedures that will make it look its best.

WEAVING IN ENDS

Weave in the loose tails to secure them and stop the knitting from ever unraveling. The same method can be used for stripes, intarsia, and stranded knitting. Always weave ends into the bumps of stitches in the same color to prevent colors appearing in the wrong places on the right side of the knitting.

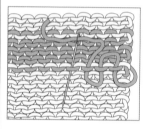 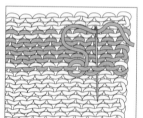

1 Thread a blunt-tipped knitter's sewing needle or a tapestry needle with a tail of yarn. On the back of the knitting, take the needle in and out of three or four stitch bumps of the same color. Here, the loops are shown loose for clarity, but you should pull the yarn gently taut as you go.

2 Work back along the bumps in the same way, but taking the yarn in the opposite direction to form loops, as shown. Cut the end short.

ADJUSTING STITCHES

Even the best color knitters will have occasional loose or distorted stitches, especially at color changes. However, a little careful tweaking can fix a good many problems.

Before blocking the knitting, lay it flat, right side up. Along the edges of color changes—especially vertical changes—there will probably be alternating looser and tighter stitches. As each stitch is linked to the next one in the same color on the same row, you can distribute any looseness more evenly along the row. Using the blunt tip of a knitter's sewing needle or tapestry needle, carefully ease the adjacent stitch to a loose one until the loose stitch looks right, then ease the next one along and so on, easing a little less yarn along each time, until all the stitches look even. Alternatively, ease the looseness into the interlocking strands on the back, then stretch the knitting gently to even out the gauge (tension).

DISGUISING MISTAKES

If you realize you have worked a stitch in the wrong color several rows back and can't bear to unravel, then you can fix it later. Duplicate stitch (Swiss darning; see page 252) can be used to hide any small (and sometimes quite large) mistakes in a knitted color pattern. You can also use this stitch to work single stitches or thin strokes of letters, or indeed to work whole letters, as in many alphabets in this book.

MISSING LINKS

If you have missed links in intarsia knitting and holes have formed, you can just sew them up. Use a knitter's sewing needle or tapestry needle and one of the ends left for weaving in, or a new length of the yarn. Carefully sew the hole closed by taking the yarn through the back of the stitches on either side and tensioning it to pull the stitches together.

BEADING

You can either completely bead letters (for example, page 26 and page 32), or use beads, or sequins, to decorate a colored letter (for example, page 77 and page 136). The technique you choose will depend on where you want to place beads. The beads need to suit the yarn—they can't be too heavy or they will stretch the stitches, and they can't be wider or longer than a knitted stitch or they will distort it.

THREADING BEADS ONTO YARN

The hole in the bead (or sequin) must be large enough for doubled yarn to pass through.

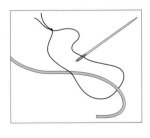

1 Thread a sewing needle with a short length of sewing cotton and knot the ends. Put the tail end of the yarn through the loop of cotton and adjust the position of the knot so that it is clear of both the yarn and the needle (that way the bead does not have to fit over the doubled yarn and the knot at the same time).

2 Slip the beads onto the needle, down the thread, and onto the yarn. Push the beads along the yarn as you work.

SLIP STITCH BEADING

This is an easy technique to work, but beads can only be placed on every alternate stitch and row, though those can be either knit or purl rows.

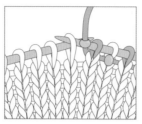

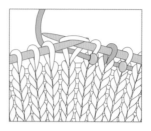

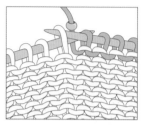

1 *On a knit row, work to the position of the bead. Bring the yarn forward between the needles, then slide a bead down the yarn so it sits right against the knitting. Slip the next stitch purlwise.*

2 *Take the yarn back between the needles, making sure the bead stays at the front. Knit the next stitch firmly. The bead is lying on a strand of yarn running across the base of the slipped stitch.*

3 *On a purl row, work to the position of the bead. Take the yarn back between the needles, slide a bead down against the knitting, and slip the next stitch purlwise. Purl the next stitch firmly.*

SLIP STITCH SEQUINS

The technique is shown here on a knit row, and the same principles apply on a purl row. Purling after the slipped stitch helps prevent the edge of the sequin from tucking into the knitting.

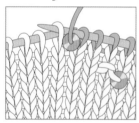

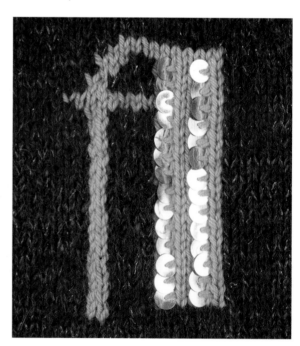

1 *Knit to the position of the sequin. Bring the yarn forward between the needles, then slide a sequin down the yarn so it sits right against the knitting. Slip the next stitch purlwise.*

2 *Purl the next stitch, then take the yarn back between the needles to continue knitting.*

KNITTED-IN BEADING

This method allows you to have a bead on every stitch on every row, but you need a tight gauge (tension). If you are placing beads on every row, they can wriggle through the knitting to the wrong side. To help prevent this, push all the beads down to the base of the stitches before starting the next row. Try to keep as many beads on the right side as possible, but if odd ones wriggle through, you can ease them back to the right side by sliding them along the yarn of their stitch once the knitting is complete.

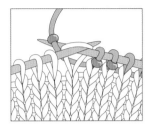 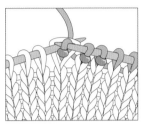 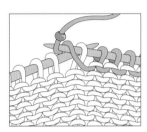 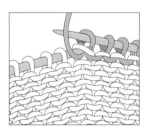

1 *On a knit row, work to the position of the bead. Slide a bead down toward the needles, then put the tip of the right-hand needle into the stitch. Wrap the yarn around the needle in the usual way, adjusting the bead position so that it's just above the right-hand needle.*

2 *Knit the stitch, making sure you draw the bead through the loop on the left-hand needle.*

3 *On a purl row, work to the position of the bead. Slide the bead down the yarn, put the right-hand needle into the stitch and wrap the yarn around the needle in the usual way. Adjust the position of the bead so that it's just above the right-hand needle.*

4 *Purl the stitch, making sure you draw the bead through with it.*

EMBROIDERY

Many embroidery stitches will work well on knitting; here are those used in this book.

CROSS-STITCH

Work cross-stitches following the natural grid of the knitted stitches (for example, page 124 and page 222).

1 *Bring the needle through and make an upward-slanting stitch the required length. Bring it out again directly below where it last went in and make another diagonal stitch to complete*

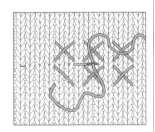

the cross. When working a series of cross-stitches, always have the top stitch sloping in the same direction.

LAZY DAISY

Single chain stitches can be grouped to form a simple flower (see page 80).

1 **Make a single chain stitch (see page 252), tying down the loop with a tiny straight stitch over the end. Bring the needle up where the first stitch started and repeat from *, fanning the stitches around to make the flower.*

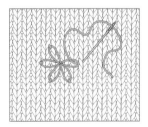

CHAIN STITCH

This stitch can be worked around tight curves so it's excellent for outlining numbers (for example, page 230), and for covering untidy knitted edges.

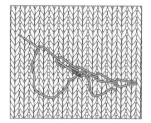

1 Bring the needle and working thread through to the front at the start of the line of chain stitch. *Take the needle back into the fabric where it came out and make a straight stitch the required length of a chain loop. Loop the working thread under the

point of the needle before pulling the needle and thread gently through to form a loop. Repeat from * to make a line of linked stitches. Anchor the last chain in the line with a tiny straight stitch over the end of the loop, as in lazy daisy (see page 251).

DUPLICATE STITCH

This is an embroidery stitch specific to knitting. It matches the stitches on the right side of stockinette (stocking) stitch and is sometimes called "Swiss darning." Duplicate stitch can be used to work whole letters (for example, page 148), decorate knitted letters (for example, page 203), or correct mistakes. Use yarn that is the same weight as that used to knit with for the best effect.

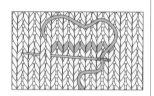

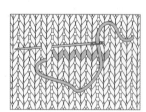

1 Work a horizontal row in whichever direction feels most comfortable. From the back, bring the needle through at the base of the stitch to be covered. Then take it under the two loops of the stitch above, being careful not to split the yarn with the needle.

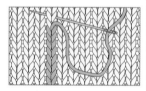

2 Pull the yarn through so that it lies flat over one "leg" of the stitch. Take the needle back through the base—where it came out—and pull the yarn through so it lies neatly over the knitted stitch. Bring the needle to the front again through the base of the next stitch along.

3 To work a vertical row, bring the needle through the base of the stitch to be covered and take it under the loops of the stitch above. Take the needle back through the base of the stitch. Bring it to the front again through the base of the stitch above.

BOBBLE

There are many ways of knitting a bobble: here is the one used in this book (for example, page 136).

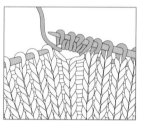

1 Work to the position of the bobble. Increase twice into the next stitch (knit into the front, then the back, the front again, and then the back again), then slip the original stitch off the left-hand needle.

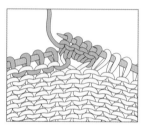

2 Turn the knitting and purl the four bobble stitches. Turn the knitting again and knit the four stitches. Turn the knitting yet again and purl the four stitches.

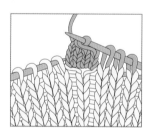

3 Turn the knitting for a final time. Slip the first two stitches knitwise onto the right-hand needle, knit the next two stitches together, then pass the two slipped stitches over the knitted one to be left with one stitch and a completed bobble.

CABLE

Straight letter strokes can be cabled to add an extra dimension to a letter (for example, page 100). Work a test before starting a project, as the results can vary depending on the width and length of the stroke. Shown here is a cable six back (C6B) and cable six front (C6F), though almost any number of stitches can be cabled.

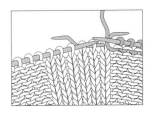

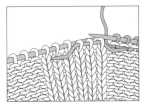

1 *For a cable six back, work to the position of the cable. Slip the next three stitches from the left-hand needle onto the cable needle. Leave this at the back of the knitting.*

4 *For a cable six front, work to the position of the cable. Slip the next three stitches from the left-hand needle onto the cable needle. Leave this at the front of the knitting.*

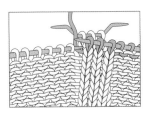

2 *Knit the next three stitches from the left-hand needle.*

5 *Knit the next three stitches from the left-hand needle.*

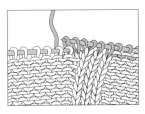

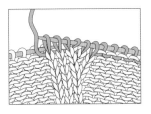

3 *Knit the three stitches that are held on the cable needle to complete the cable six back: the twist will go to the right.*

6 *Knit the three stitches that are held on the cable needle to complete the cable six front: the twist will go to the left.*

CREATE YOUR OWN WORDS

The grid below uses the same proportions as the knitting patterns shown throughout this book. Photocopy it to use when making your own words.

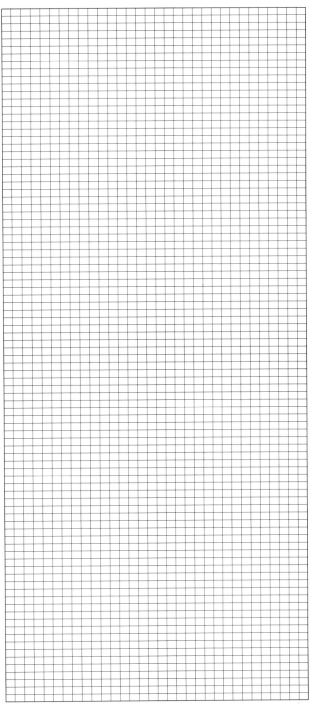

ABBREVIATIONS

A, B, C, etc.	colors as indicated in the pattern
alt	alternate
approx	approximate(ly)
beg	begin(ning)(s)
cm	centimeter(s)
cont	continue(s)
dec	decrease(s)
DK	double-knitting
foll	follow(ing)(s)
g	gram(s)
in	inch(es)
inc	increase(s)
k	knit
k2tog	knit two (or number stated) together
LH	left hand
m	meter(s)
mm	millimeters
oz	ounce(s)
p	purl
p2tog	purl two (or number stated) together
patt	pattern
rem	remain(ing)(s)
rep	repeat
rev st st	reverse stockinette (stocking) stitch
RH	right hand
RS	right side
skpo	slip one, knit one, pass slipped stitch over
sl	slip
st st	stockinette (stocking) stitch
st(s)	stitch(es)
tbl	through back loops
WS	wrong side
yd	yard(s)
yo	yarn over
*	repeat instructions between/following * as many times as instructed
[ ]	repeat instructions between [ ] as many times as instructed

YARNS

Here are the specifications for the Rowan yarns we used throughout this book.

Anchor Artiste Metallic; 80% viscose, 20% metallized polyester; 109 yd (100 m) per 1 oz (25 g) ball

Baby Merino Silk DK; 66% merino superwash wool, 34% tussah silk; 147 yd (135 m) per 1¾ oz (50 g) ball

British Sheep Breeds Fine Bouclé; 91% British wool, 9% nylon; 109 yd (100 m) per 1¾ oz (50 g) ball

Cotton Glace; 100% cotton; 125 yd (115 m) per 1¾ oz (50 g) ball

Creative Focus Worsted; 75% wool, 25% alpaca; 220 yd (200 m) per 3½ oz (100 g) ball

Felted Tweed; 50% merino wool, 25% alpaca, 25% viscose; 191 yd (175 m) per 1¾ oz (50 g) ball

Handknit Cotton; 100% cotton; 93 yd (85 m) per 1¾ oz (50 g) ball

Kid Classic; 70% lambswool, 22% kid mohair, 8% polyamide; 153 yd (140 m) per 1¾ oz (50 g) ball

Kidsilk Haze; 70% super kid mohair, 30% silk; 229 yd (210 m) per 1 oz (25 g) ball

Kidsilk Haze Glamour; 55% mohair, 22% silk, 20% nylon, 3% polyester; 177 yd (162 m) per 1 oz (25 g) ball

Kidsilk Haze Trio; 70% super kid mohair, 30% silk; 153 yd (140 m) per 1¾ oz (50 g) ball

Panama; 55% viscose, 33% cotton, 12% linen; 148 yd (135 m) per 1¾ oz (50 g) ball

Pure Wool 4ply; 100% superwash wool; 174 yd (160 m) per 1¾ oz (50 g) ball

Pure Wool DK; 100% superwash wool; 137 yd (125 m) per 1¾ oz (50 g) ball

Rowan Fine Tweed; 100% wool; 98 yd (90 m) per 1 oz (25 g) ball

Siena 4ply; 100% cotton; 153 yd (140 m) per 1¾ oz (50 g) ball

Sock yarn (we used various colors); 75% superwash new wool, 25% polyamide; 229 yd (210 m) per 1¾ oz (50 g) ball

Wool Cotton 4ply; 50% merino wool, 50% cotton; 197 yd (180 m) per 1¾ oz (50 g) ball

Wool Cotton; 50% merino wool, 50% cotton; 123 yd (113 m) per 1¾ oz (50 g) ball

INDEX

RESOURCES

UK

Rowan Yarns
Green Mill Lane
Holmfirth
West Yorkshire HD9 2DX
Tel: 01484 681881
www.knitrowan.com

Debbie Abrahams Beads
26 Church Drive
Nottingham NG5 2BA
beads@debbieabrahams.com

US

Rowan Yarns
Westminster Fibers
165 Ledge Street
Nashua, NH 03060
Tel: (800) 445 9276
www.westminsterfibers.com

Canada

Rowan Yarns
Westminster Fibers
10 Roybridge Gate, Suite 200
Vaughan, Ontario L4H 3M8
Tel: (800) 263 2354
Tel: (905) 856 3447

ACKNOWLEDGMENTS

Kate and Sarah would like to thank James Evans at Quid Publishing for offering us the

opportunity to make this book, Lucy York for editing us, Dominic Harris

for photographing all the knitting, and Tony Seddon for designing the pages.

Without the help of our knitters we would be nowhere: our thanks to

Fiona Winning, Amanda Golland, Jools Yeo, Luise Roberts, and Sophia Reed.

And much thanks to David MacLeod and Kate Buller at Rowan Yarns

for their generosity in supporting us with their beautiful yarns,

and to Debbie Abrahams for the knitting beads.